AMERICAN
STATESMEN

AMERICAN STATESMEN

An Interpretation of Our History and Heritage

BY

EDWARD HOWARD GRIGGS

Essay Index Reprint Series

BOOKS FOR LIBRARIES PRESS
FREEPORT, NEW YORK

First Published 1927
Reprinted 1970

INTERNATIONAL STANDARD BOOK NUMBER:
0-8369-1810-X

LIBRARY OF CONGRESS CATALOG CARD NUMBER:
76-121474

PRINTED IN THE UNITED STATES OF AMERICA

CONTENTS

INTRODUCTION

THIS generation of Americans faces a world of new and perplexing problems. Certain of these come from the mere expansion of the country in territory and population, with the unparalleled multiplication of machinery. Others result from the changed methods of industrial production, and the consequent drawing apart of different groups of the population in mutual antagonism. Still others are a direct heritage from the world war, which changed the whole plane of our international relations. The answer we give to many of these problems will be the permanent answer, for our whole future.

Our forefathers, one and all, believed that America was to be, not only a land of freedom and opportunity, for those who had the good fortune to dwell here, but as well a sort of beacon light to the nations of the earth. They were convinced that our experiment would challenge the liberal party all over the world, be followed by similar developments everywhere, until all nations should rise to democracy. Were these hopes vain dreams, or were they great challenging ideas that demand our following and furtherance at the present hour?

"Americanism" is on countless lips; but used often merely to express the user's prejudice and hate, toward other groups, equally American. What is Americanism? What does the American spirit mean? What is the moral leadership to which America is called, among the nations of the earth? There is no way to answer these questions justly, except by returning to our history and reinterpreting the heritage from our brief but noble past.

That is the purpose of these studies, portraying six outstanding leaders in our history, and seeking, through them, to interpret our heritage and show the challenge it carries for us today.

Washington is our first American. Patient, generous and enduring, in the face of malicious enmities and apparently hopeless conditions, never despairing, he led the loosely associated colonies through the Revolution to victory. Twice unanimously chosen President of the infant nation, his absolute integrity and selfless leadership carried the precarious Union through its initial dangers, gave it strength and permanence, and eliminated forever the possibility of a return to the monarchical system of the old world.

Second only to Washington's service was that of Franklin in making victory possible in the Revolution. The wisest and shrewdest diplomat our country has yet produced, impervious to bribes and unchanged in conduct by either flattering honors or malicious attacks, protected in spirit by his abundant humor, and through it and his wisdom steering many an apparently hopeless situation through to successful issue, he won and held the sympathy and help of France.

Discoverer and inventor, master of virile English style, humorist and moralist, he is our prototype of the self-made practical American.

Jefferson, father of American religious freedom, a Virginia gentleman, fighting consistently and successfully every form of aristocratic privilege in Virginia, a slave-holder, hating the institution of slavery, was the most many-sided and variously cultivated of all the fathers of our country. He wrote the charter of human liberties; formulated for all time the philosophy of democracy; and, as a practical statesman, disregarded his own views of the Constitution, and gave the nation that vast Western empire which assured the progress and greatness he visioned with wide imagination. Recognizing that education is the lever of democracy, he early advocated a complete system of state education, and crowned his lifework by establishing the University of Virginia.

While others initiated our institutions and formulated the Constitution, it was Hamilton who, more than all others, gave the Federal government vitality, strength and permanence. One of the truly great statesmen of all ages, a wise and far-sighted economist, the most trenchant political thinker and writer America has produced, untiringly fighting for the principles in which he believed, achieving his amazing victories by sheer force of intellect, Hamilton's tragically terminated career is one of the most brilliant in our history and fruitful in all that makes America strong and great today.

Perhaps no other American has been so universally and devotedly loved by his own people as Robert Edward Lee. A true Virginia gentleman, incarnating the beautiful chivalry of its old aristocratic life; with all of its virtues and none of its vices; opposing sectional hatreds and bitterly regretting the rift in the Union, Lee obeyed his conscience and made the only choice he could make. Holding Washington as his example and ideal, Lee hoped to achieve for his State and section the liberty and complete self-determination Washington had won for the Colonies in relation to the mother land. The greatest military genius America has produced, winner of Napoleonic victories, against seemingly impossible odds, heroic and magnanimous in defeat, as in victory, Lee devoted his closing years to healing the scars of the fratricidal conflict and educating the youth of his beloved State to be citizens of our America.

Lincoln, child of the forest, born of the poorest of the poor nomadic families of the frontier; gaunt backwoodsman, splitting rails and winning wrestling matches; with utter native integrity of character, industriously self-taught; the melancholy sombreness of his spirit tempered and sweetened by a marvelous wealth of humor; Lincoln slowly matured in self-mastery and climbed step by step, till the Nation in its most tragic crisis gave him its highest office and heaviest burden. Misunderstood, calumniated by slave-holder and Abolitionist alike, plotted against by fellow-servants of his cause, unhating, unshaken, unhastened, Lincoln held the balance true, slowly emerged the consecrated defender of "the white man's charter of liberties," the recreator of the Union, in character and spirit the prophet of that democracy America is sometime to be.

With such a constellation in our spiritual heritage, may we not be humble and proud of our America, and should we not waken and consecrate ourselves to carry on and out the greatest, most daring and most hopeful experiment in democracy mankind has attempted?

I

WASHINGTON: THE FIRST AMERICAN

TODAY, more than ever, we are awed by the marvel of America. Leaping forward, with dizzying rapidity, in business organization, invention and applied science, wealth and power; attaining a dazzling height in international leadership, yet seeking to use her power wholly for comity and peace; watch-towers of commerce rising innumerably in her countless cities; possessing more than half of the newer equipments of civilization, in use over the whole world; great, swift-growing Colossus, grossly sensual, but far-dreaming and high-visioned, brooded over by vast ideals: America is the bewildering marvel of mankind.

From the initial discovery of the Continent, onward, America the growing marvel of the world.

The wonder began with the initial discovery and early settlement of America. Never before had a whole new continent suddenly been added to the knowledge and imagination of the world, with the opportunity to transplant already highly developed civilization, to exploit its virgin resources.

Effect of suddenly adding a new continent to the known world.

Several nations were concerned in the early settlement. Spain came, largely exploring, but with settlements in the South and claims to vast territory. The French were also chiefly explorers; but settling in Canada, they extended those long lines of posts,

Nations taking part in the early settlement of America.

down through the middle wilderness, trading with the Indians to the benefit of both races. It was, however, the English, with the Scotch and Irish, and in lesser measure the Dutch and Germans, who came to live permanently in the new world: building their homes, tilling their farms, extending their hamlets ever further inland. At the time Washington was born (1732) there were some 600,000 English-speaking settlers in the colonies scattered up and down the Atlantic coast.

The English possessing the genius for colonization.

Virginia particularly attracted the English, especially those of the lesser nobility. The temperate climate, fertile soil, early introduction of negro slavery, making possible something of the aristocratic life they had known in England, and the wide demand for the staple products, tobacco and the cereals: all made Virginia alluring to the English.

Reasons why Virginia particularly attracted the English.

Washington's great-grandfather and the latter's brother came over about 1656, apparently to escape the Cromwell régime, since they were of the lesser nobility and devoted to the King and Crown. The great-grandfather was a vigorous type of man, a successful Indian fighter, winning from the Indians the name "Conotocarius" or "Devourer of Villages" in consequence. His grandson, Augustine, extended his land holdings, became interested in iron mines to the west, was twice married, having four children by his first wife and six by the second; George Washington being the eldest of the second brood, born at Wake-

Ancestry of Washington.

The family of Washington's father.

field, Westmoreland County, Virginia, February 22nd, 1732.

Washington's mother and his relation to her.

Washington's mother, Mary Ball, was a forceful, commanding personality. She seems to have had for her eldest son a strong affection, but rather of the possessive, demanding type; and as the years went by, she apparently grew increasingly querulous and complaining. While Washington fulfilled his duties toward her with scrupulous fidelity and generosity, there could have been little opportunity for great tenderness in the relationship. His letters to her sufficiently evidence this.

Consequences to Washington of his father's early death.

When Washington was a lad of eleven his father died; and this changed his whole outlook on life. Virginia had taken over the British laws on primogeniture and entail, so that estates passed regularly to the eldest son. Washington's older half-brothers had both been sent to school in England; and he doubtless would have followed had his father lived. It is true, one farm was left jointly to Washington and his mother; but she retained it, and he seems to have had no income from it during her long life-time. Thus, while welcome in his mother's home and those of his half-brothers, Washington was practically thrown upon his own resources at the age of eleven.

Meager schooling closing at sixteen.

The result was meager schooling, closing definitely at sixteen. Washington was strong in mathematics, poor in language work, of which he had very little, and particularly weak in spelling and grammar;

which doubtless will comfort many a young student of the present time.

With this limited schooling, Washington was remarkably well educated: please note the distinction between the two terms. His education came from his many-sided and incessant activities. Early he developed his interest in hunting and fishing, and he practiced those vigorous out-door activities, at every opportunity, all his life. Then came his work as surveyor, Indian fighting, with numerous expeditions through the wilderness, his career as military leader and statesman, and his life-long successful activity as farmer and business man.

Excellent education from manifold activities.

Sources of life-education.

Then, too, as a Viriginia aristocrat, Washington had constant association with the most cultivated men and women of the colony; and he studied their conversation, endeavoring to improve his own speech and written expression. Moreover, while never a rapid or wide reader, Washington was a thoughtful and earnest one; and he read solid literature. Early he had access to Lord Fairfax's good library. Later, we find him ordering books from England. Those lists make interesting reading: treatises on government, agriculture, solid histories: such were the books he read through the years.

Character of Washington's limited reading.

Washington was always sensitive regarding the defects in his schooling; and it is one of the pathetic facts of his biography, which helps to make him more human, that late in life, after he had led the country through the Revolution and been twice President of the infant nation, knowing that his writings would be published and read, he began going over the letters and other documents, written in young manhood, and carefully correcting them in grammar, spelling and style!

Mount Vernon: Washington's home from the age of sixteen.

At sixteen, he went definitely to live at the home of his half-brother, Lawrence, who had inherited the large estate which he renamed Mount Vernon, in honor of Admiral Vernon, under whom he had served in the war between England and Spain. The adjoining estate, Belvoir, was occupied by a younger member of the Fairfax family, agent for his family's great land holdings in the new world. Lawrence had married a daughter of this household, thus uniting the two families.

The valuable friendship with Lord Fairfax.

About the time Washington went to live at Mount Vernon, there came over from England, Lord Fairfax, head of the family, a sixty-year-old, cultivated, worldly, disappointed English nobleman, to look after his estates; and he went to live at Belvoir. At once a warm attachment developed between the sixty years old British nobleman and the sixteen years old George Washington. The two hunted and fished together; Washington had his first wide contact with books in Lord Fairfax's excellent library; and the nobleman was so impressed with the young Washington that he commissioned him to cross the Blue Ridge mountains and survey Lord Fairfax's great land holdings, extending up the Shenandoah valley and beyond.

At sixteen, Washington was already six feet tall:

a spare young giant. He ultimately became six feet two inches in height, with a large frame and enormous hands and feet. His gloves were usually made to order: those on the market not being large enough. He wore regularly shoes size eleven and military boots of thirteen; and his wrists and ankles were so large as everywhere to attract comment. He had the physical strength that went with this large organism. One of the stories that has come down to us, told by a comrade of the Revolution, is that Washington's military tent with its poles, required two men to lift it into the wagon for transportation; but that Washington could seize it with one hand and throw it, poles and all, into the wagon.

Washington's size and physical constitution.

At sixteen, then, Washington and a young Fairfax crossed the Blue Ridge, had weeks of adventure in the wilderness; but did the surveying so satisfactorily that Lord Fairfax was greatly pleased, crossed the Blue Ridge and built himself a hunting lodge, which he occupied as a residence for a time, and secured for Washington appointment as public surveyor. Moreover, I am told by persons living in that part of Virginia, that deeds for land today, in all that section, go back to the lines run by George Washington, at the age of sixteen: a signal illustration of the thoroughness and faithfulness with which Washington did all the work assigned to him.

Experiences in surveying for Lord Fairfax.

From sixteen to nineteen, Washington worked as public surveyor, saving his money and buying land. When he was nineteen, his brother Lawrence found

Work as public surveyor.

himself afflicted with tuberculosis; and decided to go to the West Indies in the hope of a cure, taking his younger half-brother with him. They knew little about handling tuberculosis in those days; he possibly could have gone nowhere worse; but he chose the West Indies.

The visit to the West Indies.

It was Washington's first opportunity for a look out on the big world; for the West Indies were well in advance of the mainland in cultivation. Here, Washington saw his first play upon the stage and heard his first theater music. Immediately upon arrival, the Washington brothers were invited to dine with Major Clarke. Washington says that he was reluctant to accept, as there was small-pox in the Major's family. In those days, however, a little thing such as small-pox could not stand in the way of social etiquette; so the Washington brothers accepted, dining repeatedly at Major Clarke's, and Washington promptly took the small-pox. Though speedily recovering, he was pockmarked, in consequence, for life.

Returning, Lawrence was no better; and indeed, he died a few months later, when George was twenty. He had formed such respect, as well as affection, for his younger brother that he left Washington guardian of Lawrence's young daughter; with the provision that, if she died, Washington was to inherit Mount Vernon. That death following shortly after, Washing did inherit Mount Vernon; and it became the foundation of his large fortune.

Inheritance of Mount Vernon.

Lawrence, moreover, having served in war, had

brought to Mount Vernon Adjutant Muse of the Virginia army and Jacob van Braam, a Dutch soldier of fortune. It was from the latter that Washington had his first training in sword-play and instruction in military science. Lawrence had further secured his brother's appointment on the Virginia staff, with the rank of Major. As a result, Washington, at twenty-one, was commissioned by the Governor of Virginia to proceed to the headwaters of the Ohio and warn the French commander that the French were intruding on British and Virginia rights.

Washington's early military training and associations.

The situation is easily understood: the French had extended that long line of trading posts, from Canada through the middle wilderness. Since their trade with the Indians was profitable to both races and they did not dispossess the Indians of their lands, the Indians were generally friendly to them. The English, on the other hand, were extending their farms and settlements ever further into the wilderness, pushing the Indians back, with their consequent enmity, though it was for the good of the country that the settlements should be made.

Situation of the British settlers, in relation to the French and Indians.

Washington took Van Braam, Adjutant Muse, a celebrated guide, Christopher Gist, and four woodsmen; and proceeded on horseback through the six hundred miles of wilderness. He pushed on from the headwaters of the Ohio, north within thirty miles of Lake Erie; warned the French commander; showed his shrewd native intelligence in a partially successful struggle with the French for the friend-

Washington's first expedition to the Ohio.

ship of the Indians; and was puzzled at being called by the Indians "Conotocarius": their identification of him with that earlier "Devourer of Villages", his fighting great-grandfather.

Thrilling adventures.

Leaving the others to come with the ailing horses, Washington and the guide returned on foot, with many adventures. They narrowly escaped death at the hands of treacherous Indians; were overturned from a raft in the icy waters of a river, and had to sleep all night in frozen clothes. On arrival at Williamsburg, the Governor asked for a written report. Washington had kept his *Journal* so carefully that he was able to furnish it in twenty-four hours. It was published as an official document, and widely read, not only in the Colonies, but in England and France, as it was one of the first authentic accounts of conditions in the new world for British and French eyes.

The *Journal* of of the expedition, published as an official government document.

No introspection in Washington.

That *Journal* makes interesting reading today, for one reason: there is not an introspective line in it. When one keeps a diary of vivid experiences, one is apt to put down at least occasional passages of reflection, expressing one's inner moods. It is characteristic of Washington that such a passage is hard to find in all the numerous volumes of his writings. This is notably true of the four large volumes of his surviving *Diaries*. There are bald records of the weather, his farming operations, visits and schedules of guests, even across the years when the struggle with England was developing, and his mind must have been ab-

Characteristics of the *Diaries*.

sorbed in the great problems involved. So later on, he records, day by day, his attendance at the Constitutional Convention, with no single word about the great questions so bitterly fought over in the Convention.

A culminating example of this characteristic is in the diary reference to the death of his step-daughter, Patsy Custis. Washington was deeply attached to her, and grieved over her unfortunate affliction (epilepsy). When she died in young womanhood, the diary entry for June 19, 1773, reads: "At home all day. About five o'clock poor Patcy Custis Died Suddenly."*

Character of Washington's mind.

Washington's mind was wholly objective, grasping facts, things as they are, and dominantly interested in action. It was this quality of his intellect that gave him his accurate judgment of men and events, and on the basis of his moral integrity, explains his successful leadership in so many fields.

Washington was not without humor, though he had far less of it than Franklin. The following entry for one day in the *Diary,* given in full, is characteristic in the items recorded, and is also one of the best examples of the rather dry type of humor that marked Washington:

"A Small fine Rain from No. Et. wet the Top of my Hay that had been landed last Night. It was all carted

---

* Washington, *Diaries*, Vol. II, p. 115. See Book List on pp. 348-355 for full information regarding publisher, place and date of publication of all volumes quoted.

up however to the Barn and the wet and dry separated.

"Went to a Ball at Alexandria, where Musick and Dancing was the chief Entertainment. However in a convenient Room detached for the purpose abounded great plenty of Bread and Butter, some Biscuits with Tea, and Coffee which the Drinkers of coud not Distinguish from Hot water sweetened. . . . Be it remembered that pockethandkerchiefs servd the purposes of Table Cloths and Napkins and that no Apologies were made for either.

Diary entry evidencing Washington's humor.

"The Proprietors of this Ball were Messrs. Carlyle, Laurie and Robt. Wilson, but the Doctr. not getting it conducted agreeable to his own taste would claim no share of the merit of it.

"I shall therefore distinguish this Ball by the Stile and title of the Bread and Butter Ball." *

The second Ohio expedition.

At twenty-two, Washington was again sent to the Ohio, as Lt. Colonel, second in command of an expedition to relieve the fort, which had been erected at the junction of the Monongahela and Allegheny rivers, on the site selected by Washington during the first journey. The commander's death, in the course of the expedition, left Washington in sole charge. He arrived too late to relieve the fort, which had already been surrendered; but pushed on with a detachment of troops, surprised a body of French and Indians, won the skirmish, in which the French commander and a number of soldiers were killed, and took some prisoners. It was concerning this battle that Washington wrote of his pleasure in "hearing the bul-

* Washington, Entry in *Diary* for Friday, Feb. 15th, 1760, with orthography of original: *Diaries*, Vol. I, p. 126.

lets whistling by him." Washington was a born fighter, he loved a battle; yet he so deprecated war that this is the only passage one finds in his writings expressing joy in battle, while there are numerous paragraphs in which he contrasts destructive warfare with the peaceful, constructive work of agriculture, which he regarded as the natural vocation of man.

View of war versus agriculture.

A fort was hastily built on Great Meadows—appropriately "Fort Necessity"; but Washington had too few troops, and was obliged honorably to surrender it and return. Then the British government took over the war; and Washington promptly resigned his commission. Why? Because the British military red-tape put the lowest regular British officer above the highest colonial one. Washington was singularly selfless, without self-seeking personal ambition; but he had deep reverence for the offices to which he was called; and always demanded full respect for those offices. He was unwilling, therefore, as a Virginia Colonel, to be subordinated to every British Second Lieutenant. General Braddock, however, now in command of the expedition against the French and Indians, was unwilling to lose from his forces the best fighter in Virginia, and probably in America; and he urged Washington to take a place on his personal staff, with the rank of colonel. This relieving him from the resented subordination, Washington accepted; and so accompanied Braddock on that long, slow expedition to the West. Repeatedly, Washington warned General Braddock to beware of an Indian

Relation of colonial to British officers.

Washington's modesty and dignity.

On General Braddock's staff.

Warning Braddock of an Indian ambuscade.

ambuscade; and Benjamin Franklin, twenty-six years older, and thus an apparently more authoritative counsellor, also warned him. Braddock ridiculed the warnings: said that might all be true for colonials; but those savages could not stand up a moment before British regulars. You know what happened: as the expedition reached the point where Braddock, Pennsylvania, is today, the ambuscade, of which Washington had forewarned the General, occurred. The British regulars were thrown into a wild panic, nearly as many falling as made up the entire force of French and Indians surprising them. It was the colonial officer, George Washington, who rallied the panic-stricken British regulars, had the wounded General Braddock carried off the battlefield, conducted the retreat of the British army, and read the burial service over the dead body of General Braddock.

The ill-fated Braddock campaign.

Washington's service.

It was all an illuminating experience for Washington: it taught him that British regulars could be defeated. That means more than may appear. There was at that time, among the colonists, much the same abject reverence for the British army that most of the outside world had for the German army before the World War: the notion that it was so perfectly trained and equipped that it could not be defeated. Washington learned from the Braddock expedition not only that British regulars could be defeated, but that their training really unfitted them for the conditions of warfare in the New World. It was all most instructive experience for his later career.

Lessons from the Braddock expedition.

Returning home, Washington was offered the command of the Virginia forces. He accepted; but to be relieved of subordination to British sub-officers, journeyed in state to Boston, to see General Shirley, in command of the British forces. He stopped, on the way, at Philipse Manor, on the Hudson; was greatly drawn to Mary Philipse, daughter of the family; would have courted the lady, had she been willing, which apparently she was not.

The journey to Boston.

The desired relief obtained, Washington returned to Virginia, for a couple of years of desultory Indian fighting, dealing with government incompetency, learning to control his fierce temper. Washington had a terrible temper; but so mastered it that there are but few occasions, afterwards, when that temper exploded; and then usually with adequate cause and excellent effect, as we shall see.

Further preparation of Washington for his career.

The defeat of the French in Canada led them to throw up the war; and, at twenty-six, Washington was sent again to the Ohio, to take over the abandoned Fort Duquesne; which he renamed Fort Pitt, thus giving the site and name to the present great city of Pittsburgh.

A few months before this last journey to the Ohio, Washington had ridden, with a friend, to Williamsburg, the colonial Capital, and stopped on the way to call on Martha Dandridge Custis, a handsome and wealthy young widow, with two children. Washington was instantly smitten. All his life Washington had great tenderness for the other sex. There had

Personal life.

been several early love-affairs: one for that "Lowland Beauty," to whom Washington wrote some very loving but rather clumsy verses; and who some biographers think was the girl afterwards marrying one of the Virginia Lees, and becoming the mother of Light Horse Harry Lee, Washington's beloved young comrade of the Revolution and the father of Robert E. Lee. It is, further, one of the quaint facts of Washington's later biography that, after attending any ball or other social function, especially on his presidential tours, he carefully noted down in his *Diary* the number of handsome ladies present. One reads: "There were upwards of 100 ladies. Their appearance was elegant, and many of them very handsome."* Again: "Went to an Assembly, where there was at least an hundred handsome and well dressed Ladies."* "At half after seven I went to the Assembly, where there were about 75 well dressed, and many of them very handsome ladies—among whom (as was also the case at the Salem and Boston assemblies) were a greater proportion with much blacker hair than are usually seen in the Southern States."*

Washington's appreciation of the other sex.

Diary comments of the New England journey.

The above comments are all from Washington's New England tour. On his Southern journey, he is even more enthusiastic: "Was visited about 2 o'clock, by a great number of the most respectable ladies of Charleston—the first honor of the kind I had ever

Diary entries of the Southern tour.

* Washington, *Diaries*, Vol. IV, pp. 38, 40, 45.

experienced and it was as flattering as it was singular".* "Dined with a very large Company at the Governor's, and in the evening went to a Concert at the Exchange at wch. there were at least 400 ladies the number and appearance of wch. exceeded any thing of the kind I had ever seen."* "In the evening went to a very elegant dancing Assembly at the Exchange, at which were 256 elegantly dressed and handsome ladies."* One recognizes that, North and South, all the ladies present at a social gathering were handsome, in the appreciative eyes of George Washington.

Marriage with Martha Dandridge Custis.

At the call on Martha Custis, however, Washington was completely taken. He stayed long past the hour intended, returned from the Capital as quickly as possible; engagement followed in a few days' time, and marriage, some months later, as Washington approached the age of twenty-seven. His marriage brought him a large increase of property in both land and slaves, thus further extending and assuring his growing financial fortune.

Washington as husband, and as father to his step-children and step-grandchildren.

Washington was a devoted and thoughtfully courteous husband, through all the years of his life, and an affectionate father to his step-children. When the daughter died, in young womanhood, after her long and sad affliction, Washington grieved as if she had been his own. The boy grew up to manhood, married, much earlier than his foster-father thought wise, and

* Washington, *Diaries*, Vol. IV, pp. 172, 173.

had four children. He gave his step-father considerable trouble and anxiety, during his adolescent years; and Washington handled him with as much affection as an own father could have shown, and rather more wisdom. After Jack Custis's death, the last year of the Revolution, Washington showed the same combination of affection and wisdom toward the step-grandchildren, adopting two of them as his own, after he had become convinced he was not to have a direct child. His letters to the young Washington Custis, full of wise counsel, show what serious thought he gave to the problems of the youth's restless adolescence. Compare, for instance, the following, interesting further as giving Washington's view of the wise conduct of life:

Letters to G. W. Parke Custis, who was to be Robert E. Lee's father-in-law.

Washington's rules and advice for his step-grandson.

"System in all things should be aimed at; for in execution it renders everything more easy.

"If now and then, of a morning before breakfast, you are inclined by way of change, to go out with a gun, I shall not object to it; provided you return by the hour we usually set down to that meal.

Emphasis on system and order.

"From breakfast, until about an hour before dinner (allowing for dressing and preparing for it, that you may appear decent) I shall expect you will confine yourself to your studies, and diligently attend to them; endeavoring to make yourself master of whatever is recommended to, or required of you.

"While the afternoons are short, and but little interval between rising from dinner and assembling for tea, you may employ that time in walking, or any other recreation.

"After tea, if the studies you are engaged in require

it, you will no doubt perceive the propriety and advantage of returning to them, until the hour of rest.

"Rise early, that by habit it may become familiar, agreeable, healthy and profitable. It may, for a while, be irksome to do this, but that will wear off; and the practice will produce a rich harvest forever thereafter; whether in public or private walks of life.

An important rule for family happiness!

"Make it an invariable rule to be in place (unless extraordinary circumstances prevent it) at the usual breakfasting, dining and tea hours. It is not only disagreeable, but it is also very inconvenient for servants to be running here and there, and they know not where, to summon you to them, when their duties, and attendance on the company who are seated, render it improper.

"Saturday may be appropriated to riding; to your gun, and other proper amusements.

View of the right use of time.

"Time disposed of in this manner, makes ample provision for exercise, and every useful or necessary recreation; at the same time that the hours allotted for study, *if really applied to it* instead of running up and down stairs, and wasted in conversation with anyone who will talk with you, will enable you to make considerable progress in whatever line is marked out for you, and that you may do it, is my sincere wish."*

Circumstances of Washington's first election as burgess.

The year before his marriage, Washington had been a candidate for the office of burgess, or member of the Virginia Assembly, and had been defeated. The following year he stood again; and learning by experience, adopted the conventional campaigning methods of those days. The number of constituents to be conciliated was small, as a considerable property

---

* Washington, Letter of January 7th, 1798, to George Washington Parke Custis: *Writings*, Vol. XIII, pp. 436, 437.

qualification was required to permit one to vote in colonial Virginia. Washington kept the account of his campaign expenses carefully with his own hand, as, indeed, he scrupulously kept all his accounts, through all the years. That record of campaign expenses is interesting reading today. The first item is "40 Gallons of Rum Punch", the second is "15 Gallons of Wine"; and the list goes through some fifteen items, all of drinkables. Evidently the modest flower of Washington's candidacy was not allowed to wither from the drought!

Reception by the Assembly.

This time he was elected—almost unanimously. He entered the Assembly; and, to his surprise and embarrassment, was greeted with an address of welcome and thanks, for his eminent military services to the Colony. Always a modest and even timid man, under such circumstances, Washington rose to reply, and was speechless! After waiting a moment, the presiding officer said: "Sit down, Mr. Washington, your modesty equals your valor, and that surpasses the power of any language I possess." The incident is characteristic, revealing Washington as a man of deeds, rather than words, though later he learned to use words, too, effectively, using them sometimes like bullets, as we shall see.

Washington's modesty.

Sixteen years of service as burgess.

For sixteen consecutive years Washington was a burgess in the Virginia Assembly, closing that service only to take command of the army of the Revolution. During these years, he was also on the Church Vestry, which had much to do with local government in Virginia: far too much, till Thomas Jefferson changed all that.

Through this long period, Washington was living quietly at Mount Vernon, developing his estates. It is interesting that, as farmer and business man, he showed the same grasp of objective facts, of things as they are, that marked him as military leader and statesman. Mount Vernon was a little world in itself, as indeed, a great estate had to be in those days.

Life at Mount Vernon during these years.

Washington, like nearly all the intelligent men born under it, was earnestly opposed to the institution of slavery. He recognized that it was both uneconomic and immoral. His view was that further importation of slaves should be stopped by law, and those in captivity should be gradually emancipated. In his Will, he provided that his own slaves should be freed, on the death of his widow. That will give sufficiently Washington's views on slavery. Nevertheless, again like other intelligent men born into the institution, Washington accepted it and did the best he could with it. He was a severe but just slave-master, getting the best results possible out of the uneconomic slave labor. Among his slaves and hired laborers were carpenters, masons, wheelwrights, weavers: artisans of all kinds. Washington gave constant, rigorous personal supervision to the running of his estates. His flour was accepted on the British market without inspection, recognized as the best that came from America. In spite of his long absences from home, in his country's service, Washing-

Handling of slaves and view of slavery.

Washington as farmer and business man.

ton was so successful in handling his estates and business affairs that he died worth perhaps a half million dollars, which means that he was one of the richest men in America; and all his wealth had been accumulated by intelligent labor and honest business methods.

Accumulating a large fortune.

Meantime, the storm-clouds were gathering for the great conflict that was to come. After the French and Indian war, Britain found herself heavily burdened with debt, a considerable part of which had been accumulated in the war to defend the Colonies. It seemed only just, therefore, that the colonists should be taxed to help pay this debt. To this the colonists did not object. On the contrary, they were most loyal, not only to the home land but to the King and Crown. It is usually true that colonials, seeing the home country across the distance and through the mist of sentiment, develop a peculiarly warm attachment to it. If you look for the strongest devotion to the British King today, you will find it, not in England, but in Canada; and often the Irish in America seem more enthusiastically attached to the Emerald Isle than those who still live on the "ould sod."

The gathering storm.

Attachment of the colonists to the home land.

The further view of the British statesmen, however, was that the Colonies were Crown possessions: the King owning them, or granting them to proprietors, could do as he pleased with them, through his ministers and Parliament. If he needed money, he could take it from the Colonies, by arbitrary taxation measures, without consulting the inhabitants. It was this

Causes of the Revolution.

that aroused the intense resentment of the colonists. They had come voluntarily to the new world, endured its hardships, fought the Indians, conquered the wilderness, each man forced to depend upon himself, with such compelled cooperation as he could carry out with his scattered neighbors. The result was the development of strong, free individuals, clinging most tenaciously to their rights as English freemen: those rights wrung slowly from tyranny, through a thousand years of struggle in England. It was not taxation they resented, but *taxation without representation.*

Consequences of viewing the Colonies as Crown possessions.

The claim of the colonists to the same rights as their brothers in England,

Similarly, they resented the seizing and carrying to England for trial, of men accused of crime, especially political offenses; thus denying them their traditional British right to a trial by a jury of their own peers. The home government further cynically used the colonies as a dumping ground for criminals of all types, to the exasperation and injury of the inhabitants.

To understand how these iniquitous measures could be perpetrated, one must remember that the British public service was, at the time, shockingly corrupt. The colonies were viewed largely as political "plums," to be used to reward King's favorites or successful politicians. It is probable that the British public service was then as corrupt as ours ever has been; and that is a large statement. Afterwards, Britain cleaned house, more thoroughly than we ever have;

Corruption of the British public service.

but the corruption of her public service was one cause of Britain's loss of her Colonies.

The Stamp Act of 1765.

Needing money, and acting on the theory of the Colonies as royal grants or possessions, the British government, in 1765, passed the Stamp Act, requiring taxation stamps on all legal documents, newspapers, pamphlets and other articles; and denying jury trial to offenders, at the discretion of prosecutors. Bundles of the stamped documents were sent over to the various Colonies, and agents appointed for their sale.

Effect upon the Colonies.

The result was an outburst of indignation throughout the Colonies. Public meetings of protest were held; and in some instances the stamped papers were seized and burned in public bonfires. The colonists vowed they would risk the legality of their deeds, wills and marriage licenses; but they would not buy the stamped papers. The resentment culminated in the Stamp Act Congress, called by Massachusetts and held in New York, with delegates from nine colonies. It formulated a Declaration of Rights and Grievances, with a petition to King and Parliament.

The Stamp Act Congress, meeting Oct. 7th, 1765.

Repeal of the Stamp Act, with further imposition of "taxation without representation."

The falling off in trade with the colonies was so great that British merchants brought sufficient pressure to bear on Parliament to cause the repeal of the Act; but in the rescinding, its principle was reaffirmed. Then Britain tried less direct methods. She had forbidden the colonists to manufacture articles made in Britain or to purchase these and other imports, except from British merchants, and transported in British ships. Then the needed commodities were taxed and sent over: tea, widely used in the colonies, was a conspicuous example.

Again there was an uproar of protest. Washington's own vigorous statement well illustrates the colonial attitude:

> "What is it we are contending against? Is it against paying the duty of three pence per pound on tea because burdensome? No, it is the right only we have all along disputed. * * * I think the Parliament of Great Britain hath no more right to put their hands into my pocket, without my consent, than I have to put my hands into yours for money".*

Attitude of Washington.

In May, 1769, the Virginia Assembly passed resolutions of protest against the British treatment of Massachusetts. The Assembly was promptly dissolved by the Royal Governor; but the members met at Raleigh's Tavern, near by, and passed a series of resolutions, of which the chief item was an agreement not to buy tea or other taxed articles. Many, of course, did not fulfill the agreement; they wanted tea, shrugged their shoulders and bought it; but Washington kept the resolution with consistent fidelity.

Resolutions of the Virginia burgesses in 1769.

The storm gathered rapidly. In December, 1773, came the Boston "Tea Party": not content with refusing to buy the tea, a band of masked men boarded the British ships in Boston harbor, and threw the

The Boston "Tea Party."

* Washington, in Letter to Bryan Fairfax, Mt. Vernon, July 20, 1774: *Writings*, Vol. II, pp. 422-424.

boxes of taxed tea into the water. This was direct violation of law; and early in 1774 Britain closed the Port of Boston and sent troops over to occupy the City.

Call for a union of the Colonies.

Virginia joined with Massachusetts in calling for a union of the Colonies. Representatives from all counties of Virginia met at Williamsburg, August 1st, 1774, to choose delegates for a Continental Congress. It was here that Washington made what was described as, "The most eloquent speech ever made." It is so brief it can be quoted entire. Washington stood up and said:

Washington's most eloquent speech.

> "I will raise a thousand men, subsist them at my own expense, and march myself at their head for the relief of Boston".*

That was his "most eloquent speech": a man of deeds, rather than words; but able to use words truly like bullets, when he wished to use them.

The first Continental Congress.

Washington was chosen, with Patrick Henry and others, a delegate to the first Continental Congress, which began sitting in Philadelphia, September, 1774. It drew up a Declaration of Colonial Rights, its Addresses to the King and People of Great Britain; and the delegates returned home. Washington spent the next months raising and drilling troops: he knew that war was coming.

Early in 1775, a Convention was held at Richmond, to choose delegates for a second Continental

* Ford, *The True George Washington*, p. 268.

Congress. Washington was present and heard Patrick Henry's most flaming speech. Again chosen a delegate, he went to Philadelphia, arriving in early May. Lexington had already been fought. Washington's first act was to call on the already aged Benjamin Franklin. He then went to the Congress; and it was John Adams, of Massachusetts, who realizing that Boston was the storm-center, and that something must be done to win the full support of the Southern Colonies, urged the appointment of Washington as Commander-in-Chief of the American forces. Congress accepted the proposal and appointed him. Washington was very modest about accepting: he wished a better man had been chosen; but, appointed, he would accept, on condition that he receive no pay for his services, but only a reimbursement of such funds as he might expend in the cause.

The second Congress.

Washington chosen Commander-in-Chief. Attitude in accepting.

He hastened across the country toward Boston, arriving at Cambridge, July 2nd, 1775. Bunker Hill had already been fought. When Washington learned of the battle, he asked, "Did they fight?"; and when told that they did fight, that those raw minute men stood up and drove the British regulars back, time after time, until exhausted ammunition compelled retreat, Washington breathed a sigh of relief. He was sure now that, however long and bloody the struggle might be, the end was to be complete independence.

Bunker Hill: "Did they fight?"

So on July 3rd, 1775, traditionally under the Old Elm, on Cambridge Common, Washington took command of the "Army of the Revolution." The phrase sounds big; but think what that army was: raw minute men, volunteering for one month, two months, at most three months. When the month or two was up, they went home to till their farms, look after their families, while other men came up, volunteering for the next month or two. Imagine making an army out of stuff like that! They had splendid courage, but no discipline; and then, they elected their officers. Now, you can do that in politics, with considerable cost, but you cannot do it in war. Then, too, they had no powder! If the British had not been so dilatory, they could have wiped out or scattered Washington's little army before it was sufficiently equipped to fight.

Taking command. Character of the "Army of the Revolution."

Delays and preparations.

Emissaries were sent through the Colonies. What powder there was, was gathered together; powder mills were established. The few guns, captured by Ethan Allan, at Ticonderoga, were hurried across the country to Boston: it was eight months before Washington felt strong enough to make the first move. In March, 1776, he was ready. On the night of the 4th, he started a cannonade to deceive the British; swiftly moved his troops up to Dorchester Heights; during the dark hours, entrenchments were hastily constructed; and the next morning Lord Howe found Washington's guns frowning over the city of Boston. Futile efforts were made to dislodge the Americans. Lord Howe realized that he was

Dorchester Heights.

Evacuation of Boston, March 17th, 1776.

trapped; and on March 17th, took ship with his army and sailed away.

It has always interested me that the evacuation of Boston occurred on St. Patrick's Day. Evacuation Day is, as you know, a State Holiday in Massachusetts; and Boston, as everyone is aware, has a large Irish population. The resulting joint celebration of Evacuation Day and St. Patrick's Day in Boston, is something long to be remembered. One really wonders, sometimes, whether certain of those celebrating do not actually believe that St. Patrick drove the British out of Boston, as he drove the snakes out of Ireland!

Well, Lord Howe had sailed away. It was Washington's problem to guess whither; and he guessed rightly: New York: that was to be the next point of attack. So Washington hurried across the country, his army following; but Washington went on, from New York to Philadelphia, to urge his views of the struggle on the Continental Congress.

Washington's view of the conflict and its significance.

Washington, our first American, was already thinking in terms of a *great, united and independent* America. Understand, most men did not think that way at the time. John Adams and Samuel Adams: yes; Thomas Jefferson, the young stripling Hamilton, some delegates of the Continental Congress: yes; but most men, even patriots, were thinking, "We will get rid of these iniquitous taxes, and quit." That was particularly the attitude of the well to do. You know, Wealth doesn't like war, anyway, unless it is unduly profiting by it: there is too much interference with business. Moreover, the idea of a republic had not yet come to general consciousness. There was wide devotion to the King and Crown. So the common attitude was, we will fight to get these unjust taxes removed and our rights as English freemen restored, and stop. Not so George Washington: he was convinced that the struggle must be fought through to complete independence.

Attitude of wealth toward the war.

He and those who thought with him urged their views on the Continental Congress, to final success; and the Declaration of Independence was adopted by the delegates and signed; traditionally, on the late afternoon of July 4th, 1776. It was the charter of American liberties, the birth right of the infant nation. Five days later, Washington read it to his troops on Long Island, amid great enthusiasm.

The Declaration of Independence.

Lord Howe had landed 30,000 troops on Long Island, well trained and equipped to the minute. Washington had, perhaps, 20,000 poorly trained, inadequately equipped, a fourth of them unfit for service. He had to risk a battle. Why? Because he was not only military leader, but head of the American cause, and was compelled to consider other than purely military factors. The battle was required to strengthen the American morale, and awaken the people to the fact that a war was on. So Washington risked the Battle of Long Island, in September; and was completely defeated; his whole army being left in danger of destruction.

The battle of Long Island.

Fortunately, there followed a night of dense fog. Washington commandeered every boat in the bay; and the whole army was got across the river, to New York and temporary safety, during the dark hours of the night. Nine thousand men crossed in eight hours, Washington leaving Brooklyn in the last boat.

Escape of the defeated army.

The British moved up the river; and began cannonading about where 34th Street is now. The Americans were driven to panic. Washington rode among the fleeing troops, rallied them; and Aaron Burr, a young officer, knowing a goat path over the hills, led them up to the wilderness of Haarlem Heights; while Lord Howe landed and went to dinner with Mrs. Murray, on Murray Hill.

There followed the Battle of Haarlem Heights, the fighting centering near where Grant's tomb stands today, when again Washington proved that British regulars could be defeated.

Haarlem Heights.

Lord Howe spent several weeks trying to outflank Washington; but he was dealing with too shrewd a military strategist. Washington moved swiftly across to White Plains, where a drawn battle followed.

White Plains.

Then Washington, with 5,000 men, crossed the Hudson to protect Philadelphia. He had wished to surrender Fort Washington, but Congress forbade it: an early instance of the interference of politicians with military affairs, usually so disastrous. Thus the Fort was taken, and 3000 men unnecessarily lost to the American cause. Meanwhile Lord Cornwallis and 6000 men scaled the Palisades, captured the supplies at Fort Lee, and followed the trail of the American army.

The masterly retreat across New Jersey.

Washington's retreat across New Jersey was a strategic masterpiece. Again and again he got his little army across one and another of the four New Jersey rivers just in time, finally over the Delaware to temporary safety. With his losses and the expiration of enlistments, his force had dwindled to 3000 men. The American cause seemed lost; and many, in New York and New Jersey, even patriots, were accepting Lord Howe's offer of amnesty. Even members of the Continental Congress gave up hope. Not so, George Washington: at this darkest hour, he wrote to his brother in Virginia:

Washington's view at the darkest hour.

Letter to a brother in Virginia.

> "You can form no idea of the perplexity of my situation. No man, I believe, ever had a greater choice of difficulties, and less means to extricate himself from them. However, under a full persuasion of the justice of our cause, I cannot entertain an Idea, that it will finally sink, tho' it may remain for some time under a cloud."*

Two days later he wrote the Continental Congress, having almost exceeded his authority, in striving to save the cause:

Letter to Congress Dec. 20th, 1776.

The soul of Washington.

> "It may be thought that I am going a good deal out of the line of my duty, to adopt these measures, or to advise thus freely. A character to lose, an estate

---

* Washington, in Letter to his brother, John Augustine Washington. Camp, near the Falls of Trenton, Dec. 18, 1776: *Writings*, Vol. V, pp. 111, 112.

to forfeit, the inestimable blessing of liberty at stake, and a life devoted, must be my excuse."*

Those words are the soul of George Washington.

He saw, however, that something must be done, or the cause was lost; and he planned what he hoped would be a decisive blow, for Christmas Eve. Since Congress dealt directly with the generals under him, he did not have adequate authority, to court martial, for instance, those disobeying him. The result was that four generals failed him. Gates, who hated him, anyway, and afterwards conspired for his disgrace and dismissal, deliberately disobeyed orders, and went to see Congress. Putnam remained in Philadelphia. A third general marched away from the assigned field, instead of toward it; while a fourth remained in camp. Only General John Sullivan obeyed orders and advanced along the river on the Jersey shore. Washington, as every school boy knows, on Christmas Eve, 1776, in a storm of sleet and rain, with the Delaware filled with blocks of floating ice, got his own little army across the river to the Jersey side. By four o'clock, Christmas morning, all his troops were landed. Sullivan sent a message that his men's arms were wet, and they could not fight. Washington sent back word: "Tell your general, then, to use the bayonet. Trenton must be taken."

Crossing the Delaware.

Trenton was occupied by Hessians: mercenary

* Washington, in a letter to the President of Congress. Camp, above Trenton Falls, Dec. 20, 1776: *Writings*, Vol. V, p. 116.

troops, rented by the Landgrave of Hesse-Cassel and other German princes, to the British King. Mercenaries are usually the most brutal of soldiers. They have no interest in the cause, on either side, but are out for money, plunder, loot. The Hessians had been particularly cruel to the inhabitants, and were bitterly hated. Those in Trenton had celebrated Christmas Eve in royal fashion and gone to bed, mostly drunk. Their commander, Colonel Rahl, it is said, had received a warning letter from a New Jersey Tory; but, in the celebration, had put it in his pocket, to read the next morning; and that morning, at eight o'clock, Washington struck. He completely surprised the Hessians, won a brilliant victory, took a thousand prisoners and eleven cannon; and got his little army back across the river again to safety.

The battle of Trenton.

At this point, Lord Cornwallis disembarked 7000 men, and started across New Jersey, to wipe out Washington's miserable little army. Did you ever hear words like those? Yes, early in the World War, the Kaiser, you recall, sent word to his generals at the front, to "Destroy General French's contemptible little British army." It was the same attitude in the two instances.

Cornwallis crossing New Jersey to destroy Washington's small army.

Washington waited at the Assanpink River. Cornwallis attempted to storm the bridge; was repulsed, and decided to wait until the next morning. That was all that Washington wanted. He has usually been regarded as a Fabian in military affairs, always fighting a retreating battle. I believe that is an ut-

Character of Washington as a military captain.

ter misreading of his character. He was a Fabian only when he could be nothing else; but when he had a chance, when he had half a chance, he struck with Napoleonic swiftness and audacity. So, at the Assanpink, he left his camp fires burning to deceive the British; moved up the river and crossed above; came around the British force and struck at Princeton. Three regiments had been left here, by Cornwallis, as rear guard, with the troops retreating to Princeton after the battle of Trenton. Washington surprised them; won a complete victory; and the country's cause was saved.

The battle of Princeton.

Frederick the Great is reported to have said that this New York-New Jersey campaign of Washington's was "the greatest campaign of the century." Well, Frederick the Great knew all there was to be known about military affairs. Whether he made the statement or not, the campaign was certainly a masterpiece. It won, for Washington, five months breathing space, with head-quarters at Morristown, New Jersey, to whip a new army into shape. It strengthened the morale of the people. It wakened, finally, the British to the fact that a war was really on. Hitherto, they had supposed that they were putting down sporadic insurrections; now they realized that they had a war to fight through; and at last adopted a comprehensive plan.

Significance of the New York-New Jersey campaign. View of Frederick the Great.

The British plan to split the country.

Better than any other modern people, the British have followed the old Roman maxim, "Divide and conquer." That was the plan now adopted; Burgoyne was sent down from the North, along Lake Champlain; Lord Howe was to handle the southern end; the aim being to split the country, on the line of the Hudson, and then conquer, in turn, the New England and the Southern Colonies.

The Burgoyne invasion.

Washington instantly saw the significance of the British strategy; made plans to resist the Burgoyne invasion, which were carried out by General Schuyler. At the last moment, however, Congress superseded Schuyler with Gates, who received the surrender, got the glory, and lost his head, in consequence, as we shall see.

Brandywine Creek.

Meantime, Howe with 100 ships and 18,000 soldiers, had sailed away; and, again, Washington had to guess whither. Once more he guessed rightly: Philadelphia: that would be the next point of attack. So he dropped down to the Delaware, marched through Philadelphia, to hearten the patriots and cow the Tories; and on September 11, 1777, risked a battle at Brandywine Creek. Howe had 18,000, perfectly equipped; Washington 11,000, ragged and motley. He was completely defeated. He held the British twelve days, coming twenty-six miles; but they were too strong, and on September 26th, Philadelphia was occupied.

Taking of Philadelphia.

Someone said to Franklin, in Paris, "So Howe has taken Philadelphia"; and Franklin, in one of those happy and pregnant witticisms, responded, "O no, Philadelphia has taken Howe"! That was just it: not only that the British officers, enjoying themselves among the Tory families of Philadelphia, neglected the campaign, but that the British plan of dividing their forces, and occupying one town and city after another, left too few men in the field to crush Washington's army, as they might otherwise have done.

The battle of Germantown.

On October 3rd, Washington surprised the enemy at Germantown: a battle admirably planned, but only partially successful. That he could fight at all is amazing; and the same month, Burgoyne surrendered his entire army of 5000 men, in the North, to General Gates. Congress ordered Washington to attack Howe in Philadelphia; and Washington refused, knowing that he had not men enough to do it successfully.

Results of Burgoyne's surrender to General Gates.

The result of this situation was that Gates, whose victory was merely the conclusion of General Schuyler's carrying out of Washington's plans, seemed to be the successful hero, while Washington apparently had failed. Gates was sure that he was the great man of America. Even members of the Continental Congress were deceived. The consequence was that Gates conspired with an adventurer, Conway, to get Washington dismissed and disgraced, and Gates appointed to the supreme command, with Conway as his right hand man. That "Conway Cabal", as we call it, almost succeeded! It was only Washington's absolute integrity and frank, straight-forward dealing that weathered the storm; but he did weather it. Conway was dismissed; and disappeared from the scene of history. Gates survived until the collapse of

The "Conway Cabal."

his disgraceful campaign in the South, when he, too, went the way of dishonorable schemers.

The bitter Winter at Valley Forge.

These events happened, moreover, during the darkest Winter of the war: that terrible Winter of ice and snow, 1777-78, when Washington had headquarters at Valley Forge. The soldiers were ragged and shoeless, leaving blood-stains on the snow, as they went from place to place. Washington literally wept over his men; made frantic appeals to Congress; but jealousies, incapacity and want of money gave little response. That an army stayed together at all, that terrible Winter, was due to the personal devotion of the men to George Washington, the first American.

Officers at Valley Forge.

Toward the close of the Winter the skies began to brighten. Washington, taking matters into his own hands, appointed General Nathanael Greene Quartermaster General. Supplies began to come in. There was a wonderful group of officers with Washington, that Winter at Valley Forge: La Fayette, twenty years old, Hamilton, twenty one, Light Horse Harry Lee, twenty-two, Benedict Arnold, Wayne, Knox, De Kalb, Stirling, Sullivan. Baron Steuben came over from Germany, with the last word in military training under Frederick the Great. He helped to whip an army into shape. A cavalry regiment was formed for Light Horse Harry Lee. The American skies were brightening.

The British in Philadelphia.

The British officers, meantime, were spending the Winter in a round of social pleasures, among the great Tory families of Philadelphia. In the Spring,

Lord Howe was recalled, and Clinton sent to replace him; and a beautiful Hall of Farewell was constructed, planned, if you please, by Captain André, later the Major André of the Arnold treason. The same night that this celebration was held in Philadelphia, Washington's troops crossed the Schuylkill and attacked the British outposts; and the same month news had come that France had definitely signed the treaty of alliance, recognizing our independence and joining us in the war against Britain. It was the turning point of the war. Most Americans, in fact, thought that France would now do the work for us; but not Washington. He saw that, if victory were to be worth while, we must win it for ourselves; otherwise, we should merely be vassals of France, instead of England, and in worse condition than before.

The French alliance as the turning point of the war.

The French alliance strengthened our morale and gave us desperately needed money; beyond that, there was little active help, till near the close of the war. On the other hand, the alliance brought new difficulties, which Washington met with consummate wisdom and skill.

Clinton, in view of the French alliance, decided to evacuate Philadelphia and withdraw to New York; and Washington thought he saw the opportunity for the decisive blow he had long been seeking to strike. He planned it for Monmouth Court House, New Jersey. General Charles Lee was to execute a rear attack, with Washington supporting it. Charles Lee

Defection of General Charles Lee.

had earlier been an officer in the British army; and had deep admiration for British regulars, with jealousy and distrust of Washington. Whether from fear or treachery, he deliberately disobeyed orders, ordering a retreat and marching away from the field, instead of toward it. The British fell upon his rear, and drove his troops to panic rout. Washington, learning the disastrous news, spurred his horse forward; amid a hail of bullets rallied the panic-stricken troops; gave General Charles Lee a stinging reprimand one would have loved to hear: one of the rare cases where Washington's naturally fierce temper exploded, with adequate cause and excellent result; and won a brilliant victory out of what promised to be utter defeat. Lee's defection, however, robbed him of the larger fruits of that victory; for Clinton got the bulk of his army off to New York and safety.

Battle of Monmouth.

Washington moved up to the Hudson again. There followed a year of skirmish fighting; the British sending maurauding parties into New Jersey and Connecticut, treating the inhabitants with merciless cruelty. Then they moved up the river, and took Stony Point and Verplanck Point. It looked as if they were again attempting to carry out their old plan, and split the country on the line of the Hudson.

The year with headquarters again on the Hudson.

The story is that Washington said to Wayne—"Mad Anthony" Wayne—"Will you storm Stony Point"; and Wayne responded, "I'll storm Hell, if you will plan it!" Well, Washington planned it. Stony Point was taken; then Verplanck Point.

Light Horse Harry Lee took Paulus Hook, now Jersey City: the American cause seemed brightening.

Character and career of Benedict Arnold.

The nadir was reached with the treason of Benedict Arnold. Arnold was a leader of daring courage. He had really saved his country's cause, in one of the early crises, with his little group of men, in the North. After the evacuation by Clinton, Washington left Arnold in command at Philadelphia. He married the daughter of a Tory family; was afterwards accused of wrong doing; brought before a court martial, sentenced only to a reprimand; but the sense of injury rankled in his breast. He was, moreover, selfishly ambitious, without Washington's beautiful modesty. The American cause seemed doomed, anyway; and he decided to sell us out. He induced Washington, who completely trusted him, to appoint him to the command of West Point; conspired to surrender it, on condition of receiving a large sum of money and a generalship in the British army; thus enabling the British to carry out their long cherished plan of splitting the country on the line of the Hudson. The correspondence between Arnold and Lord Clinton was carried by Major André. All arrangements were made; and Arnold was waiting for a chance to complete the surrender.

Circumstances of the Arnold treason.

It came in September, 1780, when Washington went to Hartford, Conn. Rochambeau, the second French Admiral to cross to help us, had been bottled up, by the British, at Newport. He would not land his 5000 men; was waiting for the reenforcing fleet, which the British prevented leaving the harbour of Brest, in France.

Washington's trip to meet Admiral Rochambeau at Hartford, Conn.

It was Hamilton who suggested to Washington: "We cannot go to see Rochambeau, and he will not come to see us; but can't we meet him half-way?" Washington liked the idea; arrangements for a conference at Hartford were made; and Washington, Hamilton and other aides started on horseback.

Major André's trip up the Hudson, for a final conference with Arnold.

As soon as they had gone, Arnold sent word that the hour for consummating the treason had come. Major André sailed up the Hudson, in the British war ship, Vulture, and dropped anchor in "Mother's Lap", as the bay just above Croton Point is still quaintly called. Leaving the ship, Major André crossed in a small boat to the west shore, and spent the night, conferring with Arnold, in the woods near Stony Point.

Just here is a bit of local history, contributed by our local Westchester County authority, which bridges a small gap in the histories, and seems to be authentic.

Our house stands on a plateau, looking across Mother's Lap and Croton Point, twenty miles down the Hudson. When the Vulture dropped anchor, two men, a half-breed Indian and a white man, are said to have been making cider, about where the house stands today: the place is still covered with apple orchards. They dropped their cider works; hitched up their team; drove to Peekskill, eight miles up the river, got the only available cannon; took it out and placed it in the woods, near the end of Croton Point. At dawn they fired one shot, and hit a spar of the British vessel. Here the histories take it up: the captain, believing his ship menaced by a masked battery, weighed anchor, and dropped down behind one of the great Hudson headlands. Major André, returning, could not find his ship; went back, crossed at Peekskill; came down by land, and was captured behind Tarrytown. It has always interested me that our home had probably this romantic connection with the frustration of the worst treason of the war.

The Vulture dropping down the river, causing Major André to return by land.

Washington and his aides reached the river in the early morning, returning from Hartford. Washington, who wanted to examine the West Point fortifications, said to Hamilton: "You young men go in and have breakfast with Mrs. Arnold; you are all in love with her, anyway!" During the breakfast, a messenger came with a paper which he placed in Arnold's hands: the American officer, to whom Major André had been turned over by the men arresting him, had stupidly sent André's letter direct to Arnold. Reading it, Arnold turned ashen gray, excused himself, got in a small boat, and was rowed away to the British war ship and shameful safety. A few moments later, a second breathless messenger came, with the treason papers found on Major André. These were placed in Hamilton's hands. It was Hamilton who gave them to Washington, on his return from the fortifications, Hamilton to whom Washington made his one despairing comment, "Whom can we trust

Frustration of the worst treason of the war.

now!" Washington took the needed measures for the protection of West Point; spent the night walking to and fro in the little room in the Inn; and the worst treason of the war was frustrated.

The French army joining Washington in July, 1781.

A few months later Washington had his opportunity for the decisive blow he had long been seeking to strike. Rochambeau finally lent his five thousand French soldiers, who joined Washington at Dobbs Ferry, early in July, 1781. To conceal his plan from the British, Washington began operations as if for an attack on New York; and then hastened South with the combined armies. The British had been carrying on a campaign in the Southern Colonies, which had gone against us, until Washington secured the appointment of General Nathanael Greene to the command. With La Fayette's help, Greene had driven the British into Virginia, where they were entrenched at Yorktown. Washington, having prevailed upon the French Admiral De Grasse to cut off the retreat by sea of the British, with the combined American and French armies, attacked them, storming the two redoubts; and on October 19th, 1781, Cornwallis surrendered his entire army of seven thousand men.

Hastening South for the decisive blow.

Yorktown.

Some days later, Clinton arrived in the bay with thirty five ships and seven thousand troops; but finding what had happened, turned about and sailed back to New York.

Washington's plans for continuing the struggle.

Most Americans believed the war was now over; but not Washington. He urged preparations and began planning for another campaign. Having made arrangements to protect the Southern Colonies from further British attack, he was called to Eltham by the death of his step-son, Jack Custis, who left a widow and four children. Going on to Philadelphia, Washington urged upon Congress the needed measures for continuing the conflict.

The Cornwallis surrender as really ending the war.

The war really was over, however. Britain was tired of it, and discouraged at the futility of six years of costly conflict. There had been a growth of sentiment recognizing the justice of the colonial cause, giving liberal statesmen increasing influence in England's councils. The King was eventually compelled to yield; and Britain finally acceded to the American demand for independence.

The dark period between the close of fighting and final peace.

It was a year and a half before peace was published; two years until the definite treaty was signed, and the British evacuated New York. The interim was a desperate time. Once the fighting had stopped, Congress found it almost impossible to get any more money, and so proposed to disband the troops unpaid. The result was a movement in the army to resort to force. It was only Washington's personal influence with his officers, in his earnest address to them at Newburgh on the Hudson, that forestalled that mutinous step. Washington was, meantime, urging Congress to just treatment of the army.

Congress and the army.

The movement to make Washington king.

Then came an underground plan among the officers to make Washington king. Now, understand, our people were not yet committed clearly to a Republic. They had fought for independence from

Britain; and were accustomed to the kingship idea, having only just shaken themselves loose from their absentee landlord king, across the water. Everyone saw the need for some stronger authority than the now nerveless and unsupported Continental Congress. The army had the power to enforce its wishes. All Washington needed to do was to do and say nothing; and he would have been made King of America, with no danger of the consequences that followed Napoleon's similar assumption of imperial power in France. When Washington learned of the plan, however, he peremptorily forbade it; showed his intense devotion to the principle of the Republic; and today, that we live in a Republic is due to George Washington, the first American!

Why we live in a Republic.

In November, 1783, the British left New York. Washington entered; and a farewell dinner was given him by his officers, at Fraunce's Tavern. It was a solemn occasion: there were tears in every eye as each officer clasped the hand of his beloved chief in silent farewell. Washington started South; stopped at Philadelphia to adjust his accounts with the Continental Congress. He had expended some seventy-five thousand dollars of his own money in the American cause. It would be necessary to multiply that five or ten times to get its equivalent in current wealth. This money was repaid Washington; but neither he nor his heirs ever received one cent for his eight years of service as Commander-in-Chief of the American forces.

The farewell to military service, and return to Mount Vernon.

From Philadelphia, he went on to Annapolis, where the Continental Congress was then assembled; and on December 23rd was received by the Congress, and with a solemn and brief address, resigned his commission. Thence he proceeded to Mount Vernon, arriving Christmas Eve, 1783, having not seen his home for eight years, except for three days, on his way to Yorktown in September, 1781.

With a sense of glad release, Washington resumed his life at Mount Vernon, as a Virginia country gentleman; but, of course, he could not escape public affairs. Things were going from bad to worse with the country, in those difficult years between the close of the war and the establishment of the federal government. Hamilton did the active work leading to the forming of a strong central government; but Washington influenced statesmen to a recognition of the need for it. He wrote letters to public men throughout the land. The burden of his counsel was expressed in the letter to the Governors of the States, written as the army was about to be disbanded. Since Washington supposed he was retiring permanently from public life, he spoke of this long, wise document as his legacy. In it, he characterized the situation, faced by the Country at the close of the Revolution.

Washington's service in moulding public opinion in favor of a federal government.

The letter to the Governors of the States: Washington's "Legacy."

> "It appears to me there is an option still left to the United States of America, that it is in their choice, and depends upon their conduct, whether they will be respectable and prosperous, or contemptible and miserable, as a nation. This is the time of their political

The dilemma at the close of the Revolution.

probation; this is the moment when the eyes of the whole world are turned upon them; this is the moment to establish or ruin their national character for ever; this is the favorable moment to give such a tone to our federal government, as will enable it to answer the ends of its institution, or this may be the ill-fated moment for relaxing the powers of the Union, annihilating the cement of the confederation, and exposing us to become the sport of European politics, which may play one State against another, to prevent their growing importance, and to serve their own interested purposes. For, according to the system of policy the States shall adopt at this moment, they will stand or fall; and by their confirmation or lapse it is yet to be decided, whether the revolution must ultimately be considered as a blessing or a curse; a blessing or a curse, not to the present age alone, for with our fate will the destiny of unborn millions be involved."*

Washington's view of the need for a strong central government.

In the same document, he urged as the first condition of the very existence of the nation, "An indissoluble union of the States under one federal head."† In a typical letter to John Jay, he said:

The burden of Washington's counsel.

"I do not conceive we can exist long as a nation without having lodged somewhere a power, which will pervade the whole Union in as energetic a manner as the authority of the State Governments extends over the several States. . . .

Letter to John Jay in 1783.

What astonishing changes a few years are capable of producing. I am told that even respectable characters speak of a monarchical form of government with-

* Washington, in Circular Letter to the Governors of all the States, on disbanding the Army, from Headquarters, Newburg, 8 June, 1783: *Writings*, Vol. X, pp. 256, 257.

† Ibid, p. 257.

out horror. From thinking proceeds speaking; then to acting is but a single step. But how irrevocable and tremendous! What a triumph for our enemies to verify their predictions! What a triumph for the advocates of despotism to find, that we are incapable of governing ourselves, and that systems founded on the basis of equal liberty are merely ideal and fallacious! Would to God, that wise measures may be taken in time to avert the consequences we have but too much reason to apprehend." *

Admirable psychology!

Hamilton finally succeeded in calling the Constitutional Convention to meet in Philadelphia, in 1787. Washington was chosen a delegate from Virginia; went reluctantly; was chosen presiding officer, and spoke but once from the floor; but his ideas deeply influenced the delegates.

The Constitutional Convention.

When, after the long wrangling, the compromise Constitution was finally signed, and accepted by eleven states, the first election was held under it. When the votes of the electoral college were counted, April 6, 1789, it was discovered that every vote was for Washington for President. In Washington's time, there was just one political party in the United States: it was the party of George Washington!

Washington's unanimous election as first President.

Washington was very reluctant to accept. His view was: "I may be something of a military man, but I am not a statesman; and this is not my job." Letters came to him from statesmen throughout the country, urging his acceptance, telling him he was

Attitude in accepting, and service as President.

* Washington, in Letter to John Jay, Mount Vernon, 1 August, 1786: *Writings*, Vol. XI, pp. 53-55.

the one man who could make the new government a living reality. Washington yielded; went to New York, then the capital; and immediately set about making the new presidential office worthy of respect. He personally planned the whole system of etiquette for the treatment of the President. His journey into New England was to impress the people with the fact that he was President of the whole nation; and his little contretemps with John Hancock, in Massachusetts, showed how tenacious he was that the President of all the people should be recognized as superior to the Governor of any fraction of the people.

The great first Cabinet.

His first Cabinet comprised: Jefferson, Secretary of State; Hamilton, for the Treasury; Knox, for War; and Randolph, Attorney General: a great Cabinet. He held the balance fairly between his leading Secretaries, Jefferson and Hamilton; but favored increasingly every one of Hamilton's vital measures to make the new government a living, growing organism. What those measures were, we shall study in the great career of Hamilton, who initiated them and fought them through to victory.

Washington's support of Hamilton's measures for strengthening the Federal Government.

When the first Congress assembled, Washington addressed it in person, both in his Inaugural and subsequently. John Adams followed his example; but Jefferson, who had a throat defect which prevented his speaking in public, sent in a written message. Other Presidents followed the lead of Jefferson, until Woodrow Wilson, who knew our history more intimately than any other President, rightly and wisely returned to the original example of Washington, addressing Congress in person.

In his first Address to Congress, after the Inaugural, Washington's initial demand was for an adequate military establishment for defense; his last was to urge action to support general knowledge and education, with the suggestion of a national university.

The Address at the assembling of Congress, January 8th, 1790.

Recognizing America's unique problem and opportunity, Washington was strongly convinced that, while maintaining friendly intercourse and commerce with all nations, we should scrupulously avoid entanglement in European politics, with their vicious balance of power alliances. When the difficulty over the vexing Genet affair arose, Washington issued his great Neutrality Proclamation, laying, for all time, the basis of our foreign policy.

Washington's view of international relations.

The Neutrality Proclamation.

Washington earnestly wished to retire from the presidency at the conclusion of his first term; but his feeling that his work was unfinished, with the universal demand that he continue, led him to serve for a second term. The unanimous re-election naturally pleased him, and indicated the attitude of the people toward him.

Washington's unanimous re-election.

With all the popular devotion to Washington, there developed, nevertheless, increasing opposition to the rapidly growing power of the federal government. This took shape in a more and more organized party, with opposing political tenets, rallying to itself, also, those who wished to continue a fast alliance with France, and thus resented the President's for-

The gradual organization of a party of opposition.

eign policy. The result was increasing attacks upon Federalist leaders, including even Washington, and finally focussing upon him. The malicious venom of certain of these attacks would do credit to the yellowest character-assassinating journalist of the present hour.

Virulent attacks upon Washington.

Washington was bitterly hurt by these attacks, and they wakened in him alarm for the Nation's future. He dreaded political party spirit as a menace, of which he solemnly warned the people in his great Farewell Address:

Attitude toward political parties.

> "I have already intimated to you the danger of Parties in the State, with particular reference to the founding of them on Geographical discriminations. Let me now take a more comprehensive view, and warn you in the most solemn manner against the baneful effects of the Spirit of Party, generally.
>
> This Spirit, unfortunately, is inseparable from our nature, having its root in the strongest passions of the human mind. It exists under different shapes in all Governments, more or less stifled, controlled, or repressed; but, in those of the popular form, it is seen in its greatest frankness, and is truly their worst enemy.

Washington's view of the danger in the Political Party Spirit.

> * * * * * *
>
> It serves always to distract the Public Councils, and enfeeble the Public administration. It agitates the community with ill-founded jealousies and false alarms, kindles the animosity of one part against another, foments occasionally riot and insurrection. It opens the doors to foreign influence and corruption, which finds

The style in the Farewell Address reminds that Hamilton formulated it; and the views expressed are his, as well as Washington's.

a facilitated access to the Government itself through the channels of party passions."*

Steadfastly, Washington refused to be regarded as leader of a party, serving as President of all the people, with single-minded devotion to the welfare of the Nation as a whole. The amazing fact of his career as statesman is that, realist as he was, shrewdly grasping things as they are, he was without a trace of shallow political opportunism, holding to principles with inflexible integrity.

Washington a realist, devoid of opportunism, and consistently obedient to ideals.

He waved aside the urging for a third term, peremptorily refusing to consider it; thus founding the tradition of only two terms for any one President: a tradition never subsequently successfully challenged.

Decisive refusal of a third term.

His Farewell Address to the American People, on finally leaving public life, was his second and greater "Legacy", a legacy of thoughtful wisdom and solemn warning. With the passage on party spirit, already quoted, perhaps the gravest counsel, in the light of the great conflict, which was afterwards to develop, concerned the Union. His words are almost a forecast of the Civil War:

Washington's greater legacy to the Nation.

> "The Unity of Government which constitutes you one people, is also now dear to you. It is justly so; for it is a main Pillar in the Edifice of your real independence; the support of your tranquillity at home; your peace abroad; of your safety; of your prosperity in

View of importance of the Union; warning to preserve it.

---

* Washington, in his *Farewell Address: Writings,* Vol. XIII, pp. 301-304.

every shape; of that very Liberty, which you so highly prize. But as it is easy to foresee, that, from different causes, and from different quarters, much pains will be taken, many artifices employed, to weaken in your minds the conviction of this truth; as this is the point in your political fortress against which the batteries of internal and external enemies will be most constantly and actively (though often covertly and insidiously) directed, it is of infinite moment that you should properly estimate the immense value of your national Union to your collective and individual happiness; that you should cherish a cordial, habitual, and immoveable attachment to it: accustoming yourselves to think and speak of it as of the Palladium of your political safety and prosperity; watching for its preservation with jealous anxiety; discountenancing whatever may suggest even a suspicion that it can in any event be abandoned, and indignantly frowning upon the first dawning of every attempt to alienate any portion of our Country from the rest, or to enfeeble the sacred ties which now link together the various parts."*

Almost a prophesy of the situation Lincoln faced.

Retiring again to the life of a country gentleman, at Mount Vernon, Washington was now the foremost man in America, indeed in the world. In consequence, his home was thronged with guests from all over the land and Europe, as well. He himself described the house as rather like a public inn, than a private dwelling. This condition, indeed, had developed increasingly from the close of the Revolution. Writing his Mother, in the winter before the Consti-

Late years at Mount Vernon.

The swarm of guests.

* Washington, in *Farewell Address: Writings,* Vol. XIII, pp. 286, 287.

tutional Convention, a letter that also throws interesting light on his relation to her, Washington said:

> "My house is at your service, and I would press you most sincerely and devoutly to accept it, but I am sure, and candor requires me to say, it will never answer your purposes in any shape whatever. For in truth it may be compared to a well resorted tavern, as scarcely any strangers who are going from north to south, or from south to north, do not spend a day or two at it. This would, were you to be an inhabitant of it, oblige you to do one of 3 things: 1st, to be always dressing to appear in company; 2nd, to come into the room in a dishabille, or 3rd, to be as it were a prisoner in your own chamber. The first you'ld not like; indeed, for a person at your time of life it would be too fatiguing. The 2nd, I should not like, because those who resort here are, as I observed before, strangers and people of the first distinction. And the 3rd, more than probably, would not be pleasing to either of us."*

Letter describing Washington's household and showing his relation to his Mother.

The increasing throng of visitors was generously welcomed, and entertained, as of old, with stately hospitality.

He was once more to be called from his retirement, however. When the threat of war with France came, over the XYZ Letters, President Adams appointed Washington Commander-in-Chief to raise an army; but the war scare blew over, and Washington returned home.

The brief late period of service as Commander-in-Chief.

In December, 1799, he had just finished his plans for the completion of Mount Vernon; and went out

* Washington in a letter to his Mother, Mt. Vernon, Feb. 15, 1787: *Writings*, Vol. XI, pp. 116, 117.

Circumstances of Washington's last illness and death.

to ride over his estate, as was his daily custom. A cold winter rain came on, and he returned chilled and wet to the skin; went to bed ill, and grew rapidly worse. He seems to have suffered from a particularly malignant form of laryngitis, which produces death by suffocation, as malignant croup sometimes does with children. We relieve that disease today by temporarily opening the wind-pipe; but probably not more than two or three physicians, in America, knew that difficult operation, at the time. The Doctors came; they bled him, taking away more than a quart of the precious blood he needed to fight the disease: they meant well; and so on December 14th, 1799, at the age of 67, Washington died, probably in much agony, practically strangled to death.

Summary of the character of Washington.

A great man, of many-sided activity, Washington evidenced the same balance, strong native intelligence and straight-forward achievement in every field. With utter integrity of character and unerring judgment of men, Washington's grasp of realities was equalled by his consistent devotion to ideas. A hearty eater and regular, temperate drinker, all his life, of impressive stature, phenomenal strength and enduring vigor, always with an eye for a handsome woman, loving the out-door sports of hunting, fishing and riding, Washington had all the natural passions strong in him, but well controlled. No lay figure, bronze or marble statue or graven image, but a vigorous, life-loving human being, Washington had, from the beginning, the vision of a great, united and independent America; and served that vision with unfaltering fidelity and selfless devotion to the day of his death. *Our first American,* he well deserved the eulogy of Light Horse Harry Lee, his beloved young comrade of the Revolution, who, invited by Congress to give the Memorial Address, spoke in it those memorable words, oft quoted, but which still define our conception of Washington, as indeed, "First in War, first in Peace, and first in the hearts of his countrymen."

The vision and service of our first American.

II

FRANKLIN: THE PRACTICAL AMERICAN

Franklin's part in making victory possible in the Revolution.

WASHINGTON led the country victoriously through the many trials of the Revolution, and inaugurated the Nation, serving his two terms as first President. Next to Washington, it was Benjamin Franklin who made success possible in the War for Independence, by winning and holding the sympathy and help of France. Entirely self-educated and self-made, the most many-sided in activity of all our great men, Franklin stands as the type of the practical American, for our whole history.

Friendship of Washington and Franklin.

The life-long friendship of Washington and Franklin is charmingly revealed in a paragraph of Franklin's Last Will. It reads:

Franklin's bequest to Washington.

> "My fine crab-tree walking-stick, with a gold head curiously wrought in the form of the Cap of Liberty, I give to my friend, and the friend of mankind, General Washington. If it were a sceptre, he has merited it, and would become it."*

The long period of history covered by Franklin's life.

Since Franklin was twenty-six years older than Washington, his life goes back much further into the Colonial period; but living to the age of eighty-

---

* Franklin, in his Last Will: *Complete Works*, Vol. X, pp. 226, 227.

four, and dying only nine years before Washington, his career covered the whole period of the Revolution, into the time of Washington's first administration.

The contrast in background of life and early environment, between the two great leaders, is impressive: Washington, the Virginia aristocrat, early a large landed proprietor and slave owner; Franklin, reared in humblest circumstances, descended, as the name indicates, from sturdy English freeholders, who had occupied the same thirty acres of land, in England, for three hundred consecutive years, the eldest son, for many generations, traditionally becoming a blacksmith.

Contrasting inheritance of Washington and Franklin.

Ancestry of Franklin.

Franklin's father, Josiah, came over from England about 1685, with his wife and three children, settling in Boston. Four more children were born, during the next four years; and then the wife died. Six months later, Josiah Franklin married again. His second wife was Abiah Folger, daughter, Franklin says, of one of the first settlers in New England, a surveyor, who wrote verses, loved books, and was a liberal in thought. By his second marriage, Josiah Franklin had ten more children, making seventeen in all. The colonies were in great need of population, in those days, and Josiah Franklin seems to have been a thoroughly patriotic citizen. Franklin was the fifteenth child and tenth son of his father, born in Milk Street, Boston, just opposite the Old South Church, January 17th, 1706. He outlived all his family, except one sister, and was the only

Josiah Franklin's family.

one of his tribe to attain distinction, achieved through his own unaided efforts. Franklin, throughout his life and in his bequests was most generous in assisting financially his numerous relatives, especially the surviving sister.

The father had developed a small soap and candle making business in Boston. He conversed well, sang, and played the violin, for his own pleasure and, we trust, that of his family. With the large brood of children, the household, if humble, must have been a happy one. Franklin's schooling was most meager: a scant two years; and then, at ten, he had to go to work in his father's shop, to help out the family. He was, however, a natural student, from the beginning. He says he could not remember when he learned to read, it was earlier than his earliest recollection. By the age of twelve, he was reading every book he could get his hands upon. His first book was *Pilgrim's Progress:* interesting, how many of our great men started with that. It so impressed him that he saved his pennies and bought all of Bunyon's writings. Having absorbed these, he traded them for Burton's *Historical Collections,* a more pretentious work. From his father's few books, he had Plutarch's *Lives,* De Foe's *Essay Upon Projects* and Cotton Mather's *Essays to Do Good.* This last, he says, deeply influenced his character.

Meager schooling.

Franklin a born student. His early reading.

For a half century of Franklin's long life we have a fascinating record in his *Autobiography.* The larger part was written during his third stay in

England, at the age of sixty-five; it was continued during his residence in France, at seventy-eight; and the concluding pages were written at eighty-two, after his return to Philadelphia. It is thus a typical autobiography, written late and telling the major life-story. It is, further, one of the really great autobiographies, in which the style is the man. To give the color of that style, let me quote a portion of the opening passage. It is addressed to his son, William:

His *Autobiography* as the great text for Franklin's life.

> "Dear Son: I have ever had pleasure in obtaining any little anecdotes of my ancestors . . . Imagining it may be equally agreeable to you to know the circumstances of my life, many of which you are yet unacquainted with, and expecting the enjoyment of a week's uninterrupted leisure in my present country retirement, I sit down to write them for you. To which I have besides some other inducements. Having emerged from the poverty and obscurity in which I was born and bred, to a state of affluence and some degree of reputation in the world, and having gone so far through life with a considerable share of felicity, the conducing means I made use of, which with the blessing of God so well succeeded, my posterity may like to know, as they may find some of them suitable to their own situations, and therefore fit to be imitated.

Opening passage of the *Autobiography*.

> That felicity, when I reflected on it, has induced me sometimes to say, that were it offered to my choice, I should have no objection to a repetition of the same life from its beginning, only asking the advantages authors have in a second edition to correct some faults of the first. So I might, besides correcting the faults, change some sinister accidents and events of it for others more favorable. But though this were denied, I should still

accept the offer. Since such a repetition is not to be expected, the next thing like living one's life over again seems to be a recollection of that life, and to make that recollection as durable as possible by putting it down in writing.

Hereby, too, I shall indulge the inclination so natural in old men, to be talking of themselves and their own past actions."*

Franklin's vital style as characteristic of the man.

Note the virile style, with full, balanced sentences: contrasting with the poor little choppy sentences, and phrases used as sentences, in much of our current writing; the apparent aim of which is to enable the tired business man to read without thinking. Franklin's vigorous writing challenges thought and stimulates reflection.

Buoyant, optimistic temperament.

One is also impressed with the warm, optimistic love of life. He would gladly live his life over again: O, eliminating some painful chapters, if permitted; but even without that privilege, he would live it again.

Franklin's abundant humor, an important element in his life equipment.

With this quality is the abundant sense of humor, the saving grace in Franklin's character: without it, he might easily have become a moral prig or a religious fanatic. Humor, which is the other side of ethical good taste, gave Franklin his sanity and balance, his instinctive sense of things in right relation.

Significance of Franklin's vanity.

In the passage quoted, note further the element of personal vanity. Yes, Franklin had that characteristic; and doubtless it helped him over many hard

---

* Franklin, opening passage of his *Autobiography,* written at sixty-five, while in England: *Complete Works,* Vol. I, pp. 29, 30.

places in the road; but he never allowed it to interfere with his devoted service of his country's cause.

Franklin did not like the soap and candle business. Early developing skill and liking for swimming and boating, Franklin wanted to go to sea; but his father forbade that. Recognizing his bookish tastes, the father wished to make him a minister of religion; but there was not money enough for the requisite education. So, as the nearest approach to a bookish career, the father decided on the printer's trade. That does not seem to be a very close approximation to a literary life; but it was the best the father could do. Thus, at twelve, Franklin was apprenticed to his brother, James, who was ten years older, and who had returned from England the year before, with a press and types, and set up a printing business in Boston. The brother was to feed, clothe and house him; Franklin's labor was to be his brother's till twenty-one, though he was to receive journeyman's wages the last year. Rather hard conditions, one would think, for a boy's start in life! One wonders sometimes what boys of these days would do were they compelled to submit to such conditions. We have lately been considering passing an amendment to the Constitution, giving an absentee body, that recently has rather discredited itself, the national Congress, the right to prohibit all labor of young people under eighteen: rather a dangerous authority to concede to such a body! Certainly, if young persons do not learn to work hard before they are eighteen, they will never learn in this life; and strong,

Apprenticed to his brother, as printer.

Conditions of the apprenticeship.

efficient character undoubtedly developed under the hard conditions of those earlier days.

Struggles for education.

Franklin now had wider access to books. He made the acquaintance of a book-stall keeper, and got the privilege of borrowing a book just as the shop closed at night, on condition of returning it exactly at the opening hour in the morning. Thus he frequently read most of the night to finish a book in time for its required return. At this time, he still felt that he ought to go to church, and his father was insistent that he should; but Franklin says he really did not have time; for Sundays, the noon hours and evenings were his only times to read.

Admirable use of the *Spectator Papers* in acquiring an English style.

He came upon a volume of the *Spectator Papers,* the third, and at that early age was already able to recognize its worth in thought and excellence of style. Franklin saw in this book an opportunity to improve his own use of English. So he would take one of the *Spectator Papers;* jot down hints of what it contained; wait until he had forgotten the original, and then write out an essay of his own from his notes. This he compared with the original, correcting the faults he discovered. He found his vocabulary meager, and thought he might have had a wider use of words had he continued his early begun habit of writing verses. Therefore he turned some of the essays into verse; and, after a time, converted them into prose again, and then made a fresh comparison with the original. Naturally, he discovered many faults; but occasionally, he modestly says, he thought he had improved somewhat upon the original; and this encouraged him to hope that he "might possibly in time come to be a tolerable English writer," of which he was "extremely ambitious." He fully achieved his hope, as we see. The whole passage, in the *Autobiography,* is recommended to any young student who wishes to improve his mastery of English.

Vegetarianism and frugality. Franklin's devotion to study.

At sixteen, Franklin was converted to Vegetarianism, chiefly on moral grounds, through a book that he read. Discovering that a frugal vegetarian diet was quiet inexpensive, Franklin proposed to his brother to give him one half of the money his food cost; and he would board himself. The brother, glad to save half the expense, of course accepted. Franklin took the one half, and boarded himself on one half of that amount, using the remaining quarter of the food expense to buy books. Surely, this is a supreme illustration of his devotion to study!

The typical development of an Eighteenth Century mind.

He now mastered Arithmetic and Navigation, Locke's great treatise on the *Human Understanding,* the *Art of Thinking* by the Port Royal authors, Xenophon's *Memorabilia of Socrates,* Shaftsbury and Collins. He had now become a religious skeptic: going through, as you see, the typical development of an active Eighteenth Century mind. It was a rather dry emancipation, with nothing of that spiritual warmth of mysticism that marked the parallel clarification of the Nineteenth Century, as led by Emerson in America and Carlyle in England; but it was a vital intellectual emancipation, none the less.

The *New England Courant.*

Meantime, his brother had started a newspaper, the *New England Courant,* the fourth to be published in America. Franklin, who had the journalistic instinct, was deeply interested in this venture. Believing that he could write as good an article as some of those appearing in the paper, Franklin tried his hand, and slipped an unsigned one under the door of the printing office by night. It was found the next morning, printed, and approved warmly by certain intellectual gentlemen. Franklin repeated the experiment several times; and finding his anonymous articles all acceptable, modestly acknowledged authorship. The brother was furious: jealous of the superior intellectual ability of the ten years younger lad. The result was various beatings, and Franklin's appeal to his father; who sided with him, but without relieving the situation, to any extent.

Early journalistic efforts.

An article, criticising the authorities, caused the brother to be thrown into jail: there was little free speech, in the Colonies, in those days. During the period of his brother's confinement, Franklin had to edit the newspaper. He continued "to give rubs to the authorities", but so skillfully that he escaped his brother's fate. At the end of a month, the brother was released, on condition that he cease publishing his newspaper. Well, he did not wish to give it up, as it was one of his best assets; so he adopted the device of issuing it under his brother Benjamin's name. To do this, he had to free Franklin publicly from his

Circumstances of Franklin's escape from his apprenticeship: "the first great erratum."

indenture papers; but he compelled the signing secretly of fresh papers.

Franklin saw his opportunity. He knew his brother would not dare tell, since he was striving, by a trick, to get around the order of the authorities. So Franklin simply took French leave: left his brother's establishment. He says this was "one of the first great errata" of his life. There were many others, as we shall see.

The flight to New York.

The brother prevented Franklin's getting another printing job in Boston; so he sold some of his books for funds, secretly took ship, and sailed away to New York.

During the voyage there was a big haul of codfish. Now Franklin, being a Bostonian, greatly liked codfish; but there was the obstacle of his vegetarian principles! When the larger fish were opened, however, he discovered that each had smaller fish in its belly. So he argued that, if the larger fish ate the little ones, it could not be so wrong for him to eat the larger ones, and dined heartily and joyously. The incident shows well the saving humor in Franklin's character: without it he might indeed easily have become a moral prig or a religious fanatic. Some of us could narrate chapters of our own youthful experience, similar to this of Franklin's, where we, too, were saved from attacks of moral measles by an abundant sense of humor.

The saving humor of Franklin.

Arriving in New York, Franklin was kindly treated; but there was no job for him there, and he

On to Philadelphia. Circumstances of the journey and arrival.

was advised to go on to Philadelphia. It was a considerable journey, from New York to Philadelphia, in those days. Franklin went by boat to Amboy, New Jersey; thence on foot to Burlington, being drenched with rain on the way. Some kindly persons took him in over night. The next morning he was taken into a rowboat, landed at the foot of Market Street, in Philadelphia.

Deborah Read's first view of Franklin.

His chest had gone around by sea; his pockets were stuffed with dirty clothes, and he was bedraggled from the trip. With one Dutch dollar left in his pocket, he started up Market Street, dropped into a bake shop and bought three rolls. Rolls turned out to be long loaves in Philadelphia. Having purchased them, Franklin did not wish to lose his money; so with one roll under each arm, and vigorously munching the third, held in both hands, he wandered on up Market Street, passing the home of the Read family, with Deborah, the daughter, standing at the door, convulsed with laughter at the comical appearance Franklin made, little dreaming she was to marry him later on. Tired with the long trip, Franklin dropped into a Quaker Meeting House; and went soundly to sleep. He seems to imply that it was a very good place to sleep!

The practical American.

The important point about Franklin is that he always lights on his feet. No matter what exigencies came, he met them, in every instance, with the shrewdness and self confidence of the practical American. He quickly found work in the printing office of one

Keimer, a religious fanatic. He early found lodging with the Read family; and while he had little spare time, he used what was available in the pleasant recreation of courting the buxom daughter. His industry and thrift attracted the favorable notice of certain influential men, in particular the Governor of the Colony, Sir William Keith. He said that Franklin was too fine a young man to be working for someone else; that he should go to Boston and get his father to put up the money, and start an independent printing office. The Governor would give him the government printing and see that all went well.

Work in Keimer's printing establishment.

Franklin joyfully took the advice; and with a strong letter from the Governor to his father, sailed around to Boston, surprising his family, who had been in entire ignorance of his whereabouts during the intervening seven months. They greeted him with open arms, all except the brother, whose establishment Franklin had abandoned. That brother never forgave him. When, however, Franklin made his proposal to his father, the latter threw up his hands: what, give a seventeen year old boy money to start in business independently? No, indeed, besides, he had no such money! So Franklin cheerfully said goodbye, and took ship back for Philadelphia.

The visit to Boston.

Here, Franklin resumed his work in Keimer's shop; but the Governor, on learning that the father had refused to furnish the money, offered to advance it, urging Franklin not to give up the plan, but to make his preparations to go to England for press and type.

The Governor's pleasantry.

Franklin arranged for passage, for himself and his friend, Ralph; but no money was forthcoming. Broaching the matter to the Governor, Franklin was assured all would be right, to take ship and there would be letters arranging everything. Franklin and Ralph got aboard, with some anxiety; well out to sea, the mail bag was opened, and there was nothing for Franklin! The Governor seems to have been a typical politician, promising anything and everything to anybody, and fulfilling little or nothing.

The voyage with Ralph to England.

Franklin thus landed in England, at eighteen, stranded, as far as his plans for a printing outfit were concerned; but again the practical American lights on his feet. He quickly got himself a job in a London printing office. His friend, Ralph, either could not or would not find work; and Franklin had to support both, until a fortunate quarrel relieved him of the further necessity. The funds advanced to Ralph and expended for him were never repaid, however.

Arriving stranded, and finding work

After arrival in England, Franklin wrote one letter to Miss Read, and then just stopped writing. This, he says, was another of his great errata. He later found a better place in Watts's large printing establishment. The other men employed thought they must drink, at frequent intervals, the heavy English ale, to be strong enough for their work; yet Franklin, who drank only water, was, to their astonishment, able to carry up a case of type in each hand, while the beer drinkers could carry but one. "The

The "Water-American."

Water-American" they called him: interesting, how far back that particular tendency goes in our history!

Franklin had the strong instinct for social uplift that marks the better type of practical American; and converted others of the young men to his water-Americanism, so that they, too, began saving their money, instead of spending it all on beer.

Social uplift.

Late in his stay in England, Franklin, through a remarkable swimming feat, attracted the attention of certain gentlemen, who promised him their sons as pupils, if he would remain and open a swimming school. He probably could have made a good deal of money, had he accepted; but he wanted to get back home, so at twenty, he sailed for Philadelphia.

Return to Philadelphia.

Arriving, he found his old flame, Deborah Read, in a sad situation. When Franklin's letters stopped, her mother, who disapproved of his courtship anyway, because of his small earnings, had urged her into marriage with a potter, Rogers. It was shortly reported that he already had a wife, elsewhere, so Deborah Read refused to live with him. Then, he accumulated many debts. In those days they had the pleasant custom of imprisoning a man for debt: apparently to make it impossible for him ever to pay it. Therefore, Rogers fled to the West Indies, to escape imprisonment, leaving poor Deborah Read neither wife nor widow. Franklin found her in this distressing situation. He was very sorry for her; but went cheerfully about his business, and after a brief period

The sad story of Deborah Read.

With Keimer again.

in another line, to work again with his old employer, Keimer.

Franklin received such high wages that he suspected Keimer was using him to train the young men, and then intended to get rid of him. To forestall this, Franklin and a young friend, Meredith, got the latter's father to advance the money, and set up an independent printing business. Meredith proving rather idle and given to drink, after a year or two, Franklin succeeded in borrowing enough money from two other friends to buy his partner out and continue alone.

At twenty-four Franklin independently in the printing business.

The young men wanted to start a newspaper; but Keimer, to forestall them, started one, which he entitled, *The Universal Instructor in all the Arts and Sciences and the Pennsylvania Gazette.* Its leading article was a reprint of a regular installment of *Chambers Dictionary,* just then being issued in England: not very exciting reading. As a result, after nine months, he had but ninety subscribers; and was glad to sell out to Franklin, in the Autumn of 1729, when Franklin was twenty-three. Thus Franklin had his newspaper, which he quickly made the best in the colonies. He dropped the heavy part of the title, and called it simply *The Pennsylvania Gazette.* It was a small affair: one sheet folded, a foot and a half by a foot in size; but it was a typical modern newspaper, containing news items, leading articles, advertisements, anecdotes, broad jokes, poems by the poet-laureate and humorous pieces. Indeed, Franklin was

Franklin's newspaper.

the first "Columnist," and the best we have had. Some of those humorous pieces, signed with amusing pseudonyms and dealing with local satire of the time, are fresh and delightful reading today.

The "Junto" for mutual self-improvement.

Meantime, with his constant desire for self-improvement, Franklin had formed the "Junto", a club of young men, meeting one evening a week. Each member, in turn, was to propose some question in Morals, Politics or Natural Philosophy. Then the whole group was to discuss the subject freely and vigorously, with direct contradiction prohibited, on penalty of a fine. The whole plan was admirable, as an instrument of education.

Starting the Subscription Library.

Since books were scarce, Franklin suggested that the members bring those they possessed to the common meeting place, so that all could have the benefit of all the books owned by the group. The plan was tried, but did not work very well, and the members took their books home. Then Franklin decided on a more ambitious plan, to start a Subscription Library. He had already learned that one should not say "I am starting something", since people would suspect one is seeking to make something out of it. So he went about saying that a number of gentlemen were thinking of starting a Subscription Library, and if those approached would like to come in, it would be possible to make room for them. The result was a large number of subscribers and a flourishing library, one of the first in the colonies. Others followed; and Franklin says:

> "These libraries have improved the general conversation of the Americans, made the common tradesmen and farmers as intelligent as most gentlemen from other countries, and perhaps have contributed in some degree to the stand so generally made throughout the Colonies in defense of their privileges."*

The founding of this Library Franklin calls his "first project of a public nature."

As we have seen, Franklin had passed through a period of typical Eighteenth Century religious skepticism. Lacking the religious sanction and with strong natural passions, in spite of his sobriety and industry, Franklin had fallen into certain vices of conduct. His statement in the *Autobiography* is very frank, as to the indiscretions into which "that hard-to-be-controlled passion of youth" had led him. Now he wished to straighten up his life in every way; and he thought the first step was to get married. Rather a prosaic basis, on which to found the greatest of life relationships; but Franklin had the limitations, as well as the excellence, of the practical American.

Early moral faults of Franklin.

He looked about for an available young woman; and the nearest at hand was a relative of the Godfrey family, with whom Franklin boarded at the time. He straightway began courting her, and she seems to have been quite willing; but Franklin asked as dowry, with the young woman, enough money to pay off the debt on his printing business: a matter of a hundred pounds—five hundred dollars—quite a sum of money

The practical American seeking a wife.

* Franklin, *Autobiography, Complete Works*, Vol. I, pp. 159, 160.

for those days. The Godfreys said they had no such amount of money. Franklin modestly suggested that they mortgage the house and raise it! In consequence, he was forbidden the house. Franklin says he was not sure whether they really wanted him to stay away, or hoped he would elope and marry the girl, without the dowry; but he was too shrewd a practical American to be caught that way. Making overtures in other places, he found the printing business regarded as a poor one, and that he could not expect a dowry, unless with a wife not otherwise agreeable. In this situation, and rather ashamed of his treatment of her, anyway, he returned to his old flame, Deborah Read, living in the deplorable circumstances already cited.

Circumstances of marriage with Deborah Read.

There were many obstacles now in the way of marriage with her: Franklin even feared he might be held for her absconding husband's debts; but they "ventured over all these difficulties", and he "took her to wife, September 1st, 1730". It is difficult to see how the union could have been other than a common law marriage, since Deborah Read's first marriage had not been legally proved invalid, nor Rogers's death confirmed.

Mrs. Franklin's thrift and industry.

His wife was an admirable helpmeet to Franklin. She was a careful and thrifty housekeeper, and aided in keeping shop. They took on a line of stationery, soap and groceries; imported, printed and sold books. After a time, Franklin opened branch establishments in other colonies. With his wife's full cooperation and their joint frugality, they were steadily growing affluent.

How luxury entered the family.

With all their thrift, Franklin says luxury did slip into the household; and he narrates its entrance so charmingly that the passage is quoted:

Charming light on Franklin's domestic life.

> "My breakfast was a long time bread and milk (no tea), and I ate it out of a twopenny earthern porringer with a pewter spoon. But mark how luxury will enter families, and make a progress, in spite of principle: being called one morning to breakfast, I found it in a China bowl, with a spoon of silver; they had been bought for me without my knowledge by my wife, and had cost her the enormous sum of three-and-twenty-shillings, for which she had no other excuse or apology to make, but that she thought *her* husband deserved a silver spoon and China bowl as well as any of his neighbors."*

Mrs. Franklin's two children.

Mrs. Franklin was an excellent mother to her two children. The promising boy died in childhood, of smallpox, to the father's deep and lasting grief. Franklin urges parents to be sure to have their children early inoculated: the terrible device, used before vaccination was developed, to forestall the scourge. The daughter grew up to womanhood, married and had children; and it is one of the ironies of history that it was her son who wrote attacks on Washington in the *Aurora* newspaper.

Attacks on Washington by Benjamin Franklin Bache.

Not long after his marriage, Franklin's son, William, was brought into the family, and reared with the other children. The British Government after-

* Franklin, *Autobiography, Complete Works*, Vol. I, p. 171.

wards made William royal Governor of New Jersey, probably in an effort to bribe Franklin to the British cause. This action did not influence Franklin, but it made William a Tory for life; and the result was a break between father and son, patched up after the Revolution, but with never again the old friendliness.

Franklin's son, William. Made Governor of New Jersey.

The looser aspects of Franklin's early personal life caused bitter criticism and attacks upon him, in Philadelphia when he had become famous. Also, Philadelphia Society never accepted Mrs. Franklin, which doubtless troubled the good lady not at all: she was as little interested in Philadelphia polite society as it was in her.

Later bitter criticism of Franklin's life.

With warm and lasting affection on both sides, the relation of Franklin and his wife was wholly a biological, domestic and business union, the wife sharing in no degree her husband's rapidly developing intellectual life. In their numerous letters, exchanged during Franklin's long absences abroad, each addresses the other as "My Dear Child". Franklin sends her gifts of clothing, china, silver and other household articles. The following is a characteristic letter, written from London, to his wife, shortly after Franklin had helped in securing the repeal of the Stamp Act:

Character of Franklin's domestic life.

"London, 6 April, 1766.

"My Dear Child:—As the Stamp Act is at length repealed, I am willing you should have a new gown, which you may suppose I did not send sooner, as I knew you would not like to be finer than your neighbors, unless in a gown of your own spinning. Had the trade between the two countries totally ceased, it was a comfort to me to recollect that I had once been clothed from head to foot in woolen and linen of my wife's manufacture, that I never was prouder of any dress in my life, and that she and her daughter might do it again if it was necessary. I told the Parliament that it was my opinion, before the old clothes of the Americans were worn out, they might have new ones of their own making. I have sent you a fine piece of Pompadour satin, fourteen yards, cost eleven shillings a yard; a silk *negligee* and petticoat of brocaded lutestring for my dear Sally, with two dozen gloves, four bottles of lavender water, and two little reels. The reels are to screw on the edge of the table, when she would wind silk or thread. The skein is to be put over them, and winds better than if held in two hands. There is also a gimcrack corkscrew, which you must get some brother gimcrack to show you the use of. In the chest is a parcel of books for my friend Mr. Coleman, and another for cousin Colbert. Pray did he receive those I sent him before? I send you also a box with three fine cheeses. Perhaps a bit of them may be left when I come home. Mrs. Stevenson has been very diligent and serviceable in getting these things together for you, and presents her best respects, as does her daughter, to both you and Sally. There are two boxes included in your bill of lading for Billy.

Characteristic letter of Franklin to his wife.

* * * * * *

"There are some droll prints in the box, which were given me by the painter, and being sent when I was not at home, were packed up without my knowledge. I think he was wrong to put in Lord Bute, who had nothing to do with the Stamp Act. But it is the fashion to abuse the nobleman, as the author of all mischief. Love to Sally and all friends. I am, my dear Debby, your affectionate husband,

"B. Franklin."*

Character of Mrs. Franklin's letters to her husband.

Mrs. Franklin's letters deal only with the children, neighborhood gossip, household affairs. Her forceful personality is evident in the vigorous freedom with which she expresses herself; but she was all but illiterate, and is the original phonetic speller. She had evidently heard an occasional long word from her learned husband's lips, and she uses it correctly, with shrewd native intelligence; but the spelling is so delightfully spontaneous that one has often to read the word several times, to be sure what it is intended to be.

The following is one of her characteristic letters; written shortly after receiving news of Franklin's arrival for his third stay in England:

A characteristic letter of April 7th, 1765.

"As I have but very little time to write as the rodes is so very bad I shall only to joyne with you in senser thanks to god for your presevevoashon and Safe a rivel o what reson have you and I to be thankful for maney meney (?) we have reseved.

"Billey and his wife is in town they came to the rases lodged at Mr. Galloway but Spente yisterday at our house and Mr. William's Brother we was att diner I sed I had not aney thing but vitels for I cold not get aney thing for a deserte but who knows but I may treet you with sum thing from Ingland and as we was at tabel Mr. Sumain (?) Came and sed the poste had gone by with the letters that the packit had brought so I had the pleshuer of treeting quite grand indeed and our littel

* Franklin, Letter to his wife from London, April 6th, 1766: *Complete Works,* Vol. III, pp. 457-459.

Company as cherful and hapey as oney in the world none excepted o my dear hough hapey am I to hear that you air safe and well hough dus your armes doe was John of servis to you is your Cold quite gon o I long to know the partic (?) hear I must levef of Salley not up as she was at the Assembly last night with her Sister and I have spook to more than twenty sense I wrote the above.

* * * * *

"aur one famely is well and sendes Duty I am told that my old naber Mrs. Emson is to be in London my love to her and give her a kis from me adoe my Dear child and take caire of youre selef for maneys sake as well as your one.

"I am your a feckshonet wife

"April 7, 1765. D. Franklin."*

To consider a more formal example of Mrs. Franklin's correspondence, read the following brief letter of introduction, given to Dr. Bond's son, for presentation to Franklin in London. It is certainly brief and effective, and must have been delivered by the bearer with much satisfaction:

A delightful letter of introduction, written by Mrs. Franklin in 1770.

"My Dear Child—The bairer of this is the Son of Dr. Phinis Bond his only son and a worthey young man he is a going to studey the Law he desired a line to you I believe you have such a number of worthey young Jentelmen as ever wente to gather I hope to give you pleshuer to see such a numbe of fine youthes from your one countrey which will be an Honour to thar parentes and Countrey.

I am my Dear child your ffeckshonot wife

Ocktober ye 11, 1770. D. Franklin."†

---

* Deborah Franklin, Letter to her husband, April 7, 1765: Franklin, *Complete Works,* Vol. III, pp. 375, 376.

† Deborah Franklin, Letter to her husband, October 11th, 1770: Franklin, *Complete Works,* Vol. IV. pp. 369, 370.

With all the biological validity, domestic warmth and business cooperation of Franklin's married life, it is characteristic of him, as the practical American in limitation as well as excellence, that there is no high spiritual relationship, in either love or friendship, during his entire life.

The limitation of the practical American.

Now married, the head of a family, his business rapidly prospering, Franklin wished to complete the straightening up of his personal character and life. So he "Conceived the bold and arduous project of arriving at moral perfection": no less! As a practical American, he planned the pursuit systematically and thoroughly. He made a list of all the virtues, in which he thought he particularly needed discipline. There were twelve; a Quaker friend suggested a thirteenth, Humility: Franklin probably would not have thought of that, had his Quaker friend not suggested it. He procured and ruled a blank book, with spaces for grading his conduct in each virtue, by the week. Under each virtue, he placed an appropriate motto.

The systematic pursuit of moral perfection.

The first virtue, in which he conceived the need of discipline, was Temperance; and under it the counsel "Eat not to dullness; drink not to elevation." Then, he thought himself too much given to garrulous talk. The second virtue was, therefore, Silence; with the legend, "Speak not but what may benefit others or yourself; avoid trifling conversation." Next was Order: a virtue Franklin never was able to acquire. Then followed: Resolution, Frugality, Industry, Sincerity, Justice, Moderation, Cleanliness, Tranquil-

Franklin's schedule of the virtues.

lity, Chastity, and finally, Humility, with the motto, "Imitate Jesus and Socrates": a high endeavor!

Significance of the virtues chosen.

Please note that, with the exception of Humility, and possibly Tranquillity, there is no high spiritual virtue among these. They are all, as Franklin interpreted them, the prudential virtues, that concern success in the practical conduct of life. Franklin realized that it would be difficult to attempt to practise all thirteen virtues at the same time. So he decided to focus on one virtue each week; which gave him, of course, considerable latitude with reference to the other twelve. The first week he practised Temperance, hoping it would become sufficiently a habit to carry over into the second week, when he centered on Silence. Similarly, he trusted that Temperance and Silence would last into the third week, when he endeavored to learn Order; and so on, through the list.

Plan for acquiring the several virtues.

The four courses in virtue each year.

Thirteen virtues, thirteen weeks; four times thirteen is fifty-two: he would have four systematic courses in the virtues each year. He made an "Order of the Day", with prescribed hours for rising, working, reading, conversing, retiring. He remade a Liturgy, earlier written, with a prayer to "Powerful Goodness", as he now called the Divine Being.

Special difficulty with "Order."

The discipline went bravely forward; but Franklin had particular difficulty with "Order"; he never could learn to keep his papers and surroundings with neatness. After some time, he began to wonder whether moral perfection was really intended for human nature. He says he was reminded of an incident occurring in his neighborhood; which may be condensed as follows: a man, going to purchase an ax, found it sharp on the edge, but otherwise rusty. The seller said, "you turn the grindstone, and I will quickly brighten it up for you." So he pressed the ax on hard, until the one turning said, "Well, I guess that will about do." "O no", said the other, "See, it is all speckled." The purchaser replied, "O well, I like it better speckled".

Story of the speckled ax.

Franklin says it was this way with the pursuit of moral perfection: he began to wonder whether, after all, a few faults were not desirable, to keep one human. Again, it was the saving grace of humor, which kept Franklin from becoming a moral pharisee.

Humor again saving Franklin from the fate of prig and pedant.

The one permanent result, from his discipline in the virtues, which Franklin emphasizes, concerned Humility. He states that his natural tendency was to be dogmatic and over-bearing in expressing his opinions. He carefully and successfully schooled himself to correct this fault. The valuable life-consequence is stated in the following passage, closing that portion of the *Autobiography* written in France at seventy eight:

Overcoming pride in opinions.

> "The modest way in which I propos'd my opinions procur'd them a readier reception and less contradictions: I had less mortification when I was found to be in the wrong, and I more easily prevail'd with others to give up their mistakes and join with me when I happened to be in the right.
>
> "And this mode, which I at first put on with some violence to natural inclination, became at length so easy,

The close of that portion of the *Autobiography* written in France, in 1784, stating one important result of the course in virtue.

and so habitual to me, that perhaps for these fifty years past no one has ever heard a dogmatical expression escape me. And to this habit (after my character of integrity) I think it principally owing that I had early so much weight with my fellow-citizens when I proposed new institutions, or alterations in the old, and so much influence in public councils when I became a member; for I was but a bad speaker, never eloquent, subject to much hesitation in my choice of words, hardly correct in language, and yet I generally carried my points.

"In reality, there is, perhaps, no one of our natural passions so hard to subdue as *pride*. Disguise it, struggle with it, beat it down, stifle it, mortify it as much as one pleases, it is still alive, and will every now and then peep out and show itself; you will see it, perhaps, often in this history; for, even if I could conceive that I had compleatly overcome it, I should probably be proud of my humility."*

The Almanac in colonial life.

Every printer had to publish his Almanac: it was the *Vade Mecum* of colonial life, hanging from a nail beside the open fire-place, in every settler's home. It gave the phases of the sun, moon and tides, bits of surviving Astrological prophesying, fragments of prose and verse: it was everybody's Handbook. The editor and compiler was given the impressive name of "Philomath", mathematical scholar or lover of mathematics. While Franklin lived with the Godfreys, Mr. Godfrey served as his philomath; after his break with the family, he had none, and decided to be his own. To this end he invented an imaginary character, Richard Saunders—"Poor Richard": possibly his remi-

Franklin's want of a Philomath.

Creation of Poor Richard.

* Franklin, *Autobiography: Complete Works*, Vol. I, pp. 188, 189.

niscences of Sir Roger de Coverley in the old volume of *Spectator Papers,* helped him here; and for twenty six years, from the age of twenty-seven to fifty-two, Franklin edited his Almanac through Poor Richard. It is significant of Franklin's literary skill that this purely fictitious character quickly became the best known man in the colonies.

The twenty-six annual issues of Poor Richard's Almanac.

Franklin's problem was to sell his Almanac; and he hit upon a brilliant, humorous device, to get a hearing. The philomath of the chief rival Almanac was a certain Titan Leeds; and Franklin had Poor Richard solemnly prophesy, as revealed by the stars, the death of Titan Leeds, at a certain hour, of a certain day, of the ensuing year. Titan Leeds was naturally furious: he replied with an excited repudiation of his announced death, upbraiding Richard Saunders for his scurrilous trick. Everybody chuckled, dropped by Franklin's shop, and bought his Almanac.

The literary hoax to sell the Almanac, carried on in the Prefaces of Poor Richard, for a period of years.

In the next year's issue, Richard Saunders gravely states that he does not know just at what hour, of what day, Titan Leeds died, but is quite sure that he is dead; for Titan Leeds was his friend, and could not possibly have written the vicious attack upon him, appearing under Titan Leeds's name. Leeds shrieked in response that he was not dead and didn't intend to die, and it was all a dirty trick, anyway. Everybody chuckled, dropped by Franklin's shop, and bought his Almanac.

The following year, Poor Richard states that Titan Leeds really is dead; but that his Ghost pretends to be living and to write Almanacs. Franklin closed the hoax with a letter, purporting to be from Titan Leeds, in the next world, to his friend, Richard Saunders, in this. The result was that Poor Richard's Almanac was brilliantly successful, selling ten thousand copies a year.

Unique superiority of Franklin's Almanac.

This was due, further, to its real superiority and unique originality: it was well worth buying! Even to the conventional data, Franklin gave an amusing turn. Note the delightful satire, not only on Astrology, but on colonial pronunciation, in the following typical forecast of the year as revealed by the stars:

A typical passage of humorous prophesy from the Almanac of 1736.

"During the first visible eclipse *Saturn* is retrograde: for which reason the crabs will go sidelong and the rope-makers backward. *Mercury* will have his share in these affairs, and so confound the speech of the people, that when a *Pennsylvanian* would say *Panther* he shall say *Painter.* When a *New Yorker* thinks to say *This* he shall say *Diss*, and the people of *New England* and *Cape May* will not be able to say *Cow* for their lives, but will be forced to say *Keow* by a certain involuntary twist in the root of their tongues. No *Connecticut man* nor *Marylander* will be able to open his mouth this year but *Sir* shall be the first or last syllable he pronounces, and sometimes both. * * *

This year the stone-blind shall see but very little; the deaf shall hear but poorly; and the dumb sha'n't speak very plain. And it's much, if my Dame *Bridget* talks at all this year. Whole flocks, herds, and droves of sheep, swine and oxen, cocks and hens, ducks and drakes, geese and ganders shall go to pot; but the mortality will not be altogether so great among cats, dogs, and horses. As to old age, 't will be incurable this year, because of the years past. And towards the Fall some people will be seized with an unaccountable inclination to roast and eat their own ears: Should this be called madness, Doctors? I think not. But the worst disease of all will be a certain most horrid, dreadful, malignant, catching, perverse and odious malady, almost epidemical, insomuch that many shall run mad upon it; I quake for very fear when I think on't: for I assure you very few will escape this disease, which is called by the learned Albromazar Lacko'mony."*

This delightful humor marked all features of the Almanac. There were verses, original and reproduced; jokes and stories, sometimes rather broad, but which pleased the frontier audience; and Franklin ransacked literature, ancient and modern, for maxims and wise sayings. In fact, the quarter of a century of Almanacs contains what is probably the greatest and most comprehensive collection of proverbial wisdom ever compiled. Some of these pungent sayings were, of course, original with Franklin, but many more were borrowed; and his skill lay especially in the selection and redressing of them. To appreciate their range, consider a few from the vast number:

Various features of the Almanac.

The amazing collection of proverbial wisdom.

"The proof of gold is fire; the proof of a woman, gold; the proof of a man, a woman."

From Franklin's own experience.

"There is no little enemy."

Shrewd observation of life.

"Three may keep a secret, if two of them are dead."

"Fish and visitors smell in three days."

The more pungent humor.

* Franklin, From Poor Richard's Almanac of 1736: *Complete Works*, Vol. I, pp. 458, 459.

Moral wisdom.

"Wealth is not his that has it, but his that enjoys it."

Social uplift.

"The noblest question in the world is, What good may I do in it?"

True today as when Franklin printed it!

"Keep your eyes wide open before marriage; half-shut afterwards."

"Industry need not wish."

Among Franklin's favorites.

"The used key is always bright."

"Three removes are as bad as a fire."

"It is hard for an empty sack to stand upright."*

Father Abraham's speech and its success over the world.

In the last issue of his Almanac, that for 1758, Franklin created another imaginary character, Father Abraham, portraying him as making a long speech at a public auction, in which he quotes many of the best maxims and proverbs Poor Richard had fathered during the quarter of a century. This humorous Valedictory of Poor Richard caught the imagination of the world. It was reprinted separately, translated into French and some other languages, read all over the world; and it helped to prepare the enthusiastic welcome accorded Franklin, afterwards, in England and France. It has been reprinted more than seventy times in England, and more than fifty in France.

Franklin as teacher of the virtues that have characterized American life.

Through the pungent ethical wisdom of Poor Richard's Almanac, with the influence of his own picturesque personality, Franklin became really the Schoolmaster of the Colonies, establishing the range of virtues which to this day have ever characterized the practical American, in ideal if not always in practice.

---

* Franklin, Typical Proverbs from Poor Richard's Almanacs: *Complete Works*, Vol. I, pp. 443-456.

Circumstances of Franklin's retirement from business at forty-two.

By the age of forty-two Franklin had become so successful that he was able to retire from active business, under a contract with his foreman, which was to pay him 1000 pounds, about $5000 a year, for the next eighteen years. This indicates how really affluent he had already become. He had established branches of his printing business in other colonies, shrewdly used his carefully saved money in buying Philadelphia real estate, and was now the successful, self-made, practical American. His own statement is that he retired from active business for study, scientific research and public service. Of these, the last became an unexpectedly large and onerous element of the latter half of his life.

Franklin's reasons for retiring from active business.

Language studies.

Meantime, Franklin continued his studies. At this period of his life, he mastered a good reading knowledge of French, then Italian and then Spanish; and, at this point, discovered that he could read Latin, without ever having studied it. That is, of course, true: anyone who reads fluently those Romance tongues can understand their common mother. Franklin's remarks on practical teaching of the languages are still instructive to the teacher of today.

Franklin's public service had begun long before his retirement from active business; and in it he shows an interesting combination of entirely unselfish devotion to the general welfare, with a frequent use of his public services to advance his private interests. As Clerk of the Assembly, he was able to secure the official printing; and when elected a member, serving ten consecutive years, he got his son, William, appointed clerk, in order to retain the government printing: the practical American! He differed from Washington in seeking the appointment of relatives to public office, but never to sinecures, or to the detriment of the service. He was Deputy Postmaster and later Postmaster General. He organized a city Watch and, at thirty, a volunteer Fire Company, which functioned efficiently for fifty-five years. He founded the long famous American Philosophical Society, which was practically an outgrowth of the earlier Junto. He established an Academy, for the youth of the Colony, from which developed the University of Pennsylvania. With Dr. Bond, he helped to found the first Hospital in America.

Amazing range of Franklin's public service.

Indefatigable in scientific investigation, Franklin's interest was less in pure Science, than in discoveries and inventions of immediate practical application. He invented, before leaving business, the Franklin Stove, that still bears his name: that iron open fireplace, economizing fuel, increasing heat and retaining the free ventilation of the room.

The inventor and practical scientist.

Belief in the value of fresh air.

Franklin was one of the early believers in fresh air, at a time when most persons were still under the superstition that night air was dangerous, and so kept their windows tightly closed. John Adams quaintly narrates an incident of a journey in 1776, when he and Franklin had to sleep in one bed in a small room, with no chimney. Adams wanted the window shut, but Franklin prevailed upon him to open it wide and jump into bed; then lectured him on the value of fresh air, until Adams fell asleep under the argument.

Franklin did not patent his stove because he wished the colonists to benefit by it; but a British ironmonger took out a patent on it, and made a fortune selling Franklin's stove to the colonists.

The wide range of Franklin's practical inventions.

Franklin invented an improved street lamp, and brightened the streets of Philadelphia; introduced mineral fertilizers in agriculture; improved the construction and draft of chimneys; made important technical changes in ships, sails, cordage: there is hardly a phase of practical life he did not touch helpfully. He invented the "Armonica", an instrument of musical glasses, playing upon it to his own delight, and taking it to England with him. His Essay on "The Peopling of Countries" contains at least the germ of Malthus's epoch-making work. He resented the bother of two sets of spectacles, for near and distant vision; so while in France, he had the lenses cut in two, and half of each fitted in the frame; and he had invented bifocal glasses. He quaintly remarked that, dining out, he could see his food better with the lower lens, and the expression of persons across the table with the upper, which helped him to understand their French.

At forty-one he began his experiments with Electricity: he was fascinated with this marvel, ground out of silk and glass; and early occupied with the problem whether it was not identical with the age-old terror of lightning. To his English correspondent,

Collinson, he suggested a testing experiment: admirable, but rather hard on the experimenter: a man was to stand on a high church tower. in a thunder storm, and hold an iron rod pointed toward the clouds. It is said that this experiment actually was carried out in France, without killing the operator! At forty-four Franklin announced his invention of the lightning rod. At forty-six he sent Collinson a description of his Kite experiment, which he is believed to have carried out in June, 1752. A kite, with an iron tip, was flown during a thunder storm; and Franklin, at the other end of the cord, with an iron key in his hand, felt the distinct shock, which proved the identity of lightning and electricity.

Experiments in Electricity.

It has recently been doubted whether Franklin actually carried out his experiment, on the ground that, if successful, it would have killed him. The argument seems silly; for surely through his kite and key, as under a tree struck by lightning, Franklin could have experienced any degree of shock, from the slightest tingle to death. I have verified this, through aviators in the government service, who tell me that, under conditions analagous to Franklin's experiment, they have experienced, during thunder storms, varying degrees of electric shock. Franklin definitely speaks, moreover, in the *Autobiography,* of the "infinite pleasure" he received in the success of an experiment "I made soon after with a kite at Philadelphia."

At any rate, the world of the time believed that Franklin carried out the experiment; and, with the invention of the lightning rod, it caught the imagination of mankind: that Franklin had dared to seize Jove's weapon, and that his invention had rendered it harmless! In France, particularly, the response was enthusiastic. Later, when Franklin went to France, cartoons were published and widely circulated, representing Franklin seated on a throne, clutching the lightning in one fist, a number of scepters in the other, a group of dethroned monarchs rolling on the ground at his feet, with, underneath, the French legend, reading: "He seized lightning from Heaven and the scepter from Tyrants." Such was the effect of Franklin's discoveries in Electricity on the enthusiastic French mind.

How Franklin's discoveries and inventions in Electricity caught the imagination of the world.

Like Washington, Franklin saw from the beginning the necessity for a union of the Colonies; and as early as 1754, during the French and Indian War, he made the first of his two plans for that union.

First plan for a union of the Colonies.

When General Braddock planned his ill-fated expedition, he proposed to commandeer horses and wagons from Pennsylvania. Franklin went to see General Braddock, urging him not to do that, since it would deeply offend the inhabitants, but rather to lease the teams. The General asked how he was to get them, and Franklin promised to raise them for him. Franklin did get together a hundred and fifty teams and wagons, advancing a thousand pounds of his own money and giving his personal bond for their safe return. When the expedition met its disaster, claims were made upon Franklin amounting in all to twenty

Franklin's service in the Braddock campaign.

Franklin, a devoted patriot.

thousand pounds, practically a hundred thousand dollars; and he would have been completely ruined, had the British government not finally paid the claims. This clearly shows how devoted a patriot Franklin was: with all his shrewdness in handling his own affairs, cheerfully risking all his hard-won wealth in the service of his country's cause.

The brief military career.

The Governor appointed Franklin a Colonel of militia, to defend the Northwest frontier of the Colony against the Indians. Franklin raised 560 men; marched to Bethlehem and Gnadenhut where stockades were built: there was no actual Indian fighting; but Franklin showed, in his brief period of military service, the same practical efficiency, evident in every task he undertook.

One characteristic incident of his short military experience deserves mention. The Chaplain came to the Colonel and complained that he could not get the men to attend Divine Service. Franklin intimated that he did not wish to suggest anything that might seem disrespectful to religion; but inquired if the clergyman had thought of issuing the daily rum ration immediately after the Service. The Chaplain had not; was impressed with the idea, which he adopted; and every man attended thereafter!

Difficulties of Pennsylvania Colony as a private grant.

Pennsylvania, as a private grant to William Penn, had special difficulties to meet. The sons of William Penn, who seem to have been quite unlike their father, had inherited the Colony, and instructed the Governor to refuse any tax bill that did not exempt the proprietary estates from taxation. See how unfair that was! Great areas of land had, of course, been sold off for farms, towns and cities; but vast tracts were still in the proprietor's hands, made valuable, increasingly, by the settlements of the Colony. The Assembly would prepare and pass a tax bill, to raise troops to protect the Colony and pay other government expenses; and the Governor would promptly veto it, because taxing rightly the proprietary estates, with all others. The only redress for the Assembly was to refuse to pay the Governor's salary: an item insignificant in comparison. The whole struggle was merely a flagrant instance of the age-old and age-long battle with privilege.

Injustice of the Penn heirs toward the Colony.

During the French and Indian War, the Assembly had to yield: the need for funds was too urgent; but toward its close, Franklin was sent to England, as a representative of the Colony, to seek to relieve the situation. He remained in England five years, from the age of fifty-one to fifty-six; and they were among the happiest years of his life. For the first time, he could enjoy constantly the society of highly cultivated men. His fame had preceded him, and he was welcomed by leaders of thought and civilization everywhere. He was given the degree of Doctor of Laws by two of the Scotch and one of the English Universities; both Yale and Harvard having previously given him the A.M. degree.

Franklin's happy five years in England.

He went to live, in London, at Mrs. Stevenson's, and her house became a second home to him. He became warmly attached to her lovely daughter, to whom he wrote some of his most charming letters, and earnestly desired that his son, William, should marry Miss Stevenson; but was as unsuccessful as match-making parents usually are. William, instead, presented Franklin with an illegitimate grandson, William Temple Franklin; and shortly afterward married a West Indian lady. The grandson was reared entirely by Franklin; and was later his secretary at the embassy in Paris.

Travels and contact with scholars.

The summers Franklin spent travelling, with his son, in England, Scotland and on the Continent. Of one such period in Scotland, when he had not only enjoyed the beautiful out-door world, but met intimately Hume, Robertson and other great scholars, he said they were "six weeks of the densest happiness I have met with in any part of my life."

The third and longest residence in England.

Franklin as representing the Colonies to the home Government.

Franklin's prestige was so great that by taking personally the responsibility that the Proprietors would not be injured, he won the first round of the fight to tax their estates. He came home in 1762; had two busy years of public service; and was again sent to England, in 1764, at the age of fifty-eight, on the business of the Colony. After a time, he was made official representative of Pennsylvania, at the home Government; and later, Georgia, Massachusetts and New Jersey made him their agent also. During this ten years' stay in England, Franklin was thus in the position of general representative of the Colonies to the British Government.

As before, Mrs. Franklin, who had terror at the thought of a sea voyage, refused to accompany or join him. At one time, Franklin would perhaps have settled in England permanently, had his wife been willing to come over. He went again to live at Mrs. Stevenson's; and resumed his delightful intercourse with intellectual leaders, continuing his own scientific experiments.

Franklin's view of the colonial problem.

Until Lexington, Franklin held to the belief that the King meant well, but was ill advised by bad ministers. He thought that the problem of the Colonies was, therefore, to get the liberal statesmen into power in England, rather than to break with the home land: the view held by the majority of Americans, at the time.

Accepting the Stamp Act and recommending Hughes as agent at Philadelphia. Consequences at home.

Using, unavailingly, all his energies to prevent the passage of the Stamp Act, once enacted, Franklin accepted it, and assumed the Colonies would peacefully submit. Asked by the British Minister to suggest the agent for Philadelphia, Franklin recommended his old friend, Hughes, who was forthwith appointed. When the news reached the Colony, there was an uproar of indignation. Franklin was accused of treachery; Hughes was compelled to resign and his house menaced; and there was even a threat to mob Franklin's house. Mrs. Franklin was urged to flee into New Jersey. She sent the daughter away; but decisively refused to go, and stayed on guard. Fortunately, the house was not attacked; so the good lady did not have to use even a rolling pin, which no doubht she could have used most effectively.

Franklin's examination, before the House of Commons, on the effects of the Stamp Act.

The resistance to the Stamp Act, with the refusal of the colonists to buy British made goods, led to an agitation in England for the repeal of the Act. Parliament held an Examination into its effects; and Franklin was asked by certain liberal statesmen to be one of those examined. Franklin accepted, recognizing the unique opportunity to serve the American cause. He was thoroughly prepared for the Examination; and he made of it a masterpiece. It is useless to quote briefly from it: one must read it as a whole, to realize Franklin's adroit skill and far-reaching wisdom. There was nothing of his customary jesting: the occasion was too serious. His replies were as frank, as they were skillful, shrewdly developing all the implications in the situation between England and her colonies. His Examination strengthened the American cause, helped to the repeal of the Act, and did much to advance Franklin's own prestige and influence in England.

Franklin's shrewd wisdom as diplomat. His right view of his relation to the British Government.

Regarding himself, rightly, not as a foreign ambassador, but as the representative of a part of the Empire to the home Government, Franklin took liberties that an ordinary ambassador would not dare to take. He has been severely criticized for this, as lacking in diplomatic tact and propriety. The criticism is wholly unwarranted. Franklin's view of his mission was exactly the correct one; and he did much to win liberal opinion to the justice of the American cause.

He even wrote political articles for the British papers; for which a conventional ambassador would be sent home at once. The articles were, of course, unsigned; but their authorship was quickly recognized. One of them was upon *"Rules for Reducing a Great Empire to a Small One."* You see the point: if England continued her policy, she would lose her colonies. Another skit purported to be *"An Edict of the King of Prussia."* In it, Franklin made the King of Prussia say that England had been colonized by the Saxons, who were his subjects, therefore England belonged to him. There followed restrictive edicts on British manufactures and commerce, absurdly paralleling those Britain enforced over the American colonies. Franklin describes the excitement in a group of British statesmen, on the appearance of the article, their exclamations that the impudent Prussian King would be over soon with an army, and then their laughing recognition of his authorship and of the "hit" that he had made.

The newspaper articles.

Franklin's humorous articles influencing public opinion to the American cause.

Having been abroad so long, however, Franklin failed to realize the extent and strength, in the colonies, of the growing demand for independence. One of the liberal statesmen, warning him of this, to prove that the repressive measures did not originate from the British Government showed him some confidential letters from Governor Hutchinson of Massachusetts, the Lieutenant Governor and others, describing the rioting, and asking that troops be sent over to put down the rebellion.

American sentiment for independence outgrowing Franklin.

Affair of the Hutchinson Letters.

Franklin's effort to conciliate sentiment toward Britain.

Franklin asked the loan of the letters, thinking that, if the Massachusetts leaders knew what had been written, their resentment toward Britain would be mollified. The letters were lent to him, on condition that they should not be copied nor allowed to get into print. Franklin sent them over to the Boston leaders, to be read and returned; and John Adams and John Hancock read them to the Assembly and to others. The Governor, Hutchinson, was a native of New England; and there developed intense indignation at what was regarded as his treachery to the Colony. The letters quickly got into print in Boston and were reprinted in London. Franklin could not explain the situation, without betraying his friend, the liberal statesman, who had lent him the letters. The result was a public scandal, culminating in a duel between two prominent British statesmen. Franklin finally came forward and took the responsibility for the publication of the letters, but, of course, without explanation.

Consequences of Franklin's action.

The consequence was that the Privy Council, to have an opportunity to attack Franklin, officially considered the Massachusetts petition for the removal of the Governor. At the sitting, Franklin was subjected to one of the most scathing arraignments any man ever received, at the hands of that master of sarcasm and vituperation, Lord Wedderburn. Franklin, clad in his red velvet suit, stood leaning against the mantel, in motionless position: an expression of imperturbable

The arraignment by Lord Wedderburn before the Privy Council.

serenity upon his face. Some thought Franklin the real victor in the ordeal.

His influence in England, however, was now at an end. He was deprived of his Postmastership of the Colonies; and was in danger of arrest. War was in sight anyway. A last futile attempt was made to bribe Franklin to the British cause. He lingered on, in semi-hiding, for a time, got secretly on a ship, and sailed for home, arriving May 5th, 1775. Lexington had already been fought; and from that event, Franklin was convinced that no composition was possible, and the struggle must be carried through to complete independence.

Return home to join wholeheartedly the struggle for independence.

His wife had died a few months before his return; and from now on his married daughter kept house for him. The day after his arrival, he was made a deputy to the second Continental Congress. In it, he prepared his second plan for a union of the Colonies, used all his influence for a declaration of independence, and was heart and soul for the war. He was made Postmaster General of the United Colonies; served as member of the Pennsylvania legislature and on the Committee of Public Safety, which carried on the executive government of the Colony. He helped to devise the obstructions to prevent the British ships coming up the Delaware river; was at Boston, in the Autumn, raising supplies for Washington's army; and in the Winter, already seventy, he was sent, with other commisioners to Canada, to try to bring Canada in on the American side. The journey failed of its

Incessant and varied services of the American cause.

Acceptance of the mission to France, at seventy.

object, but nearly killed Franklin. Then, in September, 1776, he was appointed one of three special commissioners, to go to France and seek to win her help for the American cause. Franklin is reported to have said: "I am old and good for nothing; but as the storekeepers say of their remnants of cloth, I am but a fag end, you may have me for what you please;" but there was a dozen good years of work and service in him yet.

Franklin, two years later, used again the "remnant" idea, in a letter to David Hartley:

> "Having nearly finished a long life, I set but little value on what remains of it. Like a draper when one chaffers with him for a remnant, I am ready to say: As it is only the fag end, I will not differ with you about it; take it for what you please."*

Silas Deane was already in France; Jefferson was to accompany Franklin, but declined because of his wife's illness, and Arthur Lee was chosen in his place. Franklin secretly took ship on the *Reprisal,* evaded the threatening British cruisers; and on the last stage of the voyage, his ship captured two British merchantmen, and sailed into port with those prizes, enough to pay the expenses of the embassy for a long period of time!

The French welcome to Franklin.

Franklin was welcomed in France with a universal enthusiasm, accorded no other American. The French had read Father Abraham's speech from Poor Rich-

* Franklin, in letter to David Hartley, from Paris, in 1778: *Complete Works,* Vol. VI, p. 169.

ard's Almanac, they were dazzled by Franklin's discoveries in Electricity, enthusiastic over his work as statesman: he stood out, to them, as the great man of America. The result was he exercised an influence no other man could have approximated, completely overshadowing the other commissioners.

France was already assisting us, through a private Company, not daring to do so openly, as that would have meant the war with Britain she was as yet unwilling to face. Congress, not understanding the situation, was not making fair return. Arthur Lee also misunderstood; and, jealous anyway of Franklin's overshadowing influence, wrote bitter letters to Congress, accusing his fellow commissioners of treachery. Deane came home, and was completely ruined, through the attacks and misunderstanding. Franklin said, "Spots of dirt thrown on my character I suffered while fresh to remain; I did not choose to spread by endeavoring to remove them, but relied on the vulgar adage that they would all rub off when they were dry"; and they did.

The handicap of jealousies and attacks.

John Adams was sent over to replace Deane; and was scandalized to find Franklin's papers and accounts in their usual confused disorder, and Franklin living, as guest, in the house of a French nobleman, at Passy; but he recognized, nevertheless, Franklin's complete integrity in devoted service of his country's cause. John Adams was present, at the Academy of Sciences, when Franklin and Voltaire met. The crowd, not content with Anglo-Saxon handshaking,

Franklin and John Adams.

Meeting with Voltaire.

insisted the two great men embrace French fashion, kissing each other on both cheeks; which they did. The delighted throng murmured, "How beautiful to see Solon and Sophocles embrace!": Franklin being Solon, and Voltaire, Sophocles, to the enthusiastic French sentiment.

Success of Franklin in the French alliance.

Burgoyne's surrender was the added increment, to Franklin's great personal influence, which turned the scale, and decided France to come in openly on the American side. At the signing of the treaty of alliance, February 6th, 1778, Franklin wore the old red velvet suit, in which he had suffered Lord Wedderburn's arraignment: a characteristically whimsical revenge!

Signing of the treaty in February, 1778.

Adams, on his return, advised Congress to leave but one representative at Paris; so from 1779, for his remaining six years in France, Franklin was sole plenipotentiary. Relieved of the bickerings, he was burdened with a vast range of services. He negotiated the exchange of prisoners, served as court for prize ships: he was, in fact, making international law, day by day. He was, moreover, the chief source of money for the war, skillfully negotiating those multiplied loans from France, that made victory possible. Other commissioners came over, appointed to various lands; could not get to their posts; and Franklin had to find money for them. Congress sent incessant drafts, for which Franklin had to find funds, or suffer disgrace and dishonor to his country. Finally, he wrote Congress that it must cease drawing on him. Congress

Amazing services as Ambassador.

Franklin, the chief source of money for the war.

promised; but went right on issuing the drafts, and antedating them. Somehow, without forfeiting the friendship of France, Franklin obtained the loans and met them. This aspect of his service alone is phenomenal, and proves him a great diplomat.

Social life and charming flirtations.

Amid these incessant labors, Franklin found time to dine out, six nights a week, and entertain the important Americans in Paris on the seventh. Also, he found leisure to carry on charming flirtations with French ladies of the old régime. Madame Helvetius was particularly devoted to him, embracing him publicly and enthusiastically, whenever she met him at a ball or festival, much to the scandal of puritanical Mrs. John Adams; who wrote home that she had never witnessed anything so vulgar; but Franklin liked it! Another of these love passages was with the charming young matron, Madame Brillon, for whom Franklin wrote certain of his most delightful little Allegories and Essays. Even Countess d'Houdetot—Rousseau's Countess d'Houdetot—gave a pompous festival in his honor, greeting him with fulsome and flattering verses. Franklin's vanity was tickled; but he went right on serving the American cause, with unwearied fidelity. It may be said that these flirtations went just as far as the ladies were willing; which, apparently, was not very far, with the seventy-five years old Franklin.

For the graver aspect of his personal life, consider the following portion of a letter to Washington, written in March, 1780, at a rather dark period of the war. It contains one of Franklin's expressions, frequent in his letters of this period, of his feeling that his life and work were nearly over; but is even more remarkable for the closing enthusiastic prophesy of America's recovery and progress, after the war:

Evidence of friendship and appreciation for Washington.

"You would, on this side of the sea, enjoy the great reputation you have acquired, pure and free from those little shades that the jealousy and envy of a man's countrymen and contemporaries are ever endeavoring to cast over living merit. Here you would know and enjoy what posterity will say of Washington. For a thousand leagues have nearly the same effect with a thousand years. The feeble voice of those grovelling passions cannot extend so far either in time or distance. At present I enjoy that pleasure for you; as I frequently hear the old generals of this martial country, who study the maps of America and mark upon them all your operaions, speak with sincere approbation and great applause of your conduct; and join in giving you the character of one of the greatest captains of the age.

View of America's future. Franklin never doubting final victory in the war for independence.

"I must soon quit this scene, but you may live to see our country flourish, as it will amazingly and rapidly after the war is over; like a field of young Indian corn, which long fair weather and sunshine had enfeebled and discolored, and which in that weak state, by a thundergust of violent wind, hail, and rain, seemed to be threatened with absolute destruction; yet the storm being past, it recovers fresh verdure, shoots up with double vigor, and delights the eye, not of its owner only, but of every observing traveller."*

Adams and Jay came over, to join Franklin in

* Franklin, in letter to Washington of March, 1780: *Complete Works*, Vol. VII, pp. 26, 27.

negotiating the peace with Britain of 1782. They brought instructions from Congress that nothing was to be done without consulting the French Minister; but insisted, over Franklin's protest, that these instructions must be disregarded and the peace privately arranged. It was the protesting Franklin who had, afterwards, the task of conciliating the justly offended French Minister, Vergennes; which he accomplished successfully.

Preliminary peace articles signed at Paris, Nov. 30th, 1782.

Franklin's part in the peace treaty.

Franklin urged the other commissioners to demand the cession of Canada, as over against compensation to Tories. Adams and Jay, in the mood of post-war hatred, insisted that not a dollar of damages should be paid a Tory; and Franklin was over-ruled. Had he had his way, it is likely Britain would have yielded. She had possessed Canada only since the French and Indian War; and it was Franklin who, at the close of that War, had urged the British statesmen to ask the cession of Canada from France, rather than the Guadeloupe Islands. Canada was still largely French in population, and its value not yet appreciated in Britain. Thus, if Franklin had had his way, it is probable that Canada would have been, from the beginning of our nation, an integral part of the United States of America. This is mentioned only to indicate how far-visioned a statesman Franklin was.

Franklin's views with reference to Canada.

Why Canada remained a British possession.

Franklin's departure from France, in July, 1785, was as triumphal as his reception nine years before. The King lent his royal litter to take Franklin to the sea-coast; there were throngs of cheering populace all

Return to Philadelphia at seventy-nine.

along the route. He came home to his house on Market Street, Philadelphia, to live there surrounded by children and grandchildren. There was a mulberry tree in the back yard, under which he could sit and meditate, read or dream over his full memories.

His days of public service were not over, however. On his return, he was made President of the governing Council of Pennsylvania, holding the office for three years. At eighty-one, he was chosen a member of the Constitutional Convention, which met, in Philadelphia, in 1787. He did not attempt to speak from the floor, but wrote his speeches, and they were read by his Pennsylvania colleague; and are thus the only ones, of the Convention, which have come down to us just as given. It was, moreover, Franklin, always the conciliator, who settled the worst controversy of the wrangling Convention. The small States feared being swamped by the larger ones, if they went into an indissoluble Union. It was Franklin who suggested that, in the House, representation should be by population, and in the Senate, by States; and that is why, to this day, little Delaware, Rhode Island or Maryland has its two Senators, side by side with great New York, Pennsylvania or Illinois.

Delegate to the Constitutional Convention.

Franklin's happy solution of the worst controversy of the Convention.

Behind the Presiding Officer of the Convention, Washington, was a picture of the sun. When the long Convention drew to its end, Franklin turned to a colleague, and said that he had always been puzzled by that picture of the sun, not knowing whether it was the rising or the setting sun; but now that the

The characteristic closing witticism of Franklin's public life.

Constitution was adopted and signed, he was sure it was the Rising Sun of the nation's future. With this happy and pregnant witticism, Franklin's public life appropriately closes. He lingered on, for a few years of failing health, afflicted by a complication of diseases, and died, April 17th, 1790, eighty-four years old.

Death at the age of eighty-four.

Of vigorous and enduring physical constitution and strong natural passions, entirely self educated and self made, most many-sided in ceaseless activities, scientist, moralist, journalist, business man, inventor, humorist and philosopher, the greatest diplomat America has so far produced, schoolmaster of the colonists, establishing the type of virtue that has characterized us ever since, in ideal if not in conduct, Franklin is one of the most picturesque figures in our history and, in virtues and faults, the type, for all time, of the Practical American: one of the really great men in all our past.

Summary of Franklin.

III

JEFFERSON: THE DEMOCRATIC AMERICAN

Significance of Jefferson and Hamilton in our history.

IN WASHINGTON and Franklin, we have studied the great struggle for independence, and the making of a nation out of the scattered colonies. In Jefferson and Hamilton, we turn to leaders of high importance in the Revolution, but whose careers culminated in the first phases of development of the new Government, and in whom came the initial cleavage of political philosophy, which was to divide the Nation for more than a half-century and culminate in the Civil War.

Ancestry of Jefferson.

Born at Shadwell, Albemarle County, Virginia, April 13th, 1743, Jefferson was eleven years younger than Washington, and thirty-seven years younger than Franklin, who was, indeed, the patriarch of the Revolution. On his father's side, Jefferson was of Welsh descent. According to the tradition Jefferson gives in his fragmentary *Autobiography,* the ancestor came from near Mt. Snowdon, in Wales, in the earliest days of the Virginia Colony. Jefferson's father, Peter Jefferson, surveyor, engineer, burgess, was a man of great energy and remarkable stature and strength. The tradition was that he could lift a hogshead of tobacco, with each hand, at the same time,

The forceful personality and liberal convictions of Jefferson's father.

while other men found it difficult to lift one with both hands. He was a liberal in politics and religion, in contrast to his aristocratic neighbors; and with limited schooling, had read thoughtfully and somewhat widely. Though dying when his son, Thomas, was a boy of fourteen, the son's intellectual development was so precocious that he was already deeply influenced by his father's opinions. Through life, he retained deep reverence for his father's memory; and his father was the first strong influence, determining Jefferson's life-long liberalism in politics and religion.

Influence of his father's opinions on Jefferson.

Peter Jefferson went West from the more settled portion of Virginia, a hundred miles into the wilderness, bought a thousand acres of land, on the banks of the Rivanna, and built himself a temporary cabin. He returned and married Jane Randolph, of the great Scotch Randolph family, that had become eminent and powerful in Virginia; and took his bride west, to his new home. There was no site on his thousand acres, which he considered entirely satisfactory for a permanent dwelling; so he bought one from his dearest friend and nearest neighbor, William Randolph, for "the largest bowl of punch"; and on it erected the home he called Shadwell. It was here Thomas Jefferson was born: the third child and first son of his father.

Peter Jefferson's estate on the Rivanna.

Jefferson's mother.

Shadwell.

Jefferson differed from others of our great statesmen in having an excellent schooling. He was thoroughly prepared for college; and entered William and Mary, at the Colonial Capital, Williamsburg, at

Jefferson's thorough schooling. Entering William and Mary College at seventeen.

Jefferson, an eager and life-long student, becoming widely cultivated.

the age of seventeen. A natural student and scholar, he seems to have been equally proficient in mathematics, the languages, ancient and modern, and in the natural sciences; and continued his studies in all three fields, throughout his life.

Life and associations at Williamsburg, the Colonial Capital.

Williamsburg was then a small town, perhaps a thousand inhabitants, with unpaved streets, a dozen gentlemen's estates scattered through the countryside; but it was a remarkable cultural center, nevertheless. The chief college building and the Capital building had been designed by Sir Christopher Wren, architect of St. Paul's in London. It is noteworthy, what a list of eminent leaders has come from that little college: members of the Revolutionary Committees, of the Continental Congress, Presidents of the United States, Judges of the first Courts.

Jefferson's remarkable early development is evident in the fact that he was welcomed as the fourth in an unusual group of men, who dined together two or three times a week. The leader was the worldly and cultivated Governor, Fauquier. The others were Wythe, leader of the Virginia Bar, and Dr. Small, the chief liberal scholar in Virginia, and the second great influence in liberalizing Jefferson's opinions. That these eminent men welcomed the young collegian as dinner companion is a signal tribute to Jefferson's cultivation and conversation. At this time, Jefferson was rather a dandy in dress, and a lover of fine riding horses, which he had kept with scrupulous cleanness.

Of Dr. Small's influence upon him, Jefferson says:

"Dr. William Small of Scotland, was then Professor of Mathematics, a man profound in most of the useful branches of science, with a happy talent of communication, correct and gentlemanly manners, and an enlarged and liberal mind. He, most happily for me, became soon attached to me, and made me his daily companion when not engaged in the school; and from his conversation I got my first views of the expansion of science, and of the system of things in which we are placed. Fortunately, the philosophical chair became vacant soon after my arrival at college, and he was appointed to fill it *per interim:* and he was the first who ever gave, in that college, regular lectures in Ethics, Rhetoric and Belles Lettres. He returned to Europe in 1762, having previously filled up the measure of his goodness to me, by procuring for me, from his most intimate friend, George Wythe, a reception as a student of law, under his direction, and introduced me to the acquaintance and familiar table of Governor Fauquier, the ablest man who had ever filled that office."*

Jefferson's statement of Dr. Small's influence upon him.

Leaving college at nineteen, Jefferson spent five years studying law with Wythe, the above mentioned leading lawyer in Virginia; and at twenty-four, was admitted to practice. He was immediately successful. During his first year he had sixty-eight cases: an almost unequalled record for a young lawyer. The point is, the Virginia aristocrats were in constant litigation over land and boundaries; and Jefferson seems to have been the favorite young lawyer, to whom they gave their cases. He was wholly an office lawyer: a defect in the throat prevented his ever speaking in public,

Studying law.

* Jefferson, *Autobiography: Writings,* Vol. I, pp. 3, 4.

even in a Court room. This should be remembered, with reference to his later career. During his seven years of law practice, Jefferson practically doubled his large inherited property; and he was now one of the richest young men in Virginia. At thirty-two, Jefferson transferred his remaining cases to his friend, Edmund Randolph, to serve in the activities of the Revolution, and never practised law again.

The successful seven years of law practice.

Meantime, from 1769 to 1774, he had served every year as burgess, together with Washington. In 1774, he was elected to the Convention to plan the union of the Colonies; and sent a series of resolutions. These were not adopted, as they were in advance of public opinion of the time, but were printed in a pamphlet, entitled *A Summary View of the Rights of America,* and widely read throughout the Colonies. That pamphlet makes interesting reading today. In it, Jefferson held that the British colonization of America was exactly parallel to the Saxon settlement of England: Franklin's idea in his *Edict of the King of Prussia.* Of the American colonists he said, "For themselves they fought, for themselves they conquered, and for themselves alone they have the right to hold." He denied all right on the part of Britain to restrict the trade and manufactures of the Colonies, and claimed for them entire freedom of self-government. You will recognize that these principles, while in advance of the hour, were just those, for which the colonists fought through the Revolution; evidencing

Service as Burgess.

Summary of the Rights of America.

how far-visioned Jefferson was, as political philosopher.

It was during his period of law practice, at Williamsburg, that Jefferson's personal life was permanently established. Like Washington, Jefferson had early shown a warm interest in the opposite sex. There had been a number of youthful love affairs. At Williamsburg, however, one of Jefferson's legal associates was John Wayles, possessed of a very beautiful estate, on the edge of town, "The Forest", and, more important, of a lovely daughter, a young widow without children, Martha Skelton, belle of the neighborhood, well educated, accomplished in music. Jefferson, all his life, was a lover of music. Early, he procured an unusual violin, under peculiar circumstances, carried it everywhere with him—to Paris, to the Capital, as President—and played upon it, to his own satisfaction. Well, there were duets at the Forest; from the musical companionship, there developed a warm, tender love relationship; and on New Year's Day, 1772, as Jefferson approached the age of twenty-nine, he and Martha Skelton were married. She was then twenty-three years old. A few days later, he started with his bride, on the hundred mile drive to "Monticello", the home he had begun building two years before.

Jefferson's marriage with Martha Skelton.

Monticello—little mountain—as the Italian name indicates, rises, an almost perfect cone, about six hundred feet above the surrounding countryside, sloping down to the banks of the Rivanna, with marvellous

Monticello.

views, over the rolling hills, to the majestic line of the Blue Ridge. On the summit of the little mountain, Jefferson had his mansion half-erected; living with his bride, for a time, in a small brick building, afterwards part of the slave quarters; and then moving into the still unfinished great house. It was, indeed, thirty-two years, from its beginning, before Monticello was finally completed.

The mansion. Jefferson, his own architect.

Jefferson was his own architect. A devoted student of architecture and lover of the Classic type, he planned the stately home on Greek lines. The Portico rose the full height of the structure, with majestic Doric columns. The west rooms also rose to the roof; but in the interior, Jefferson used the lighter and more graceful Ionic style. It was the finest mansion in that part of Virginia, and in majestic simplicity and dignity, one of the most satisfying dwellings ever erected on American soil. Here Jefferson entertained, with more than the generous Southern hospitality. The dinners and wines of Monticello were famous.

Monticello, a world in itself.

Even more than Mount Vernon under Washington, Monticello was a little world in itself. It had to be, for it was further away from the more settled portion of Virginia. Jefferson was opposed to slavery, more bitterly even than Washington. There are many passages, in his various writings, expressing his view of the institution. The following is a typical paragraph, from the *Notes on Virginia*:

"There must doubtless be an unhappy influence on the manners of our people produced by the existence of slavery among us. The whole commerce between master and slave is a perpetual exercise of the most boisterous passions, and most unremitting despotism on the one part, and degrading submission on the other. Our children see this and learn to imitate it. * * * With the morals of the people, their industry also is destroyed. For in a warm climate, no man will labor for himself who can make another labor for him. This is so true, that of the proprietors of slaves a very small proportion indeed are ever seen to labor. And can the liberties of a nation be thought secure when we have removed their only firm basis, a conviction in the minds of the people that these liberties are of the gift of God? that they are not to be violated but with his wrath? Indeed, I tremble for my country when I reflect that God is just; that his justice cannot sleep forever."*

Jefferson's views of slavery.

The only fault in limiting the statement to a warm climate!

No Abolitionist ever stated the case more impressively.

With that attitude toward it, Jefferson, like Washington and other intelligent men born into the institution of slavery, accepted it and did the best he could with it. Among his slaves, were artisans of all kinds. The bricks for Monticello were made on the estate. The nails for the mansion were wrought by slaves: indeed, the sale of wrought nails was one of the sources of income for the estate.

Life at Monticello.

At the time of his marriage, Jefferson had about five thousand acres of land. The death of his wife's father, the following year, brought him forty thousand more acres and a hundred and thirty-five more slaves. This again practically doubled his property.

The large inheritance from John Wayles and its consequences.

* Jefferson, *Notes on Virginia: Writings,* Vol. II, pp. 225-227.

In his father-in-law's lands was the Natural Bridge of Virginia, about eighty miles from Monticello. Jefferson loved that beautiful phenomenon; dreamed of building a hermitage there, where he could retire, for study and meditation; but that plan was never carried out.

This inheritance from his wife's father was not an unmixed blessing, for the lands were heavily mortgaged; and in the end Jefferson paid the mortgage practically three times over: having to pay it with British gold in London, and collect the money in the depreciating Continental currency. This was one of the causes of the collapse of Jefferson's financial fortunes, later on.

Character of Jefferson as husband and father.

Jefferson's marriage, the result of a warm and tender love-affair, remained a beautiful love-affair through the ten years of his wife's life. He was a devoted husband and a tender father to his children. There were six, only two daughters surviving infancy. These two grew to maturity and married; the younger dying early, while the elder lived through a long life-time and was the mother of eleven children. Jefferson's letters to his daughters are tender in affection and wise in kindly counsel. It is interesting that the democratic Jefferson was anxious, above all, that his daughters should have the manners of cultivated gentlewomen.

The tradition is that when Jefferson's wife was dying, in September, 1782, she held up her fingers to the number of the children she was leaving behind, and said she could not bear to think of any other woman being the mother of her children. Jefferson promised his dying wife that he would never marry again; and kept the promise faithfully to the end. There may have been other love-affairs—apparently there were—but he never married again.

The faithfully kept promise to the dying wife.

It is interesting that Jefferson was not the successful farmer and business man that Washington was, although he gave equally careful attention to details of management. It is true that the ravaging of his estates during the Revolution and the multiplied paying of his father-in-law's mortgage contributed to the later collapse of Jefferson's financial fortunes; and then, through his wife's early death, there was no Martha to supervise the estate during the long periods of absence, as in Washington's case. Beyond all this, however, it must be admitted that Jefferson did not have the practical business success of Washington. Was it that Jefferson was more the idealist, dreamer, experimenter, without that consistent grasp of objective facts, of things as they are, that was the dominant characteristic of Washington's mind? Jefferson introduced new varieties of plants, sending the seeds widely through the Southern Colonies. He imported improved breeds of domestic animals. He sought to develop olive culture and improved rice culture, in the South. He carried out rotation of crops: a great advance in farming, at that time. In it all, he was the progressive experimenter, in the interest of the

Jefferson as farmer and business man.

Contrast with Washington.

Progressive measures in agriculture.

general welfare, rather than the consistently successful business man.

Jefferson taking his seat in the second Continental Congress, June 21st, 1775.

Jefferson was a member of the Convention at Richmond, to choose delegates to the second Continental Congress. He heard Patrick Henry's most eloquent speech; and was chosen an alternate delegate to the Congress. As the one he was to replace could not serve, Jefferson was sent to the Congress. He had drawn up the Virginia answer to Lord North's Propositions, and took it with him to the Continental Congress, which approved it. Though there were but two members of the Congress younger than Jefferson, he was asked to prepare the reply of the Congress to the Propositions; which means that his remarkable literary gift was already widely recognized.

Drafting the answers, both of Virginia and of the Congress, to Lord North's Propositions.

In May, 1776, the Virginia Assembly passed resolutions of independence, and sent a copy of them, by Richard Henry Lee, to the Continental Congress, with the request that Congress take similar action. After extended debate, the Virginia motion carried; and Jefferson was appointed on the Committee to prepare the Declaration. The other members of the Committee requested Jefferson to draft it; and he did so, spending eighteen days at the task. His draft, approved by the members of the Committee, was bitterly attacked from some quarters in the Congress; but with the elision of some passages, and a few changes, mostly improvements, it was accepted by the Congress, substantially as written by Jefferson, and signed by the delegates, on the late afternoon of July

Virginia's Resolutions of Independence.

Jefferson appointed to draft the Declaration of Independence.

4th, 1776. It was read publicly in Independence Square, Philadelphia, at noon, on July 8th. That evening, the King's Coat of Arms was brought from the State apartments and publicly burned. There were similar scenes throughout the colonies, the Declaration really launching the Revolution.

The Declaration accepted by the Congress, and signed by the delegates, July 4th, 1776, thus launching the Revolution.

Jefferson thus became the author of the Nation's birthright, the charter of our liberties. Lincoln loved to call it, "The White Man's Charter of Freedom", using the phrase until it became a political campaign cry. To get more fully Lincoln's view of the Declaration, note the passage in his letter to the Boston Committee, inviting him to the celebration of Jefferson's birthday in 1859:

> "All honor to Jefferson—to the man who, in the concrete pressure of a struggle for national independence by a single people, had the coolness, forecast, and capacity to introduce into a mere revolutionary document an abstract truth, applicable to all men and all times, and so to embalm it there that today and in all coming days it shall be a rebuke and a stumbling-block to the very harbingers of reappearing tyranny and oppression."*

Lincoln's view of the significance of the Declaration.

Such was Lincoln's view of the Declaration of Independence, as written by Thomas Jefferson, stated during the year between Lincoln's candidacy for the Senate and his election to the Presidency, under the auspices of the political party born to fight the party founded by Thomas Jefferson.

---

* Lincoln, in Letter to the Boston Committee, Springfield, Ills., April 6th, 1859: *Writings* Vol. V, p. 26.

Lincoln regarding Jefferson as our most distinguished political leader.

In the campaign of 1854, in his speech at Peoria, replying to Senator Douglas, Lincoln had said:

> "Mr. Jefferson—the author of the Declaration of Independence, and otherwise a chief factor in the Revolution— . . . who was, is, and perhaps will continue to be, the most distinguished politician of our history." *

Permanent significance of the charter of American liberties.

Lincoln's words on the Declaration are worth pondering today, when so many half-formed scholars patronizingly dispose of the Declaration as a "tissue of glittering generalities." Rightly understood, that is just what it is: a fabric of resplendent general ideas—the only basis on which men can widely unite. They can never agree on questions of special policy. It is only such a program of large, permanently true general conceptions that furnishes a sound basis of union. Exactly the same criticism was made on President Wilson's famous Fourteen Points; and they had just the same excellence, formulating a program of shining general ideas, on which the struggling nations could unite. Indeed, it is because President Wilson was so faithful to the great ideas of Thomas Jefferson, and applied them with such wisdom to international relations, that History will doubtless regard him as the outstanding American president since Lincoln.

President Wilson's Fourteen Points as arousing the same criticism and having the same excellence as the Declaration.

If Jefferson had done nothing else than write the Declaration of Independence, his fame would have been sufficiently established as the philosopher of democracy.

* Lincoln, in speech at Peoria, Ills., Oct. 16th, 1854: *Writings*, Vol. II, p. 180.

In October, 1776, Jefferson was appointed, with Franklin and Silas Deane, as Commissioner to go to France and seek to bring France in on the American side. Because of his wife's illness, Jefferson declined the appointment and went home to Virginia, where he was elected a member of the Virginia Legislature and appointed at the head of a Committee to revise the Virginia statutes. As an independent commonwealth, Virginia wished to reform its whole body of legislation and take a fresh start. The other members of the Committee did little work, so that the revision was the labor of Jefferson. He had previously collected the colonial statutes, during the period of his law practice, and many of them had survived only because of this.

Jefferson's great service in the revision of the Virginia statutes.

This work of Jefferson's was far more important than easily appears. Virginia was burdened with a mass of ill advised legislation: some of it atrocious in in character; other parts lifted over from England. She had, for instance, taken over the British laws on primogeniture and entail, with the result that a powerful landed aristocracy was rapidly growing up in Virginia, similar to that in England. Jefferson's first aim was to eliminate this whole body of legislation fostering aristocracy, and substitute the principle of division of estates among all the children of a family in each generation. This was carried the same year, 1776, with the result of stopping largely the growth of a landed aristocracy in Virginia, but

Eliminating laws on primogeniture and entail.

with the further consequence that Jefferson had the life-long hatred of many of the aristocrats.

Glaring injustice and oppression of the Colonial laws on religion.

Still more important was Jefferson's work in relation to the Virginia laws on religion. It is difficult for anyone, not intimately familiar with colonial history, to realize how atrocious many of those laws were. Virginia, so largely settled by British aristocrats, had taken over the established Church of England, and given it even more arbitrary authority in the Colony. All persons, whatever their faith, were compelled to pay tithes to the established Church. Baptists, Methodists, Quakers, Presbyterians were forbidden to teach school or hold religious services, on penalty of arrest and fine. Roman Catholics could not teach school, hold religious services, own a horse, carry a gun or give testimony in a court of law. Celebration of the Mass was punishable by death. It was a felony to deny the doctrine of the Trinity. A father could be legally deprived of his children, if he did not accept the tenets of the Church of England. For treating a Church of England clergyman with disrespect (and under their habit of life in Virginia, some of them perhaps deserved such treatment) the offender was publicly whipped and compelled to ask pardon in Church on three successive Sundays. For failure to attend the exposition of the Catechism, one was fined a week's provisions; for a second offense, the same and whipping; for a third offense, these two punishments and imprisonment. All persons were required to give an account of their faith to the Church of England Clergyman. If they refused, they were publicly whipped. For a second refusal, the same and public acknowledgement in Church. For a third refusal, one was publicly whipped every day until one did make acknowledgement in Church.

Now please note that you cannot make a bad law respectable by enacting it. This is emphasized because there is a fraction of our population, rather noisy at present, insisting that, the moment a law gets on the statute books, it thereby becomes venerable, and demands the respect as well as obedience of every citizen. That is distinctly not true. It is just as much the duty of good citizenship to protest against unjust laws and seek to have them abrogated, as it is to respect and obey just laws. The chief advantage of enforcing a bad law is to arouse public opinion to its swift elimination. A law may be so bad that it is well that it is not regularly enforced. It was a good thing that these atrocious statutes on religion were not always enforced in colonial Virginia. For instance, was it not well that George Washington, who was a liberal in religion, and of whom the Church of England clergyman frequently complained to Mrs. Washington, because of his neglect of certain of the above observances, was not publicly whipped every day, for failing to give an account of his conscience to the Church of England clergyman?

What is good citizenship in relation to unjust laws?

Jefferson fought for the elimination of this whole mass of wicked legislation. The fight lasted ten years. At the end of that time, Jefferson's friends

Jefferson's successful fight.

in the legislature secured the repeal of all the old laws on religion, and the substitution of Jefferson's great statute on religious freedom. It is so brief that the whole main item may be quoted:

The great Statute on Religious Freedom.

> "*Be it therefore enacted by the General Assembly,* That no man shall be compelled to frequent or support any religious worship, place or ministry whatsoever, nor shall be enforced, restrained, molested, or burthened in his body or goods, nor shall otherwise suffer on account of his religious opinions or belief; but that all men shall be free to profess, and by argument to maintain, their opinions in matters of religion, and that the same shall in no wise diminish, enlarge, or affect their civil capacities."*

Jefferson, the Father of American religious freedom.

This was not the earliest statute on religious freedom in America; but it is one of the simplest and noblest; and the great personal prestige of Jefferson made it peculiarly influential in the national councils. That we have a similar guaranty, in those first great amendments to the Constitution, is due in large measure to the influence of Jefferson. He thus deserves, more than any other individual, to be called the Father of American religious liberty, of that permanent separation of the State from all Church establishments, with untrammeled freedom of belief, speech and worship, guaranteed in the Nation's charter.

Today, we witness a wide recrudescence of religious and racial prejudice and intolerance, with sinis-

---

* Jefferson, from the *Act for Establishing Religious Freedom,* passed by the Virginia Assembly, 1786: *Writings,* Vol. II, pp. 302, 303.

ter renewed attempts to suppress by prohibitory legislation the open study and free discussion of scientific facts and laws, under the absurd delusion that there can be a conflict between true religion and science, which is merely the faithful recording of reality. This much may be said: whenever there is a conflict between science and what calls itself religion, it is never science that passes. The anti-evolution laws of several States are an ugly symptom of our reversion back well toward the spirit of the Spanish Inquisition. In a time such as this, surely Jefferson's great liberal ideas need reaffirmation and loyal following, as never before in our history. Truly the conduct of many who call upon his name and claim to be his followers is in flagrant violation of the principles Jefferson taught.

Significance of Jeffersons's liberal ideas for present day America.

The third item in Jefferson's revision of the Virginia statutes was education. He was one of the earliest American statesmen to recognize the responsibility of the State in the education of the citizen, under democracy, and the first to see fully that responsibility. He planned a complete system of state education for Virginia, crowned by a university. Unfortunately, this plan was rejected by the Legislature. The only part of it Jefferson succeeded in fighting through, in his late years, was the establishment of the University of Virginia.

The rejected program on public education.

The fourth item in Jefferson's great program was the elimination of slavery. The plan was, with the stopping of further importation of slaves, to declare

The plan for eliminating slavery.

free all born after a certain date, and deport them at a proper age. It is interesting that Jefferson held deportation to be as necessary as emancipation. His own statement is:

Jefferson believing in deportation, as well as emancipation.

> "The principles of the amendment were agreed on, that is to say, the freedom of all born after a certain day, and deportation at a proper age. But it was found that the public mind would not yet bear the proposition, nor will it bear it even at this day. Yet the day is not distant when it must bear and adopt it, or worse will follow. Nothing is more certainly written in the book of fate, than that these people are to be free; nor is it less certain that the two races, equally free, cannot live in the same government. Nature, habit, opinion have drawn indelible lines of distinction between them. It is still in our power to direct the process of emancipation and deportation, peaceably, and in such slow degree, as that the evil will wear off insensibly, and their place be, *pari passu*, filled up by free white laborers. If, on the contrary, it is left to force itself on, human nature must shudder at the prospect held up."*

Almost a forecast of the Civil War!

It is noteworthy that Lincoln agreed with his master, Jefferson, on the wisdom of deportation, as well as emancipation.

The only element of this plan which carried was the prohibition, in 1778, of the further importation of slaves into Virginia.

The one item concerning slavery that carried.

The final feature of the program was the revision of the penal system. The colonial laws contained much that was barbarous and based literally on the

* Jefferson, *Autobiography: Writings,* Vol. I, pp. 72, 73.

"eye for an eye, and tooth for a tooth" principle. Jefferson prepared a code, based on the more humane European models, restricting capital punishment, and aiming at the reformation of the offender. The gradual adoption of this, ultimately eliminated the mass of merely revengeful laws. This reform, alone, justifies Jefferson's fame as the philosopher of democracy.

Significance of Jefferson's revision of the penal system.

Jefferson summed up the significance of his revision of the Virginia laws in these words:

> "I considered four of these bills, passed or reported, as forming a system by which every fibre would be eradicated of ancient or future aristocracy; and a foundation laid for a government truly republican. The repeal of the laws of entail would prevent the accumulation and perpetuation of wealth, in select families, and preserve the soil of the country from being daily more and more absorbed in mort-main. The abolition of primogeniture, and equal partition of inheritances, removed the feudal and unnatural distinctions which made one member of every family rich, and all the rest poor, substituting equal partition, the best of all Agrarian laws. The restoration of the rights of conscience relieved the people from taxation for the support of a religion not theirs; for the establishment was truly of the religion of the rich, the dissenting sects being entirely composed of the less wealthy people; and these, by the bill for a general education, would be qualified to understand their rights, to maintain them, and to exercise with intelligence their parts in self-government; and all this would be effected, without the violation of a single natural right of any one individual citizen."*

Jefferson's own view of the aim and value of his work in revising the Virginia statutes.

The correlation of different elements in Jefferson's program of democracy.

* Jefferson, *Autobiography: Writings*, Vol. I, pp. 73, 74.

Jefferson's two terms as Governor of Virginia.

During the darkest period of the War for Independence, Jefferson served two terms as Governor of Virginia. At this time, Virginia was overrun and ravished by British troops, especially by those under the command of Benedict Arnold, who behaved with a cruelty only a traitor will show toward the people he has betrayed. The legislature had to flee from Richmond, which was ravaged, to Charlottesville, and narrowly escaped capture. Jefferson, himself, just avoided capture, by fleeing from Monticello, as the British were coming up the hill. The beautiful mansion was fortunately spared by the British commander, Tarleton, but Jefferson's other estates were ravaged and the buildings burned; which was a further cause for the later ruin of his financial fortunes.

Ravaging of Virginia by the British.

The criticism of Jefferson and its effect upon him.

Jefferson was severely criticized for not having taken, as Governor, stronger and more efficient measures for resisting the British invasion. The Legislature, in 1782, passed a resolution exonerating him; but he regarded the attacks as wholly unjust, and his bitterness over them lasted to the end of his days.

The *Notes on Virginia.*

It was at this period of his life that Jefferson wrote his *Notes on Virginia.* The book was written primarily to inform one of his friends, a French nobleman, of the conditions and life in the new world. Jefferson modestly printed it in a private edition of two hundred copies. One of these got translated into garbled French and published abroad. To protect himself, Jefferson published a complete edition in London. He need not have been so modest about the work; for it is truly a great book. It not only gave a general review of Virginia, in her then vast territory, of the topography, mineral wealth, fauna and flora, slaves and Indians, institutions and laws, but contains as well much of his social and political philosophy, with passages of literary beauty and wisdom which are delightful reading today. Jefferson collected and analyzed his material with the instincts and labor at once of the scholar, the literary man and the philosopher. The *Notes on Virginia* did much to advance his fame, at home and abroad, and to prepare the way for his warm welcome in France.

Remarkable character of Jefferson's work.

Advancing reputation as a man of letters.

In 1783, Jefferson was again a member of the Continental Congress. He was at the head of the Committee to consider the treaty of peace. His report on a Monetary System gave the basis for our present currency, though Gouverneur Morris first advocated the decimal system. More important still was Jefferson's service in formulating the plan of government for the Northwest Territory. Virginia's claim to that vast region extending from the Ohio to Wisconsin, and including the present states of Ohio, Indiana, Michigan and Illinois, was ceded to Congress and Jefferson presented the deed. His plan for government provided that slavery should cease in the territory after 1800. Defeated at first, this measure carried in 1787; slavery being thus prohibited by law, in the Northwest Territory after 1800; and that made Union victory possible in the Civil War. Jefferson's original bill further provided that slavery should be

Services in the Continental Congress of 1783.

Significance of Jefferson's bill forbidding slavery in the Northwest Territory.

prohibited, from the same date, in the southwest territory. This was permanently rejected by the Congress: had it carried, there would have been no Civil War. This is mentioned to indicate how far-visioned a statesman Jefferson was, with reference to the greatest issue that was afterwards to divide the Nation.

The happy five years in France, 1784-1789.

In 1784, at forty-one, Jefferson was again asked to go to France, as associate with Franklin and John Adams, to negotiate commercial treaties with European powers. His wife had died in the meantime: there was nothing now to hold him to Monticello, and he accepted. After a year, he was made successor to Franklin as Minister to France. He remained in France five years, among the happiest of his life. He was welcomed with an enthusiasm, second only to that accorded Franklin. His fame as statesman had preceded him; the French had read his *Notes on Virginia.* His wit, cultivated conversation, aristocratic manners and quick mastery of a fluent speaking of the French tongue made him a welcome member of that brilliant, worldly circle, gathered at the Court of the last King Louis and Marie Antoinette. He took an elegant establishment in Paris and entertained with easy hospitality, finding his chief difficulty in living on his nine thousand dollars salary, with the reduced revenues of his Virginia estates, ravaged by the War. His elder daughter went over with him; and he sent, shortly after arrival, for the younger. He formed many friendships with brilliant women and men.

Jefferson as diplomat.

Associations with Paris society.

The impression made upon him by the artificial French society, feverishly dancing on the brink of revolution, is expressed in his numerous letters, of which the following is a characteristic example:

A characteristic letter, giving Jefferson's view of French society, in contrast to the conditions prevailing in America.

"Behold me at length on the vaunted scene of Europe! * * * You are, perhaps, curious to know how this new scene has struck a savage of the mountains of America. Not advantageously, I assure you. I find the general state of humanity here most deplorable. The truth of Voltaire's observation, offers itself perpetually, that every man here must be either the hammer or the anvil. It is a true picture of that country to which they say we shall pass hereafter, and where we are to see God and his angels in splendor, and crowds of the damned trampled under their feet. While the great mass of the people are thus suffering under physical and moral oppression, I have endeavored to examine more nearly the condition of the great, to appreciate the true value of the circumstances in their situation, which dazzle the bulk of spectators, and, especially, to compare it with that degree of happiness which is enjoyed in America, by every class of people. Intrigues of love occupy the younger, and those of ambition, the elder part of the great. Conjugal love having no existence among them, domestic happiness, of which that is the basis, is utterly unknown. In lieu of this, are substituted pursuits which nourish and invigorate all our bad passions, and which offer only moments of ecstacy amidst days and months of restlessness and torment. Much, very much inferior, this, to the tranquil, permanent felicity with which domestic society in America blesses most of its inhabitants; leaving them to follow steadily those pursuits which health and reason ap-

The philosopher of democracy.

prove, and rendering truly delicious the intervals of those pursuits.

Pungent application to present day America!

Jefferson a lover of the arts.

"In science, the mass of the people are two centuries behind ours; their literati, half a dozen years before us. Books, really good, acquire just reputation in that time, and so become known to us, and communicate to us all their advances in knowledge. Is not this delay compensated, by our being placed out of the reach of that swarm of nonsensical publications which issues daily from a thousand presses, and perishes almost in issuing? * * * Were I to proceed to tell you how much I enjoy their architecture, sculpture, painting, music, I should want words. It is in these arts they shine. The last of them, particularly, is an enjoyment, the deprivation of which with us, cannot be calculated."*

While Jefferson fulfilled his duties as diplomat with scrupulous fidelity, and was entirely at home with the aristocrats of the old régime, his instincts and settled convictions alike fitted him fully to appreciate the aims of those leaders who were bringing on the French Revolution. La Fayette was one of his most intimate life-long friends.

Influence of the American Revolution on France.

France was deeply influenced by our example. We had fought through the Revolution successfully and got rid of kings: why should not she? Of course, there was a difference: our King was an absentee landlord; while theirs lived among them, exercising supremely autocratic power; and then, there was a wide difference in the temperament and character of

* Jefferson, in letter to Charles Bellini, Paris, September 30, 1785: *Writings,* Vol. V, pp. 152-4.

the two peoples. Nevertheless, the French Revolution was profoundly stimulated by ours.

Here in America, the desperate conditions of the years following the War, impressed our statesmen—Washington, Hamilton and the rest—with the need of a strong, authoritative central government. As the French Revolution began, they saw chiefly its bloodshed and destructive lawlessness, and drew away from it, in strong disapproval, turning sympathetically to the British example and practice in government. Jefferson, remote from the situation at home and so less influenced by it, and prepared by temperament and political philosophy to understand the hopes of the leaders of the French Revolution, was, alone among our statesmen, able to see across the initial bloodshed to its final meaning. For this, he was bitterly attacked at the time; and slavish biographers have echoed the criticisms to the present hour; but they are wrong; for the view Thomas Jefferson took of the ultimate significance of the French Revolution is the one held by every liberal scholar in the world today. The Bastille fell before his return from France; so he saw the actual beginnings of the Revolution.

Jefferson's view of the French Revolution.

Jefferson's years in Paris gave him life-long love and devotion to France and the French people. After reviewing his experience in the *Autobiography,* he said:

> "I cannot leave this great and good country (France), without expressing my sense of its pre-emi-

Jefferson's permanent love for France.

nence of character among the nations of the earth. A more benevolent people I have never known, nor greater warmth and devotedness in their select friendships. Their kindness and accommodation to strangers is unparalleled, and the hospitality of Paris is beyond anything I had conceived to be practicable in a large city. Their eminence, too, in science, the communicative dispositions of their scientific men, the politeness of the general manners, the ease and vivacity of their conversation, give a charm to their society, to be found nowhere else."*

His intense Americanism, increased by his residence abroad.

With this feeling permanently for France, Jefferson came home in October, 1789, only the more wholeheartedly American. His residence abroad had increased his love for his home land and made him idealize it. This is expressed in numerous letters from Paris. For instance, to his friend, James Monroe, he had written:

Letter to James Monroe, expressing Jefferson's view of the effect of foreign residence.

"I sincerely wish you may find it convenient to come here; the pleasure of the trip will be less than you expect, but the utility greater. It will make you adore your own country, its soil, its climate, its equality, liberty, laws, people and manners. My God! how little do my countrymen know what precious blessings they are in possession of, and which no other people on earth enjoy. I confess I had no idea of it myself." †

Jefferson's advice, based upon his experience, that the best way to waken love of one's own land is to live

* Jefferson, *Autobiography: Writings*, Vol. I, p. 159.

† Jefferson, in a letter to James Monroe, Paris, June 17, 1785: *Writings*, Vol. V, p. 21.

abroad awhile, is just as true today as when Jefferson gave it to Monroe.

Formulating the principles of the Monroe Doctrine.

Jefferson returned believing in America for Americans, deprecating free immigration, advocating the complete detachment of America from European politics and conflicts, formulating the principles Monroe afterwards promulgated in what we know as the Monroe Doctrine. Monroe proclaimed it; but Jefferson formulated it.

Jefferson's intention to return to France, and embarrassment at Washington's invitation to become Secretary of State.

Jefferson had expected, on his return, to retire to spend some time at Monticello and go back to France. To his surprise and embarrassment, he found that Washington wanted him, as Secretary of State, in the newly formed Federal Government. His experience abroad had increased Jefferson's strong belief in the need for a union of the States. He held that "The politics of Europe render it indispensably necessary that, with respect to everything external, we be one nation only, firmly hooped together. Interior government is what each State should keep to itself." * He followed, with deep interest and increasing approval, the formulation of the Constitution, in which his friend, James Madison, had so important a part. His two criticisms of the Constitution, as signed, were that it contained no bill of rights and no prohibition of the repeated re-election of a President: both valid objections. His view is best expressed in a letter from Paris, to A. Donald:

Jefferson's belief in a union of States and substantial approval of the Constitution, adopted in his absence.

His two objections to the Constitution.

* Jefferson, in letter to James Madison, Paris, February 8, 1786: *Writings,* Vol. VI, p. 278.

The letter giving Jefferson's matured view of the Constitution.

"I wish with all my soul, that the nine first conventions may accept the new constitution, because this will secure to us the good it contains, which I think great and important. But I equally wish, that the four latest conventions, whichever they be, may refuse to accede to it, till a declaration of rights be annexed. This would probably command the offer of such a declaration, and thus give to the whole fabric, perhaps, as much perfection as anyone of that kind ever had. By a declaration of rights, I mean one which shall stipulate freedom of religion, freedom of the press, freedom of commerce against monopolies, trial by juries in all cases, no suspensions of the habeas corpus, no standing armies. These are the fetters against doing evil, which no honest government should decline. There is another strong feature in the new Constitution, which I as strongly dislike. That is, the perpetual re-eligibility of the President. Of this I expect no amendment at present, because I do not see that anybody has objected to it on your side the water. * * * We must take care, however, that neither this, nor any other objection to the new form, produces a schism in our Union. That would be an incurable evil, because near friends falling out, never re-unite cordially; whereas, all of us going together, we shall be sure to cure the evils of our new Constitution, before they do great harm."*

The Amendments answering Jefferson's chief objection to the Constitution.

Eleven States had ratified the Nation's charter before Jefferson left France; and the ten great Amendments, which answered his chief objection to it, were proposed at the first session of Congress, shortly after his return. He was reluctant, nevertheless, to as-

* Jefferson, in letter to A. Donald, Paris, Feb. 7, 1788: *Writings*, Vol. VI, pp. 425, 426.

sume the duties of Secretary of State; but yielding to Washington's reiterated wish, he accepted, taking office in March, 1790.

Assuming office as Secretary of State, in March, 1790.

The most important problem of foreign relations, Jefferson had to handle as Secretary of State, was the Genet affair. France, under the Directorate, declared war on Britain; and as the treaty of alliance, of 1778, had never been repealed, assumed that we would enter the war on the side of France. Citizen Genet was sent over; and landed at Charleston, South Carolina, in April, 1793. He came North, greeted with wild enthusiasm by the French-loving populace, enlisting men to fight against Britain, arranged for the French consuls to act as courts for prize ships brought into American ports, and even made plans for fitting out privateers to sail from our ports and prey on British commerce.

The Genet affair.

Conduct of Citizen Genet on arriving in America.

With the intense popular sympathy for France, the result was the serious embarrassment of the Government. We were a young, struggling country, burdened with the devastation and debts of the Revolution, in no condition to go to war, and with no reason for it, except the old French friendship.

The consequence was a split in the Cabinet. Hamilton, Knox and Randolph, with whom Washington agreed, held that France had declared a war of aggression, while the treaty was for an alliance for mutual defense, and that our treaty had been made with King Louis; and since he had lost his throne and head, and an entirely different government had been

Opposing views in the Administration.

established as a result of the French Revolution, the treaty was automatically abrogated. This was perhaps the technically correct view, and certainly the view expedient for American interests.

Jefferson, loving France passionately and welcoming her Revolution, hating Britain and regarding his colleagues in the government as servile toward her, argued just the opposite. He held that the treaty had been made in good faith; France had loyally fulfilled her part under it, during our Revolutionary War; we were not concerned with domestic changes in France; and the treaty was, therefore, still binding. This was the more generous and the more moral view, though inconsistent with practical American interests.

Jefferson's treatment of Citizen Genet.

Jefferson therefore welcomed Citizen Genet, had conferences with him and sought to further his plans. When, however, Genet arrogantly announced his intention to appeal, across the head of the beloved President, Washington, to the people of the United States, Jefferson shared the universal indignation, would have nothing more to do with Genet and his schemes, and from that time supported Washington's policy. The result of these circumstances, however, was that Washington's great Neutrality Proclamation was drafted, not by Jefferson, the Secretary of State, but by Randolph, the Attorney General. It might be added that Citizen Genet did not go back to France: he married a daughter of Governor Clin-

The Neutrality Proclamation, furnishing the permanent basis for our foreign policy.

ton, of New York, and settled down in New York City, to innocuous citizenship.

During the early period of Jefferson's service as Secretary of State, he was on entirely friendly terms with Washington's great Secretary of the Treasury, Hamilton. When in his fight to make the Federal government a living reality, Hamilton was threatened with defeat on his key-measure, for the assumption of state debts by the Federal Government, he came to Jefferson and proposed that if Jefferson would give him the needed Virginia votes for assumption, he would furnish enough Federalist votes to place the new Capital where Jefferson and the other southern leaders wanted it: where it is today. Otherwise, the Capital would have gone to New York or Philadelphia, as the majority of votes favored one of those places.

Jefferson's relations with Hamilton.

The political bargain on Assumption and the Capital.

At that time, Jefferson was not opposed to Hamilton's measure, probably not recognizing the consequences it carried. Also, Jefferson did not realize the feeling in the South, and thought it would be well for the Federal Government to take over the State debts. So he cheerfully agreed. In July, 1790, came the vote on the Capital; and Hamilton carried out his part of the bargain. In August, the final vote came on assumption. Jefferson, true to his side of the agreement, furnished the needed Virginia votes; and Hamilton's key measure carried by a slight margin. That is why the Capital is at Washington; and *that is why* there was a government in it, strong enough to survive the Civil War and function effectively to the present hour.

Reasons for the break with Hamilton.

As time went on, however, Jefferson drew back, in increasing alarm, from the rapidly growing power of the Federal Government, under Hamilton's vigorous fostering with Washington's sanction. To understand this, one must remember the fundamental contrast between the two men. Hamilton was forceful and aggressive, rather loving a fight. Jefferson was pacific and conciliatory, disliking a quarrel, but holding tenaciously to his opinions. Hamilton, moreover, believed, by temperament and conviction, in the strongest government possible consistent with liberty. Jefferson, equally by temperament and conviction, believed in the least government possible, consistent with law and order. He held that when government goes much beyond the police functions of protecting life and property and enforcing contracts, it is in danger of passing over into tyranny.

Contrast in the two great leaders, in temperament and philosophy.

Jefferson never understood Hamilton's funding scheme, and failed to appreciate the moral significance of his plans for paying the Nation's debt, unjustly regarding these measures as a mere device to gain partisan adherents for the Federalist group. He sincerely believed that the Treasury Department was corrupting the Congress, and that the government was going headlong toward monarchy.

The result was a growing rupture between Jefferson and Hamilton: the fundamental opposition in conviction finally becoming bitter personal enmity.

Jefferson fostered, or at least approved, the increasingly bitter attacks upon Hamilton, finally directly arraigning him and his policies in letters to the President. When he found, however, that Washington continued to favor every one of Hamilton's measures for strengthening the power and authority of the central government, he resigned at the end of 1793, and went home, with mingled relief and disgust, to Virginia.

Resignation from the Cabinet in 1793.

Late in his life, Jefferson wrote out gossipy, anecdotal reminiscences, for which he had kept notes at the time, of his experiences as member of Washington's Cabinet. He called them *Anas;* and left them to be published after his death. In the *Anas,* with the reiterated charge that Hamilton governed by corruption, Jefferson says that Hamilton tricked him into the bargain on the Capital and assumption; that he had recently returned from France, did not understand the situation, and was deceived. That was not true: Jefferson was not tricked. He experienced a sincere change in conviction; and should have so stated it. Leaving for publication, after death, these *Anas,* with their unjustly sinister reflections on a great associate, long since dead, is the darkest stain upon Jefferson's high career.

Character of the *Anas.*

The instance is mentioned as the most flagrant example of Jefferson's gravest fault, occasional unfairness to individuals, with tenacious holding to personal resentment. Always close to the heart of the people, with almost a divining power in relation to the

Jefferson's worst fault.

Significance of Jefferson's lack of humor.

popular attitude, Jefferson was sometimes unjust to persons. One wonders whether this fault came partly from his lack of that abundant sense of humor, possessed by Hamilton and Washington, and still more by Franklin and Lincoln, among our great statesmen. Wit, Jefferson had, repartee, intellectual cleverness; but he was without that genial humor that gives perspective and their right values to great and small.

Jefferson's preference for agriculture.

Jefferson was delighted to get back to Monticello and resume his life as a country gentleman. He always called himself a farmer; and regarded agriculture as the natural vocation of man, desiring, indeed, to keep the whole country agricultural, as the only life consistent with sobriety and morality. He went so far as to regard yellow fever as a desirable scourge, a blessing in disguise, since he held it would forever prevent men living in cities.

Vice President.

When the election of 1796 occurred and the votes of the electoral college were counted, it was found, Washington having refused to stand, that John Adams had the largest number of votes for President, and Jefferson the next number. According to the Constitution at that time, Adams automatically became President and Jefferson Vice President: the one a strong Federalist; the other, the outstanding opponent of the growing Federal power. Adams and Jefferson, though with a period of estrangement, remained friends to the end of their joint lives; and some of Jefferson's loveliest letters were written to

John and Samuel Adams. President Adams was, however, dominating, sure of his own opinions, denying Jefferson any real share in the government. Jefferson therefore spent his term as Vice President in consolidating the elements of opposition to the rapidly growing power of the central government. He was thus the founder of the first consciously formed political party, since the Federalists were forced into a party by Jefferson's organized opposition. Jefferson named his organization the Republican party. It was afterwards called the Republican-Democratic, and finally the Democratic party. It is the party that has had the longest life of any in the United States; that has repeatedly returned to the principles formulated by Jefferson; and that, in spite of the apparent results of certain recent elections, is alive, vigorous and flourishing at the present time.

Organizing the longest-lived political party in the United States.

During Adams's administration occurred the trouble with France over the *"XYZ Letters"*, in which the French cynically demanded bribes of large sums of money, before even seeing President Adams's special commissioners. The publication of the *Letters* over here caused nation-wide indignation and a general demand for war. The scare subsided however. The Directorate fell, succeeded by Napoleon, who showed better sense in his dealings. As a result of it all, the Federalist leaders in office lost their heads, and enacted most unwise legislation, the Alien and Sedition Laws, which doomed their party.

Effect on the Federalists of the war scare over the *XYZ Letters.*

Those Federalist leaders had made the central government: it was a natural mistake for them to regard attacks upon themselves as attacks upon the government. That is by no means the only time in our history when men in office have regarded criticism of themselves as criticism of the government; but in no other instance had the mistake so much excuse. In this mood, the Alien laws were passed, providing fourteen years before an immigrant could become a naturalized citizen; and during that long period the President could deport the immigrant at will, without legal action, merely declaring him dangerous or undesirable: a grave abuse of power. The Sedition laws were worse: for conspiring against the Government and its measures, for interfering with its activities, or for issuing scandalous material concerning the President, Congress or the government departments, the penalty was severe fine and imprisonment: gag-law of the worst kind. Jefferson was furious. He drafted, in protest, a series of resolutions, which were adopted in November, 1798, by the Kentucky Legislature, and are therefore called the Kentucky Resolutions. His friend, James Madison, drafted a similar series, adopted a month later by the Legislature of the State of Virginia, and so called the Virginia Resolutions.

The unwise Alien and Sedition laws.

Jefferson's protest in the Kentucky Resolutions.

In the Kentucky Resolutions, Jefferson held that the Federal Government could rightfully exercise only such powers as were specifically assigned to it in the Constitution; that each State had the right to annul—nullify—any act of the Federal Government

Jefferson's views of State versus Nation.

not specifically warranted in the Constitution; and (most dangerous of all) each State was to be its own final judge as to when its rights had been violated: thus denying the authority of the Supreme Court finally to interpret the Constitution.

These Resolutions were a much needed protest, at the time, against the wickedness of the Alien and Sedition Laws; but they contained germs of grave trouble, which was to develop and culminate in the Civil War.

The dead lock in the election of 1800.

The situation described destroyed all chance of John Adams succeeding himself as President; and when the election of 1800 was held, and the votes of the electoral college were counted, it was found there was an equal number of votes for the two leading candidates, Jefferson and Aaron Burr, for President. This threw the election into the strongly Federalist House of Representatives. Party feeling has never been more bitter than it was then. Certain Federalists, who thought they owned the Government, talked of setting the Constitution aside and appointing a Federalist President pro tempore. Fortunately, that nefarious step was not taken.

Threats of disregarding the Constitution.

Jefferson was the outstanding leader of the opposition; and so most bitterly hated. You know it takes a great man to be greatly hated. The House was therefore inclined to give the election to Aaron Burr, which would have been a national calamity. At this point, Hamilton intervened. He and Jefferson were now personal enemies; but Hamilton recognized that

Jefferson was a patriot, and in office, would serve the country with all his wisdom and ability. On the other hand, Hamilton regarded Aaron Burr as an unscrupulous adventurer, who would be most dangerous in the presidential chair, possibly even attempting to make himself king; and Burr's later career would seem to indicate that Hamilton's distrust was not without foundation. Thus it was Alexander Hamilton who influenced enough Federalist votes in the House of Representatives to make his personal enemy, Thomas Jefferson, President of the United States. Do not forget it: it was one of the great actions of Hamilton's great career.

Hamilton's part in making Jefferson President.

Jefferson's *Inaugural Address* was a high statement of his whole program of political principles: next to the Declaration of Independence, it is perhaps his most important writing as philosopher of democracy. In it he said, "We are all Republicans —we are all Federalists." He hoped to unite the whole people behind him, as Washington had done; and he very nearly achieved it.

Statement of Jefferson's political philosophy in his Inaugural Address.

He stated in the Inaugural his conception of what government should be:

Jefferson's conception of government.

> "A wise and frugal government, which shall restrain men from injuring one another, which shall leave them otherwise free to regulate their own pursuits of industry and improvement, and shall not take from the mouth of labor the bread it has earned. This is the sum of good government. * * *
>
> "Equal and exact justice to all men, of whatever

state and persuasion, religious or political; peace, commerce, and honest friendship, with all nations—entangling alliances with none; the support of the state governments in all their rights, as the most competent administrations for our domestic concerns and the surest bulwarks against anti-republican tendencies; the preservation of the general government in its whole constitutional vigor, as the sheet anchor of our peace at home and safety abroad; a jealous care of the right of election by the people—a mild and safe corrective of abuses which are lopped by the sword of the revolution where peaceable remedies are unprovided; absolute acquiescence in the decisions of the majority—the vital principle of republics, from which there is no appeal but to force, the vital principle and immediate parent of despotism; a well-disciplined militia—our best reliance in peace and for the first moments of war, till regulars may relieve them; the supremacy of the civil over the military authority; economy in the public expense, that labor may be lightly burdened; the honest payment of our debts and sacred preservation of the public faith; encouragement of agriculture, and of commerce as its handmaid; the diffusion of information and the arraignment of all abuses at the bar of public reason; freedom of religion; freedom of the press; freedom of person under the protection of the *habeas corpus;* and trial by juries impartially selected—these principles form the bright constellation which has gone before us, and guided our steps through an age of revolution and reformation. * * * They should be the creed of our political faith—the text of civil instruction—the touchstone by which to try the services of those we trust."*

Summary of Jefferson's political principles in the Inaugural Address.

* Jefferson, from first Inaugural Address: *Writings*, Vol. III, pp. 320-322.

On the basis of these principles, which he hoped to carry out in his administration, Jefferson assumed the presidency. Three weeks after the inauguration, he wrote a letter to Samuel Adams, then seventy-eight years old, which reveals his most lovable aspect:

The charming letter to the aged Samuel Adams.

> "I addressed a letter to you, my very dear and ancient friend, on the 4th of March: not indeed to you by name, but through the medium of some of my fellow-citizens, whom occasion called on me to address. In meditating the matter of that address, I often asked myself, is this exactly in the spirit of the patriarch, Samuel Adams? Is it as he would express it? Will he approve of it? I have felt a great deal for our country in the times we have seen. * * * How much I lament that time has deprived me of your aid! It would have been a day of glory which should have called you to the first office of the administration. But give us your counsel, my friend, and give us your blessing; and be assured that there exists not in the heart of man a more faithful esteem than mine to you, and that I shall ever bear you the most affectionate veneration and respect." *

Among Jefferson's first acts, as President, was the freeing of those imprisoned under the Alien and Sedition Laws; which was right. He gave the first post in the Cabinet to his close friend and gifted disciple, James Madison; and the other members were all men of high character and education.

Jefferson's excellent cabinet.

Under the Federalist notion of owning the government, John Adams had used the last hours of his term

* Jefferson, letter to Samuel Adams, Washington, March 29th, 1801: *Writings*, Vol. X, pp. 250, 251.

to fill every office under presidential patronage: "midnight judges," certain of these appointees were called. Jefferson naturally and justly resented this; and as rapidly as he could do so, without disturbing the public service, replaced these with men of his own party. For this he has been attacked as the author of the spoils system. The criticism is unjust: he was merely correcting his predecessor's unfair use of power. One of the reasons (there were others!) for Jefferson's hatred of Chief Justice Marshall was that Marshall was one of Adams's midnight judges, and being appointed for life, Jefferson could not remove him.

Significance of removing the "midnight judges."

Believing, as Jefferson sincerely did, that Hamilton wanted a monarchy and that, politically and socially, the country was moving rapidly toward aristocracy, he sought to thwart that tendency in every possible way. He abandoned the system of etiquette Washington had prepared for behavior toward the President and abolished the weekly levees. He dressed deliberately in slipshod fashion, in contrast to his earlier dandyism; and adopted a behavior widely different from that which had given him his reputation as an unusually cultivated gentleman. His state dinners were arranged on what was called the "pell-mell" plan. The dinners themselves were excellent: Jefferson had brought over a French chef, and the wines were as famous as at Monticello; but the plan was, when dinner was announced, all present thronged into the dining room, taking any available seats, with

Efforts to thwart tendencies toward monarchy and aristocracy.

Jefferson's experiments in social democracy.

no precedence whatever, even for foreign ambassadors. The result was, a stately minister would find himself at one end of the table; while his wife, crowded out in the throng, would be seated at the other end, between two quite undesirable companions. Jefferson actually got into trouble with foreign governments, in consequence; and he finally came to see that the ordinary usages of polite society are not necessarily opposed to the principles of democracy, and returned to those usages.

The Louisiana Purchase, the outstanding achievement of Jefferson as President.

The great achievement, however, of Jefferson as President, and the supreme anomaly of his career was the Louisiana Purchase. The year that Jefferson was elected President, Spain ceded to Napoleon her claim to that vast territory, extending from New Orleans to the northwest Pacific coast. Jefferson's sympathy for France had been chilled by the rise of Napoleon out of the ashes of revolution; and he regarded Napoleon's possible possession of an American empire with grave alarm. His first thought was that "The day that France takes possession of New Orleans * * we must marry ourselves to the British fleet and nation."* His one hope of avoiding grave trouble and probably war with France was that Napoleon might recognize our paramount interest, and be willing to cede New Orleans for a price. He therefore urged our Ambassador to begin negotiations, and then sent Monroe, as special envoy, with

* Jefferson, in letter to the U. S. Minister to France, April 18th, 1802: *Writings*, Vol. X, p. 313.

private instructions and large authority for the purchase of New Orleans and the territory immediately about it; which was all he imagined he could get. Understand: Jefferson did not originate this idea: it was an old problem. As the population spread westward, there was an increasing demand for an open port at the mouth of the Mississippi, the great artery through which commerce could be carried on with the old world. Washington had been occupied with the problem; and Jefferson, as his Secretary of State, had struggled to secure free navigation. At one time, Kentucky had threatened to leave the rest of the states and form a separate nation, to attain this long-cherished desire. Jefferson merely believed the time had come for realizing it.

Earlier struggles for an open port on the Mississippi.

To Napoleon, however, the possession of this empire proved an embarrassment. He had not been able to shake England's command of the seas. All she would need to do would be to detach a portion of her fleet and army, take New Orleans; and the claim to the entire territory would be hers, and not Napoleon's. He finally offered, therefore, to sell the whole empire, for a sum which, with the assumption of American claims against France, amounted to about sixteen million dollars. For this insignificant sum of national small change, Jefferson bought that vast empire, from New Orleans to Tacoma and Seattle, which has made our greater America possible. Through Jefferson's urging, the bill was rushed

Why Napoleon sold his American empire.

through both houses of Congress in four days; and the purchase was completed.

Paradox of the Purchase, and its explanation.

Jefferson had great difficulty in settling the purchase with his own conscience, and still more in explaining it to the public. The point is, Jefferson had held, publicly and repeatedly, that the Federal government could rightfully exercise only such powers as were specifically assigned to it in the Constitution; and there was nothing in the Constitution giving the President of the United States the right to use the national funds, even with the consent of Congress, to buy an empire from a foreign potentate.

Jefferson's wisdom in meeting the practical issue.

The explanation of the paradox is that Jefferson was wiser as practical statesman than as political theorist; that as national executive he did the thing he saw was right and best for the welfare and progress of the country, and did it in direct violation of his oft-expressed opinions regarding the Constitution. He was the greater man thus to rise to the issue and solve it for the Nation's good. It is worth noting that, in office, Jefferson, Madison and Monroe all were compelled to act on the basis of Hamilton's view of the implied powers in the Constitution; which says much for that view, as well as showing how official responsibility is apt to convert liberal theorists into political realists in handling practical problems.

What executive responsibility does to political theorists.

Jefferson was intensely interested in the empire he had given the nation. He appointed his secretary, Captain Lewis, the son of his neighbor, in command of an expedition to explore the new territory. Congress gave the Lewis and Clarke expedition five thousand dollars expense money. Jefferson gave Captain Lewis the right to draw at need on the credit of the United States government: he meant to see the expedition rightly carried out. He was intensely interested in all the discoveries: fauna, flora, streams, mountains, Indian life.

Jefferson planning the Lewis and Clarke expedition, and deeply interested in its discoveries.

Jefferson was a temperamental expansionist. He wished to annex Cuba, to annex or purchase the Floridas from Spain; and indeed, got into trouble with Spain in consequence. During the periods when war with Britain loomed on the horizon, he repeatedly expressed the hope that the acquisition of Canada would be the first result, if war had to come.

The temperamental expansionist.

A further curious instance of inconsistency in the great democrat is in the fact that Jefferson's plan for the government of the Louisiana Territory was wholly autocratic, conferring on the President the powers previously held by the King of Spain, and providing for no self-government by the population. Jefferson's followers defended this, on the ground that the States owned the Territories and could do with them as they pleased: an amazing reversion to that British view of the Colonies, which fomented the Revolution! Our history, of course, is full of such inconsistencies, as notably, the limiting of "all men", in the Declaration of Independence, to white men, in its application, excluding Indians, negroes and women. Fortunately, Jefferson's plan was modified, in its adoption, and

Paradox in the imperialistic plan for governing the new territories.

soon replaced by one more in harmony with his life-long principles.

Jefferson a personal executive.

As President, Jefferson exercised personal domination and direction in all this complicated range of problems with which he had to deal. He found time, however, to continue his cultural activities: writing thoughtful letters on scientific, medical and educational questions. A culminating example is in the correspondence with Dr. Priestley, which also shows well Jefferson's earnest and liberal religious attitude.

Eager continuation of his cultural interests amid harassing presidential cares.

Significant illustration in the letters to Dr. Priestley.

Dr. Priestley sent Jefferson, in 1803, a brief comparative study of Socrates and Jesus. Jefferson wrote, expressing his pleasure, and urging a wider comparison with the ancient philosophers, saying that he had thought of writing something of the kind and even sketched the outlines in his mind:

Jefferson's view of the moral teaching of Jesus.

> "I should first take a general view of the moral doctrines of the most remarkable of the ancient philosophers. * * * I should do justice to the branches of morality they have treated well. * * * I should proceed to a view of the life, character, and doctrines of Jesus. * * * His system of morality was the most benevolent and sublime probably that has been ever taught, and consequently more perfect than those of any of the ancient philosophers. His character and doctrines have received still greater injury from those who pretend to be his special disciples, and who have disfigured and sophisticated his actions and precepts, from views of personal interest, so as to induce the unthinking part of mankind to throw off the whole system in disgust, and to pass sentence as an impostor on the most innocent, the

most benevolent, the most eloquent and sublime character that ever has been exhibited to man."*

Evidencing how deeply the subject was in his mind, ten days later he wrote to Edward Dowse, returning a sermon by Mr. Bennet, and referring to Dr. Priestley's pamphlet. Of the ancient philosophers, he said:

The letter to Dowse, further comparing the ancient philosophers with Jesus.

"Their philosophy went chiefly to the government of our passions, so far as respected ourselves, and the procuring our own tranquility. In our duties to others they were short and deficient. They extended their cares scarcely beyond our kindred and friends individually, and our country in the abstract. Jesus embraced with charity and philanthropy our neighbors, our countrymen, and the whole family of mankind. They confined themselves to actions; he pressed his sentiments into the region of our thoughts, and called for purity at the fountain head." †

January 29th, 1804, Jefferson writes again to Dr. Priestley, expressing his satisfaction that the larger comparison is to be carried out; then turning to the significance of the Louisiana Purchase, and concluding:

"Have you seen the new work of Malthus on population? It is one of the ablest I have ever seen. Although his main object is to delineate the effects of redundancy of population, and to test the poor laws of England, and other palliations for that evil, several important

Just appreciation of the great work of Malthus, then appearing.

---

* Jefferson, in letter to Dr. Priestley, April 9th, 1803: *Writings*, Vol. X, pp. 374, 375.

† Jefferson, in letter to Edward Dowse, April 19th, 1803: *Writings*, Vol. X, p. 377.

questions in political economy, allied to his subject incidentally, are treated with a masterly hand." *

The literary and philosophic statesman.

Truly Jefferson was the most many-sided in cultivation of all our great leaders, pursuing his intellectual interests, with unflagging zeal, to the end of his days.

Why Jefferson accepted a second term.

Jefferson's fame as President would have been greater had he declined a second term. He had opposed, on principle, the re-eligibility of the president; but had urged Washington to accept a second term, for the good of the country. Feeling that a second term was needed to complete his work, justify his policies and answer Federalist criticisms, he decided to follow Washington's example. He was over-

Circumstances of his election.

whelmingly elected, receiving 162 out of 176 electoral votes: one of the greatest victories in the history of American political parties. It looked as if he had really achieved his aim of uniting the whole people

The second Inaugural.

behind him. His second *Inaugural Address* was a pean of triumph, reviewing the achievement of the program laid down in the first address.

Bad results from the overwhelming majority.

The very size of his majority meant trouble, however. When a political party goes into power with too large a majority, usually the party splits behind its leaders: which should comfort the defeated! This is what happened to Jefferson: the new recruits quarreling with the older members of the party. Then, too, there were exasperating foreign complications;

* Jefferson, in letter to Dr. Priestley, Jan. 29th, 1804: *Writings*, Vol. X, pp. 447, 448.

and Jefferson met these with a vacillating weakness, strikingly in contrast with the firm attitude of his first administration.

Jefferson's obsession regarding the national debt.

To understand this, one must remember that Jefferson had one obsession. Believing that no generation has the right to bind any subsequent one, he was opposed to any funding of the national debt, which would extend the time of payment beyond the life of the generation incurring the debt. This helps explain his opposition to Hamilton's program. Now in this, without much argument it may be said, Jefferson was simply wrong. A legitimate national debt is merely a mortgage on the national farm. If one buys a farm for forty thousand dollars, giving a ten thousand dollar purchase money mortgage, and dies before the mortgage is paid; if one's heir accepts the farm, it is only right he should assume the mortgage.

What a legitimate national debt really signifies.

Of course, a farm mortgaged beyond its value is an undesirable inheritance; and a national debt that approximates the national wealth is a hideous monstrosity; but a legitimate debt is merely the mortgage on the national wealth handed on to the next generation. Those who fought through the Revolutionary War and achieved independence did it not only for themselves, but for all subsequent generations of Americans. They gave freely their blood and treasure, and borrowed money wherever they could get it, to pull the struggle through to victory. Is it not right that subsequent generations inheriting the country, its painfully achieved freedom, its institutions and wealth, should share in the payment of the debt, incurred for the good of all?

Effects of Jefferson's extreme pacifism during his second term.

Jefferson did not see this; and therefore he was obsessed with the desire to pay off the national debt before going out of office as President. To achieve this, he must not have a foreign war, or the debt would be greater than when he assumed office. Well, the Napoleonic wars were drawing out their devastating length in Europe. Hatred was increasing on every hand. England was issuing Orders in Council, claiming the right to search our ships and take out whatever she chose to declare contraband, impressing our seamen into her service. She forbade us to trade with the continent of Europe, from the Mediterranean to the North Sea, on penalty of confiscation of our ships and cargoes. Napoleon retaliated, forbidding us to trade with Britain, on the same penalty. Spain observing, said, "Well, if they can do it, why can't we?" We were slapped on one cheek, then on the other, then in the mouth; and Jefferson did nothing. Had he assumed a firm attitude, it might have meant war; but he would have had the whole people with him. As it was, to avoid any chance of increasing the national debt, and with a growing belief in peace at any price, he submitted. Finally, in the last period of his administration, the Embargo Act was rushed through Congress, forbidding American ships to leave port: a cowardly device to prevent their search and seizure and the impressing of their seamen! Early in the World War, you remember, there were leaders weak

The Embargo Act.

enough to propose similar cowardly measures to keep us out of war: rather inconsistent with national self-respect, do you not think?

New England, whence the ships mainly sailed, was furious over the Embargo law. "What," the sea captains said, "Are they not our ships? Have we not the right to risk them, if we wish? Are our sailors not free men, with the right to earn their living and risk their freedom, if they choose?" Please note that the earliest challenging of the authority of the Federal Government, and affirmation of the rights of the States over against that Government, came not from the South, but from New England: that will be made more clear when we come to Robert E. Lee.

Resentment in New England and first challenging of the Federal authority.

The result of all this was that Jefferson left office deeply humiliated, but with the heart of the people still with him. The legislatures of five states urged him to run for a third term; but Jefferson refused, thus establishing the tradition, founded by Washington, of only two terms for any President: a tradition, as has been said, never since successfully challenged by any man. Jefferson returned home, at the age of sixty-six, resuming his life at Monticello. His immediate successors in office were his friends and neighbors, Madison and Monroe, who constantly consulted him, carried on his policies and continued his influence.

Refusal of a third term and return to Monticello at sixty-six.

The last long period of Jefferson's life was spent largely in realizing a part of his cherished educational program, through founding the University of Vir-

The successful fight to establish the University of Virginia.

ginia. It was a ten-year fight. Finally, the Act was passed in 1819, and the University established, with Jefferson as Rector. It never had a president, until about twenty years ago, when yielding to the autocratic tendency in education of the time, it took a president and became an ordinary university.

Jefferson's service as architect and Rector of the University.

Jefferson was the architect of the buildings, planning them on beautiful classic lines: the simple quadrangles of stately arcades, with student rooms behind, and here and there a more impressive structure rising. It was a very inexpensive plan, but probably the most beautiful series of academic buildings then in America, and in dignified simplicity and majestic harmony, one of the most satisfying ever erected on American soil.

The curriculum Jefferson planned on liberal elective lines. The University had one of the first self-governing student bodies in America. The whole organization was singularly modern. In other words, Jefferson inaugurated, at the University of Virginia, many of those reforms carried out, three quarters of a century later, at Harvard and elsewhere in the North, and then regarded as novelties. Once more, how far-visioned Jefferson was, as educator as well as political philosopher!

View of life in old age. The letter to John Adams.

In many letters, Jefferson expressed his relief at being free from the anxious cares of active political life. The serene and mellowed attitude of his later years is well expressed in a letter to John Adams, written at seventy-three, a decade before his death:

"You ask, if I would agree to live my seventy or rather seventy-three years over again? To which I say, yea. I think with you, that it is a good world on the whole; that it has been framed on a principle of benevolence, and more pleasure than pain dealt out to us. There are, indeed (who might say nay), gloomy and hypochondriac minds, inhabitants of diseased bodies, disgusted with the present, and despairing of the future; always counting that the worst will happen, because it may happen. To these I say, how much pain have cost us the evils which have never happened! My temperament is sanguine. I steer my bark with Hope in the head, leaving Fear astern. My hopes, indeed, sometimes fail; but not oftener than the forebodings of the gloomy. There are, I acknowledge, even in the happiest life, some terrible convulsions, heavy setoffs against the opposite page of the account. I have often wondered for what good end the sensation of grief could be intended. All our other passions, within proper bounds, have an useful object. And the perfection of the moral character is, not in a stoical apathy, so hypocritically vaunted, and so untruly too, because impossible, but in a just equilibrium of all the passions. I wish the pathologists then would tell us what is the use of grief in the economy, and of what good it is the cause, proximate or remote."*

Reasons for the collapse of Jefferson's financial fortunes.

Meantime, Jefferson's financial affairs were in increasingly desperate condition. We have seen various causes for this: Jefferson's long absences from home in his service of the country, the ravaging of his estates during the Revolution, the multiplied payment

* Jefferson, in letter to John Adams, Monticello, April 8th, 1816: *Writings*, Vol. VI, pp. 575, 576.

of the heavy mortgage on his father-in-law's lands; but there was a further cause. After Washington's death, Jefferson was the most eminent man in America, recognized as such all over the world. After his retirement from the presidency, a countless stream of guests came to Monticello, from North, South, West and from all over Europe. Jefferson entertained them with the old lavish hospitality; and they literally ate and drank him out of house and home! His debts accumulated so that he was finally compelled to sacrifice his beloved library. Think what that meant: a natural student and devoted lover of books, all his long life he had been gathering together this splendid collection; and now he had to let it go. To keep it together, he sold it to Congress, which gave him the miserly sum of twenty-three thousand nine hundred and fifty dollars for it: about half what it would probably have brought at public auction. This amount proved only a slight alleviation, paying but a part of the growing debts. He turned over the running of his estates to a grandson, hoping for better results. Friends in other states raised a purse of sixteen thousand five hundred dollars, and presented it to him, which prevented his having to leave Monticello. After his death, his daughter was compelled to leave, and the estate was sold for about ten thousand dollars. Just now, there is a nation-wide movement on to buy it back, as a national monument, for a half million dollars; and yet we sometimes think we are a practical people!

Jefferson's sale of his great library.

The gift that enabled Jefferson to close his life at Monticello.

Jefferson, therefore, died at Monticello at the age of eighty-three, and strangely enough, on the Fourth of July, 1826: interesting, that he should have died on the birthday of the nation, the anniversary of the day when his great Declaration of Independence was adopted by the Continental Congress, and the new nation brought into being. Still more remarkable, Jefferson's life-long associate, friend and rival, John Adams, died the same day in Massachusetts; and almost the last words of John Adams were, "Thomas Jefferson still survives"; but Jefferson had died, a few hours earlier, at Monticello.

Death, July 4th, 1826.

He wrote his own epitaph. It is inscribed on the simple monument, that stands in the enclosure, beside the road, as you climb the slope of Monticello. It reads:

> "Here was buried
> THOMAS JEFFERSON,
> Author of the Declaration of American Independence, of the Statute of Virginia for religious freedom and Father of the University of Virginia."

Significance of Jefferson's self-written epitaph.

That was all: no word about his two terms as President, the Louisiana Purchase, his service as Ambassador, Secretary of State and Vice President. "Author of the Declaration of American Independence": the great charter of our liberties, through which the independent nation was born; "of the Statute of Virginia for religious freedom", making him the father of American religious liberty; and "Father of the University of Virginia": the first American states-

Services by which he wished to be remembered

man to recognize fully the responsibility of the State in the education of the citizen, under democracy: those were the three achievements by which he wished to be remembered.

Summary of Jefferson and his career.

Like Washington, six feet two inches tall, of robust and enduring physical constitution, with red hair, a firm, sensitive face, and thin, rather compressed lips; the most many-sided in cultivation of all our great men, an aristocrat in manner, Jefferson was a born leader, always close to the heart of the people, and the philosopher of democracy for all time. Founder of our longest-lived political party, through the Louisiana purchase virtual creator of our greater America, father of our religious freedom, idealist in political philosophy, Jefferson stands for just that range of ideas that most need re-emphasis at the present hour. Today, when the World War has left us with vastly increased tendencies toward centralization and paternalism in government, when the popular mind is obsessed with the idea of multiplied legislation as the certain cure for all moral and social ills, we particularly need to return to the great ideas of Thomas Jefferson: *freedom of speech and press, freedom in religion, freedom of person and conduct*: principles for which we must ever fight, if we are to keep the soul of democracy in our great, ever more powerful, more highly organized, centralized and authoritative Republic.

Present day significance of Jefferson's ideas.

Principles on which depends the soul of democracy.

IV

HAMILTON, AND THE MAKING OF OUR GOVERNMENT

IF WASHINGTON, more than any other leader, made possible an independent nation on the American continent, it was Hamilton who called the Convention that made the Constitution, who initiated and fought through to victory the great measures that moulded the new government into a living, growing organism. Covered with abuse and calumny because of his very excellence and fighting force, accomplishing his great work by sheer power of intellect acting on the leaders of his time, Hamilton stands out as one of the truly great statesmen in the entire history of mankind.

Hamilton the virtual creator of the Federal Government.

Hamilton was born in the island of Nevis, one of the lesser West Indies, January 11th, 1757. He was thus fourteen years younger than his great associate and rival, Jefferson, twenty-five years younger than Washington, and fifty-one years younger than Benjamin Franklin, who as we have seen, was the patriarch of the Revolution.

One of the youngest of Revolutionary leaders.

Nevis is a small island, with about fifty square miles of territory, rising over a plateau to a volcanic cone, about three thousand feet above the sea. The West

The Island of Nevis, Hamilton's birthplace.

Indies, as has been said, were well in advance of the mainland in civilization. The luxuriant soil, tropical climate, early introduction of Negro slavery, and the wide European demand for the great staples produced in the Islands, sugar, molasses and rum, developed prosperity at an early day. The planters lived in stately homes, with beautiful grounds about them, and imitated the manners of continental Europe.

Relations of the West Indies to the mainland.

The relation of the islands to the mainland was, moreover, much closer than at a later day. The easy and natural means of travel and transportation was by water. It was easier to go from the West Indies to Virginia or Massachusetts, than to go, by land, from Massachusetts to Virginia. Trade with the mainland was thus constant and intercourse close. The island Colonies of Britain had, further, to meet just the same neglect and tyranny, on the part of the home government, as those upon the continent. Hamilton was a child of eight when the Stamp Act was passed. There were on Nevis and other islands, the same scenes of public meetings of protest, with the seizing and burning of the stamped papers, as occurred on the mainland.

Hamilton devoted to the American cause from its inception.

These facts are mentioned merely to indicate that Hamilton had every right to feel, as he did feel, that he was born an American, as completely as if he had been born on the mainland. He had no sense of being apart, and was a whole-hearted patriot, devoted to the American cause from the beginning.

Behind the birth of Hamilton is a most interesting romantic story, and strange to say, we had to wait for a novelist to clear it up for us with scholarly accuracy. Until Gertrude Atherton went to the islands, examined every oldest inhabitant, looked up all the mouldering records and published her results, the biographers and historians were very hazy and uncertain regarding that story. Since Gertrude Atherton made her thorough investigation, her results have been accepted as scholarly and accurate by subsequent writers, notably by Hamilton's grandson, Allan McLane Hamilton, who published in 1910 his *Intimate Life of Alexander Hamilton,* giving Miss Atherton full credit. Hamilton's own letters, moreover, are entirely consistent with the facts as now established, and show that he was fully aware of the circumstances of his birth and ancestry. The romantic story deserves brief retelling.

Gertrude Atherton's service in ascertaining Hamilton's ancestry.

Hamilton's maternal grandfather was Dr. John Fawcett, of French Huguenot family: the name being originally Faucette, which he had changed to the English pronounciation and spelling. It is worth remembering that Hamilton had French blood: it helps to explain certain characteristics of his temperament. Dr. Fawcett bought land, became a fairly wealthy planter, married a young English girl, and lived in a great house on his country estate, associating with the fashionable society of Nevis. There were three daughters, two of whom married early. After twenty years of married life, the wife sought

The Huguenot French grandfather.

a separation from her husband; and taking her youngest daughter, Rachel, went to live apart, in a property she possessed on the neighboring island of St. Kitts.

Hamilton's mother.

Rachel Fawcett was apparently an unusually beautiful and gifted girl, finely formed, with reddish fair hair, deep gray eyes, vivacious manner and an excellent gentlewoman's education. At sixteen, she was seemingly pushed by her mother into a loveless marriage with a wealthy Dane, John Levine, who had come over to the Danish island, St. Croix, and seemed a desirable match. Levine took his bride and her mother to Copenhagen; the ladies were presented at the Danish court; then the mother returned to St. Kitts, and a little later, the couple to live on St. Croix.

The circumstances of her married life became unendurable to Rachel, however. She fled suddenly from her husband's home to her mother on St. Kitts. Her family connections were sufficiently high, so that her husband was unable to compel her return. When the child of the union was born, the father claimed and reared it. Hamilton, by the way, in one of his letters to his wife, probably written in 1782, speaks of "the death of my brother Levine", and adds, "You know the circumstances that abate my distress, yet my heart acknowledges the rights of a brother,"* proving that he knew all about the connection. John

* Hamilton, Allan McLane, *Intimate Life of Alexander Hamilton*, p. 4.

Levine secured some sort of legal separation from his wife, which did not permit her to marry again. Her mother's death occurring shortly, Rachel was left, still a girl of nineteen, living alone on St. Kitts, in this anomalous situation, neither wife nor widow.

Hamilton's Scotch father.

There came to the island, seeking his fortune in the new world, James Hamilton, younger son of the great Scotch Hamilton family, affable, handsome, well educated, a good conversationalist. He and Rachel Levine came to love each other very deeply and wished to marry. She could not obtain a divorce, however, except by act of Parliament; and Parliament was too far away, and she was without the requisite influence. The two young persons decided, therefore, to accept the fact of marriage and unite their lives, since they could not overcome all the legal obstacles. Under the circumstances and ethics of the time, it should probably be regarded as a common law marriage, since it was accepted as a permanent life union on both sides. They went to live on Rachel's inherited property in the island of Nevis; and while there was some criticism, the families of the two young persons stood by them loyally; and they were soon accepted in the best society of the islands. Two children were born of this union: Alexander Hamilton in 1757, as we have seen, and his brother, James, five years later.

Circumstances of the union of Rachel Levine and James Hamilton.

The father, however, with all his education and charm of manner, seems to have been one of those men who are unable to find satisfactory business adjustment in life. He was unsuccessful in one position after another. Finally, his devoted wife sold her inherited property and gave him her whole capital to start in business independently. He took it, and failed again, making his family penniless. Lytton, the husband of one of Rachel's sisters, gave him a manager's position on an estate in St. Croix, whither the family removed. In this work, also, he was not successful; and when his son, Alexander, was a boy of nine, James Hamilton left for St. Vincent, hoping to better his condition. He was able to earn but a meager salary; and Rachel took her two children and went to live in the home of her sister, Mrs. Lytton. She was too proud, too sensitive, however, to endure the situation of her life: she had suffered bitterly under the anomalous circumstances of her marriage anyway; and when she was but thirty-two and her son, Alexander, a lad of eleven, she died.

James Hamilton's business failures.

Death of his mother when Hamilton was but eleven.

Hamilton was thus left, at eleven, practically doubly orphaned; for it is doubtful if he ever saw his father again. In his later life, when Hamilton had become famous in our country, he wrote affectionate letters to his father and brother in the islands, sending gifts of money, and urging the father to come to New York and spend his last years with his son there. The father had agreed to do so; but frail health and warfare on the sea postponed this, and he died in St. Vincent, with the plan unfulfilled. In his later years, Hamilton also sent money to his aunts, who were then in reduced circumstances. From

Hamilton's later relations with his father and family.

the age of eleven, however, Hamilton was thrown upon his own resources. He could, of course, continue to live in the home of his aunt; but he had his mother's pride and sensitiveness, and wished to support himself.

Early education.

From his mother, Hamilton had acquired an excellent speaking and reading knowledge of French, which was a great asset to him later on. Rev. Hugh Knox, recognizing the boy's precocious intellect, had already tutored him in certain of the conventional academic subjects. Hamilton was, moreover, a born student, with a richly gifted and intensely active mind. He was already reading widely and deeply in history and allied fields, and he continued an eager student all his life.

Work in the store of Nicholas Cruger from twelve to fifteen.

At twelve, Hamilton went to work in the general store of Nicholas Cruger, doing the ordinary tasks of a clerkship and casting up accounts. He did not like the work, but it must have been excellent training for his subsequent career. It was done so faithfully, however, that when, the following year, Nicholas Cruger was called to the mainland, for some months' time, he left this boy of thirteen in entire charge of the business, during his absence: a signal tribute to the fidelity and thoroughness with which Hamilton fulfilled the tasks assigned him.

So his life went on to the age of fifteen. That year, one of those terrible hurricanes that frequently devastate the West Indies swept the island. St. Croix suffered frightful loss of life and property.

Hamilton's account of the hurricane.

The young Hamilton wrote an account of the disaster, which was published in a newspaper in St. Kitts, and received much favorable comment. It was, indeed, a remarkable literary production for a youth of fifteen. It awakened his relatives to recognize that he had too good a mind to spend his life in an island clerkship; and they raised enough money to send him to the mainland for a college education.

To the mainland for a college education.

Still under sixteen, Hamilton sailed for Boston, landed at that port, made his way to New York and into the edge of New Jersey, and entered a secondary school, at Elizabethtown, to complete his preparation for college. His high family connections gave him letters of introduction to certain eminent New York and New Jersey statesmen; and these recognized at once his intellectual ability and promise. In fact, during his period in the secondary school, Hamilton lived in the home of one of the prominent New Jersey political leaders, Elias Boudinot.

In the preparatory school at Elizabethtown, New Jersey.

After a few months, he felt himself ready for college, and wished to enter Princeton. He had limited funds, and knew that he could study intensely and rapidly; so apparently he asked the Princeton authorities if they would let him go through as fast as he could. Well, there were pedants and martinets in those days, just as there are today: one wonders why a college student must do time, after he has done all the work; but it was so then and it is so now. The Princeton authorities refused, saying he must go through in conventional fashion. Hamilton therefore

Circumstances of entering King's College, New York City.

turned his back on Princeton, and tried King's College, New York City, the germ from which Columbia University has developed. King's College had a Tory president and two professors: very different from the vast educational machine, Columbia University has become today. This small faculty was quite willing Hamilton should go through as fast as possible; so he entered King's College.

Hamilton's education.

He remained in college hardly two years, leaving to join the army of the Revolution; but do not imagine he did only two years' work. With his precocious, awakened intellect, he was reading with passionate eagerness in the fields of history, government and statesmanship. Then, too, leaving college did not close his student years: he continued a student always, becoming one of the best educated men in America, perhaps in the world, of his time.

First services of the Revolution.

When Hamilton was seventeen and a half years old, a mass meeting was held in the City Hall Park, New York. Hamilton made an address, which certain eminent men present recognized as masterly; and shared, from that time, the expectation of a great future for him.

A pamphleteering age.

The chief method of influencing public opinion, in those days, corresponding to our use of newspapers and magazines, was by issuing pamphlets. It was a pamphleteering age. A Rev. Dr. Seabury, an intense Tory, issued one, severely attacking the Continental Congress. Hamilton, not yet eighteen, replied with a fourteen thousand word pamphlet, *The Continental*

Hamilton's mature ideas of government in the pamphlets issued at seventeen and eighteen.

Congress Vindicated. Dr. Seabury came back with *Congress Canvassed by a Westchester Farmer;* and again Hamilton, now eighteen, answered with a long pamphlet, equivalent to a small volume, *The Farmer Refuted.* In these early writings, Hamilton outlines his permanent philosophy of government, evidencing the precocity of his intellectual development. At the same time, these pamphlets show how completely he had accepted the prevalent ideas of natural rights, on which the Revolution proceeded. Nothing that Jefferson wrote in the Declaration of Independence affirms those rights more clearly than the following passage from *The Farmer Refuted*:

His acceptance of the democratic conception of government, based on the theory of the rights of man.

"The origin of all civil government, justly established, must be a voluntary compact between the rulers and the ruled, and must be liable to such limitations as are necessary for the security of the *absolute rights* of the latter; for what original title can any man, or set of men, have to govern others, except their own consent? To usurp dominion over a people in their own despite, or to grasp at a more extensive power than they are willing to entrust, is to violate that law of nature which gives every man a right to his personal liberty, and can therefore confer no obligation to obedience."*

The mob at Dr. Cooper's.

While whole-heartedly devoted to the Revolutionary cause, Hamilton deprecated the rioting that was taking place. For instance, Dr. Cooper, President of King's College, was an intense Tory; and there was a plot to mob his home. Hamilton, hearing of the plan, proceeded in advance of the mob to Dr.

* Hamilton, in *The Farmer Refuted: Works*, Vol. I, p. 63.

Cooper's dwelling, mounted the steps, and when the rioters arrived, addressed them, urging them to observe law and order. Dr. Cooper stuck his head out of an upstairs window; and recognizing who was speaking, but not hearing the words, shrieked, "Don't listen to that fellow, he's crazy!" Rather grotesque: Hamilton endeavoring to save Dr. Cooper's life; and Dr. Cooper responding as cited! Hamilton smiled, continued speaking, held the mob till Dr. Cooper got out of the house by the back door, was rowed out to a British ship, and carried to England and safety: England where he should have stayed!

Hamilton's belief in authoritative government.

Again, a mob out of Connecticut attacked Rivington's Press, which had published Tory pamphlets, broke up the presses and wrecked the establishment. Hamilton wrote a letter to John Jay, member of the Continental Congress, vigorously opposing such methods in the service of the American cause and urging that rioters be punished.

Temperamental contrast between Hamilton and Jefferson.

The point is: Hamilton believed, temperamentally and by conviction, in law and order first, and freedom afterwards. Jefferson, if you wish the initial contrast between the two men, believed, equally by temperament and conviction, in freedom first, and law and order afterwards. Hamilton's is far the safer theory of society: I agree with Jefferson.

Commissioned as Captain of Artillery in March, 1776.

Knowing that war was coming, Hamilton studied intensely military science; and when the New York authorities sanctioned the raising of armed forces, applied for a commission as captain of artillery. The authorities were surprised at this stripling of nineteen wanting to be a captain of artillery; and put him through a severe examination, which he passed brilliantly, proving that he had mastered the whole field and was prepared to serve. He was granted his commission the same week that Washington caused the British evacuation of Boston.

Hamilton used all the rest of the money, he had been given for his college education, in raising and equipping his artillery company; and that money was never paid back to Hamilton, nor to his family after his death. His widow did receive, in her necessity, payment of his back pay as officer; but these funds, used to organize and equip his company, were never repaid.

The service of Hamilton's Company.

Hamilton trained his men so thoroughly, that his company was one of the few entirely dependable ones Washington had, early in the War. He was given the rear guard service in the retreat across the river, after the battle of Long Island. He was at Haarlem Heights, where apparently Washington's personal attention was first called to him, and in the battle of White Plains. He accompanied Washington on the retreat across New Jersey; and it was his dependable company that had again and again the rear guard service, in crossing one and another of those New Jersey rivers. He shared in the victories of Trenton and Princeton; and when these won for Washington that five months' breathing space at Morristown, he asked Hamilton to give up his commission as captain of artillery, take a position on Washington's personal staff, with the rank of colonel, and serve as Washington's secretary.

Reasons why Washington urged Hamilton to become his Secretary.

Washington may have been partly moved to this by the fact that he had already recognized Hamilton's brilliant intellect and also his reckless daring in the field; and realizing that Hamilton could hardly live very long if he remained in active military service, he may have wished to save this great mind for the nation's need, later on. Besides this, Washington, always sensitive about the defects in his early schooling, wanted someone else to express his ideas for him. Those ideas had come to entire clearness: Washington knew what he wished to say; but he was sensitive over his grammar, spelling and style.

The four years of service as Washington's brain and voice.

Hamilton did not wish to accept. His strongest ambition, strange to say, was in the military field. His great work as statesman was done to serve the nation's need, from a sense of duty, with a minimum of personal ambition; but he was keenly ambitious in his military career. Nevertheless, he accepted: why? Because he recognized that he could serve the country's cause best that way. So for four years, Hamilton served as Washington's brain, voice and pen, laboring incessantly, writing those innumerable letters to the Continental Congress, to generals in the field, to commanders of the opposing armies, to statesmen throughout the colonies.

The contrast between the two men is impressive: Washington, twenty-five years the elder, six feet two

Contrast of Washington and Hamilton.

in height, a tall giant, with those enormous hands and feet, wrists and ankles; Hamilton, a little man, five feet seven, with finely formed hands and feet, a handsome figure, sandy red hair, piercing blue-gray eyes, a straight classic nose, and red-white Scotch complexion. Washington came to feel for his young associate a truly fatherly affection. Indeed, Washington seems to have had a warmer affection for Hamilton than for any other of his young companions of the Revolution, with the possible exception of Light Horse Harry Lee of Virginia.

Hamilton's engagement to Elizabeth Schuyler.

It was during Hamilton's period of service as Washington's secretary, that his personal life was permanently established. In the autumn of 1777, he was sent on a mission to General Gates; and stayed, in Albany, at the home of General Schuyler, head of one of the great New York landed families, of Dutch descent, and a close friend of Washington's. Here Hamilton met, for the first time, Elizabeth, the second daughter of the family, just twenty, a petite brunette, with charming manner and dark, lovely eyes. Then, in the winter of 1779 and 80, when Washington again had headquarters at Morristown, General Schuyler, at that time a member of the Continental Congress, took a house at Morristown, to be nearer his family. Hamilton was constantly carrying messages between Washington and General Schuyler, on business of state, he was a frequent guest in the Schuyler home; and a warm, deep love affair quickly developed between him and Elizabeth Schuyler. She was some seven months younger than Hamilton. General Schuyler warmly welcomed the engagement, having come to feel for Hamilton much the same fatherly affection Washington had.

It was during the period of their engagement that the Benedict Arnold treason occurred. You will recall it was Hamilton into whose hands the treason papers were placed; Hamilton who gave them to Washington and heard his one comment; Hamilton who had the task of comforting the hysterical Mrs. Arnold, which no doubt he did very effectively; and it is from Hamilton's letters to his fiancée, her father, and to Laurens, that we have our best account of the trial and execution of Major André, afterwards.

Hamilton's personal life.

About a month after the Arnold treason, Hamilton and Elizabeth Schuyler were married. The marriage, the result of a warm and passionate love affair, remained a deep relationship to the end of Hamilton's life. He was a tender and loving father to his eight children, their companion in every leisure hour, playing with them, even in their childhood days, upon the nursery floor, bitterly resenting the long absences from home his service of the country's cause necessitated. His wife was devoted to him with utter loyalty, through his life time and during her long widowhood, in spite of certain infidelities, which Hamilton's strong and not always controlled passions afterwards caused.

A few months after Hamilton's marriage a break occurred with Washington: that it was not permanent was due to Washington's generous magnanimity.

Circumstances of the temporary break with Washington.

The circumstances are sufficiently interesting to deserve narration. Hamilton was hastening from one office to another with a message for some general, passed the foot of a stairway, and Washington, from the top, called down to him. Hamilton responded, went on and delivered his message, and returning, was stopped for a few moments' conversation by La Fayette. Reaching the foot of the staircase again, Washington, still standing at the top, in one of those rare occasions when Washington did not control his naturally fierce temper, exclaimed, "Colonel Hamilton, you have kept me waiting for ten minutes: you treat me with disrespect, Sir!" Hamilton, from the bottom of the stairway, responded, "Sir, I am unaware of it, but since you think so, we part."

Washington went into his office, realized at once that he had spoken hastily and unjustly, and with that beautiful magnanimity that makes him so lovable and human, sent a general to Hamilton, with what was practically an apology, from the chief to the subordinate, urging Hamilton not to leave his service.

Hamilton's desire to resume active military service.

Hamilton was insistent: he would not remain. Probably he welcomed the opportunity to go: for with his keenest ambition in the military field, and recognizing that the war was drawing into its last phase, he was anxious to get into active service before the fighting stopped. Besides this, however, Hamilton had something of that personal touchiness which a great man who is physically small sometimes shows. One wonders about that characteristic. It is rarely, if ever, found in a great man who is large in stature; but sometimes, perhaps often, it is seen in a truly great man of small size. Can it be an instinctive effort to throw out a protection Nature has not given? Whatever the explanation, Hamilton had something of that quality; so his decision to go was unalterable.

Fault in character.

A little later, Hamilton wrote Washington, asking for an appointment in the field. This put Washington in a quandary. Hamilton had been out of active service four years. To appoint him over officers who had been fighting during that period, would be unfair and cause heart burnings. On the other hand, if not appointed, Washington feared Hamilton would take it as a personal matter, because of their quarrel. So Washington sat down and wrote Hamilton a frank, manly letter, explaining the situation, telling him he would like to appoint him, but these were the reasons why he could not, and hoping Hamilton would not take it personally. Hamilton replied with an equally manly letter, saying that he understood perfectly, but that, if Washington had a chance to appoint him, wouldn't he please do so.

A few months later, the opportunity came: when Rochambeau lent those five thousand French soldiers and Washington, with the combined armies, hastened south to Virginia. Hamilton was given the command of a regiment of light infantry, and accompanied Washington. At Yorktown, there were two redoubts to be stormed. The larger was assigned to the French. A large body of the troops moved slowly forward,

Hamilton's appointment as Colonel of a regiment of Infantry.

was discovered by the British, and the fort was taken only after a sanguinary conflict.

Brilliant military service at Yorktown.

The smaller redoubt was assigned to Hamilton to capture. He crept swiftly forward, with a small body of men, had himself lifted on the shoulders of his soldiers, and leaped over among the British, followed by his men: a most daring and dangerous act. The result was, the fort was taken with hardly any loss. Washington described this feat as one of rare coolness, firmness and intrepidity. Hamilton had his military opportunity late; but you see what good use he made of it.

Turning to the law as a life vocation.

With the surrender of Cornwallis, the war was at an end; and Hamilton was out of a job. He had no money and no vocation. He was married, and his eldest child, Philip, was born a few months after Yorktown. He did not wish to live on his father-in-law. What was he to do? He turned naturally to the law. That was where his interest centered: in the great problems of government and society which law embodies; and it was in that field he had read most widely. So he went to Albany, and isolated himself for five months. At the end of that time, he passed brilliantly his examinations for the Bar, was admitted to practice; and in the meantime, had compiled a *Manual of Practice,* just to fix his ideas, which served several generations of lawyers helpfully. Surely that can hardly be equalled, as an example of precocious and gifted youthful intelligence and intense work; and understand, he was admitted to the Bar, not

A brilliant mind, with marvelous power of work.

through favoritism, but because he had mastered the whole field and was ready.

He wished to begin practice in New York City; but the British occupancy continued till the autumn of 1783, and he had to wait. He recommended to the Treasurer of the Continental Congress, Morris, the appointment of superintendents to collect the requisitions from the states. Morris liked the idea, and straightway appointed Hamilton for New York. He accepted reluctantly: it was a thankless task; but he fulfilled it faithfully.

Hamilton's aim and service as a member of the Continental Congress.

In 1782, Hamilton was a member of the Continental Congress. His whole effort, during his term of service, was to strengthen the authority of that weak government. The situation was going from bad to worse. By 1780 the Continental currency was down to forty to one, by official action. The following year it had reached 175 to 1. Meantime, state notes were three to one. That was because the states could lay taxes; the Congress could not. All Congress could do was to assess the states their quotas, and then hope they would respond. As long as the war was on there was an acute reason for the states to do as well as possible; but when the actual fighting stopped, there was not the same pressure. For instance, in 1782, the year that Hamilton served in the Continental Congress, Rhode Island did best among the states, paying one-fourth of her assigned quota. Pennsylvania paid one-fifth, Massachusetts one-eighth, Virginia one-twelfth, New York one twentieth,

Weakness of Congress. Effect of no taxing power.

Relation of the States to Congress.

New Hampshire one-one hundred and twenty-first, North Carolina and Georgia nothing. Imagine, running a government under conditions such as those!

Hamilton realized, more clearly than anyone else, that the only hope lay in establishing a stronger central government. He had stated his view the year that the war was concluded:

Early statement of Hamilton's conception of the Union.

> "There is something noble and magnificent in the perspective of a great Federal Republic, closely linked in the pursuit of a common interest, tranquil and prosperous at home, respectable abroad; but there is something proportionally diminutive and contemptible in the prospect of a number of petty States, with the appearance only of union, jarring, jealous, and perverse, without any determined direction, fluctuating and unhappy at home, weak and insignificant by their dissensions in the eyes of other nations."*

First calls for a Convention to make a Constitution.

In 1780, Hamilton had suggested a Constitutional Convention. In 1782, through the New York Legislature, he issued a definite call for one; but the time was not ripe, and he had to wait.

Beginning law practice. Qualities that made Hamilton a leader at the bar.

In the interim, the British evacuated New York in the autumn of 1783. Hamilton immediately moved to the city, and opened a law office on Wall Street. He strode quickly to the head of the profession. His marvelously gifted mind, power of intense and incessant work, ability to sheer down to the fundamental principles of a case, and genius for concise, logical statement made him a master at the Bar.

---

* Hamilton, in *The Continentalist*, published in 1781: *Works*, Vol. I, pp. 286, 287.

At the same time, his complete disregard of public opinion and devotion to principle, even when it was abstract principles of government, are shown in one of the earliest cases he took.

In the treaty of peace with Britain, Congress had agreed that no action would be taken against Tories or British subjects, who had occupied American property, during the periods of British occupancy of our towns and cities. Under the mood of post-war hatred, the New York Legislature, in 1783, passed a law that such action could be taken, making royalists liable for arrears of rent. Thus the state law was in direct violation to the treaty made with Britain, by Congress, for the whole country. Hamilton at once saw the point: is the government of all the people to prevail, or the government of part of the people?

Hamilton's devotion to principle.

The first case to come up, under this conflict of legislation, was that of a poor widow, whose property had been occupied by British subjects during the period of British control of New York. They had duly paid their rent, as designated by the British authorities; and under the treaty no action could be taken against them. Under the New York statute, the widow sued for her arrears of rent over again. Public opinion was strongly in her favor: she was a poor widow and everybody wanted to kick a Tory in those days.

Hamilton took the unpopular case of the British subjects; made an argument so trenchant and convincing, so unanswerable in logic and moral basis, that the judge said there was only one possible way

The first victory for Nation versus State.

to settle the case, and decided it in favor of Hamilton's clients. Hamilton had won the first round of the fight of Nation versus State. There was a public uproar against Hamilton: he was threatened with assassination and with duels; but he carried the fight to the public in the *Phocion* pamphlets. Hamilton's opponents won a sweeping victory in the next election: one price he paid for devotion to principle.

The price Hamilton paid for victory.

Cause of the Phocion Letters.

Hamilton's two letters signed "Phocion", and addressed to "The Considerate Citizens of New York", in 1784, were inspired by this unreasoning bitterness toward Tories, and the widely favored proposal to confiscate all their property. He trenchantly observed:

A statement that the prejudiced and intolerant everywhere might well take to heart!

> "There is a bigotry in politics as well as in religions, equally pernicious in both. * * *
>
> "It is remarkable, though not extraordinary, that those characters, throughout the States, who have been principally instrumental in the revolution, are the most opposed to persecuting measures."*

Hamilton prophet in vision as well as realist in practice.

In the second *Phocion Letter,* Hamilton gave an impressive diagnosis of the situation created by the victorious War for Independence: the unparalleled opportunity and resulting responsibility, and the threatened tragedy, if the opportunity should not be taken and the obligation fulfilled. The whole great passage proves that Hamilton was not only the supremely practical statesman, but that he could be, on occasion, the seer, as far-visioned as Jefferson or any

* Hamilton, in *Phocion Letters*: *Works,* Vol. IV, pp. 284, 285.

other. The noble words are still vitally pregnant for the America that has issued, again victorious, from the World War:

The responsibility upon the States, following the Revolution.

"Those who are at present entrusted with power, in all these infant republics, hold the most sacred deposit that ever was confided to human hands. * * *

Effects of good and bad government.

"If we set out with justice, moderation, liberality, and a scrupulous regard to the Constitution, the government will acquire a spirit and tone productive of permanent blessings to the community. If, on the contrary, the public councils are guided by humor, passion, and prejudice; if from resentment to individuals, or a dread of partial inconveniences, the Constitution is slighted, or explained away, upon every frivolous pretext, the future spirit of government will be feeble, distracted, and arbitrary. The rights of the subject will be the sport of every party vicissitude. * * *

America's opportunity to be the beacon light to mankind.

"The world has its eye upon America. The noble struggle we have made in the cause of liberty has occasioned a kind of revolution in human sentiment. The influence of our example has penetrated the gloomy regions of despotism, and has pointed the way to enquiries which may shake it to its deepest foundations.

* * * * *

"To ripen enquiry into action, it remains for us to justify the revolution by its fruits.

"If the consequences prove that we really have asserted the cause of human happiness, what may not be expected from so illustrious an example? In a greater or less degree the world will bless and imitate.

The contrasting tragic possibility.

"But if experience, in this instance, verifies the lesson long taught by the enemies of liberty, that the bulk of mankind are not fit to govern themselves, * * * we shall then see the final triumph of despotism over liberty.

How Hamilton's diagnosis and prophcsy apply to the America of today!

* * * With the greatest advantages for promoting it that ever a people had, we shall have betrayed the cause of human nature."*

With this dilemma, faced by the country in those bitter post-war years, conditions had to grow worse before they could get better. Under democracy, the people will get the worst government they are willing to tolerate; and under democracy, the people can get the best government they are willing to work for. That principle should be remembered: it is the key to the functioning of democracy. When therefore, conditions become very bad, there is always hope that the people will be aroused to make them better; which ought to comfort us in dark days. So it was with the country during those desperate years following the close of the war. Congress was increasingly feeble and migratory. England was passing such Orders in Council as she chose, and doing as she pleased with our shipping on the high seas. Algerine pirates were seizing our ships as prizes, and selling our seamen into slavery. Finally the merchants of the country were aroused by their increasing losses. You know, when the business interests get really stirred up, they can bring strong pressure to bear on the politicians. Thus, not Massachusetts, New York or Pennsylvania, but *Virginia* issued a call for a Commercial Convention, to meet in Annapolis, September, 1786, to see what could be done to relieve the situation.

The key to the functioning of democracy.

The Commercial Convention of 1786.

* Hamilton, from the second *Phocion Letter,* to the Considerate Citizens of New York, in 1784: *Works,* Vol. IV, pp. 288-290.

Hamilton saw his opportunity, and got himself elected a delegate to the Annapolis Convention. When it met, Hamilton rose and made a stirring address, in which he urged the calling of a second Convention, to meet in Philadelphia, in May of the following year, to make a Constitution. His resolution was unanimously adopted, though the language was altered to placate certain delegates: it was to be a Convention "to revise the Articles of Confederation"; but it was the Constitutional Convention just the same. Thus Hamilton called the Convention that made the Constitution.

Hamilton calling the Constitutional Convention.

He hastened home to bring New York in line. That was more difficult than might be imagined, for the reason that Governor Clinton had New York in his pocket. To understand that, one must remember that a considerable property qualification was required for voting in those days. For instance, when New York State had 325,000 population, there were only about 12,500 voters in the State. It can easily be seen how a successful politician, in league with the great landed families, could get that small constituency united behind him. Governor Clinton had accomplished that. The Governor was a strong state sovereignty man: probably on principle: let him have the benefit of the doubt; but all his interest was on that side. If New York refused to sign a constitution and remained a separate empire, Governor Clinton was czar in his own régime. If New York entered a union of the States, under a strong central government, Governor

Governor Clinton and New York State politics.

Clinton descended to the position of a satrap, merely a governor of a part of the nation.

The three New York delegates to the Constitutional Convention.

Hamilton succeeded in getting himself elected one of the three delegates from New York to the Constitutional Convention; but his associates, Yates and Lansing, were Clinton henchmen and strong state sovereignty men. When the Convention began by abrogating the old Articles of Confederation, Yates and Lansing simply turned their backs on it and went home, and would have nothing more to do with it, leaving Hamilton sole representative from New York. Hamilton had his heavy law practice. He went from New York to Philadelphia and from Philadelphia to New York. He did not take a very active part in the Convention; partly because he was only a minority representative from New York, but probably more because he saw it was not necessary. He seems to have asked for more than he wanted, to get as much as he could. When, after the months of wrangling, the Constitution was made and signed by the delegates: our compromise Constitution, great as it is, which completely satisfied nobody, but which most of the delegates believed was the best compromise they could achieve; and the first copy of it reached New York City, there appeared, the same day, a virulent attack upon it, from the pen of Governor Clinton, in the Governor's official newspaper.

Hamilton's part in the Convention.

Governor Clinton's attack on the Constitution.

The *Federalist* papers.

Hamilton saw that something must be done; and in a sloop, coming down the river from Albany to New

York, he wrote the first of the *Federalist* papers. The opening passage reads:

Opening appeal in the *Federalist*, to the people of New York State.

> "*To the People of the State of New York:*
>
> "After an unequivocal experience of the inefficiency of the subsisting federal government, you are called upon to deliberate on a new Constitution for the United States of America. The subject speaks its own importance; comprehending in its consequences nothing less than the existence of the UNION, the safety and welfare of the parts of which it is composed, the fate of an empire in many respects the most interesting in the world. It has been frequently remarked that it seems to have been reserved to the people of this country, by their conduct and example, to decide the important question, whether societies of men are really capable or not of establishing good government from reflection and choice, or whether they are forever destined to depend for their political constitutions on accident and force. If there be any truth in the remark, the crisis at which we are arrived may with propriety be regarded as the era in which that decision is to be made; and a wrong election of the part we shall act may, in this view, deserve to be considered as the general misfortune of mankind."*

Hamilton's view of the crisis faced by our people. Recognition that the solution was for mankind.

Hamilton appealed to Jay and Madison to help him in the critical fight. Jay wrote a few papers, Madison a considerable number, more philosophical in character; but it was Hamilton who took up in detail every power conferred by the Constitution, and argued its significance and value, and who considered one by one the objections raised against it, answering them conclusively. The bulk, thus, of that thick,

The part of Jay and Madison in the *Federalist*.

Hamilton's major part and the amazing thoroughness of his work.

* Hamilton, opening passage of the first paper in *The Federalist: Works*, Vol. XI, pp. 3, 4.

large volume of *Federalist* papers was written wholly by Hamilton, in a few months' time, in the intervals of his law practice.

Fighting for a union of the people in a Nation.

One weakness of the Continental Congress had been that its members voted only as State delegations, not unlike the procedure of a political party convention under the unit rule. Hamilton fought hard for a truly national Union, as against a federation of States, with the government's authority flowing from the people and not from the States. He said in number 22:

Hamilton's reiterated belief in the first principle of democracy: self-government by the people.

> "It has not a little contributed to the infirmities of the existing federal system, that it never had a ratification by the *people*. * * * The fabric of American empire ought to rest on the solid basis of the *consent of the people*. The streams of national power ought to flow immediately from that pure, original fountain of all legitimate authority." *

Believing that the national government should exercise unhampered authority, he argued:

> "A government ought to contain in itself every power requisite to the full accomplishment of the objects committed to its care, and to the complete execution of the trusts for which it is responsible, free from every other control but a regard to the public good and to the sense of the people." †

The *Federalist* papers giving the program of Hamilton's great work as statesman.

Hamilton laid down, in the Federalist papers, the whole program for a strong, unhampered, truly na-

---

* Hamilton, in No. 22 of *The Federalist: Works*, Vol. XI, pp. 179, 180.

† Hamilton, in No. 31 of *The Federalist: Works*, Vol. XI, p. 241.

tional government, which afterwards he was to fight through to victory.

The concluding words of the last paper were a solemn warning:

The closing warning.

> "I acknowledge that I cannot entertain an equal tranquillity with those who affect to treat the dangers of a longer continuance in our present situation as imaginary. A nation, without a national government, is, in my view, an awful spectacle. The establishment of a Constitution, in time of profound peace, by the voluntary consent of a whole people, is a prodigy, to the completion of which I look forward with trembling anxiety. I can reconcile it to no rules of prudence to let go the hold we now have, in so arduous an enterprise, upon seven out of the thirteen States, and after having passed over so considerable a part of the ground, to recommence the course. I dread the more the consequences of new attempts, because I know that powerful individuals, in this and in other States, are enemies to a general national government in every possible shape."*

Hamilton's sincerity and utter devotion to the cause.

It is hard to see how anyone can read Hamilton's writings, and not recognize his entire sincerity and pure-minded devotion to the welfare of the people and the nation, as he saw it. That we became a Nation, and not a collection of loosely associated, mutually jealous and contending States, is due to Hamilton more than to any other man or group of men.

Why the United States is a nation.

Among all his writings, the *Federalist* essays rank high. They won completely New York City and Westchester County to the Constitution, influenced

What the *Federalist* essays achieved.

* Hamilton, concluding passage in No. 85, the last paper of *The Federalist: Works,* Vol. XII, pp. 345, 346.

voters throughout the state and in other states; and the volume remains a great, permanent classic on government, vital and interesting at the present hour.

Hamilton's service in the Poughkeepsie Convention.

In 1788, New York State held a Convention at Poughkeepsie, to decide whether or not New York should accept the Constitution and enter the Union. There were fifty-seven delegates; and when the Convention met, forty-six were opposed, and only eleven in favor of entering the Union. It looked as if Governor Clinton had won in advance, hands down. The debate lasted three weeks. Hamilton spoke nearly every day, and sometimes almost all day; and the sheer force of the man's intellect, acting on the intellects of those other men, won the fight. It is true he used a whip: he threatened that if New York refused to enter the Union, New York City and Westchester County would leave the rest of the State, form a separate commonwealth, and enter anyway. That helped; but it was mainly his dominating intellect and unanswerable logic that won, in the final vote, thirty for the Constitution, against twenty-seven opposed. Thus Alexander Hamilton put New York in the Union; and more than anybody else, he made the Union.

Putting New York in the Union.

The celebration.

The celebration in New York City was planned by L'Enfant, who laid out the City of Washington, D. C. When the great float, the ship marked "Hamilton" came by, the crowd went wild with enthusiasm. For a considerable time afterwards, New York City was called, by both the friends and enemies of Hamilton,

"Hamiltoniana": not such a bad name: one almost wishes it might have lasted.

The first election under the new Constitution followed, with every vote of the electoral college for George Washington for first President. You will recall Washington's reluctance to serve, and the letters he received from statesmen all over the country, urging his acceptance. Hamilton wrote what was perhaps the strongest letter of all. The young man wrote to his senior, the secretary to his chief to the effect: you must accept, you have no right to decline; you are the one man who can lead the country safely forward and make the new government a living reality. Washington replied, recognizing the justice of Hamilton's arguments and saying he would accept. Then, a little later, he said, "But you must be my Secretary of the Treasury".

Hamilton's influence in Washington's acceptance of the Presidency.

It was the worst job of the Union. It has always been a thankless task: it was worse then than it has ever been since, or could be imagined ever again to be. Hamilton knew that, if he accepted, he would be criticized, vilified, abused. He accepted: why? Because he knew he was the one man who could do that work and carry the problem through.

Appointment and acceptance as Secretary of the Treasury.

Think of the task he faced: a hideous internal debt, for which the government had not had value received, since the debt had been accumulated under a rapidly depreciating currency. Besides this, was an almost equally terrible external debt. We had borrowed money wherever we could get it, chiefly from France.

Hamilton's colossal task.

Then we borrowed more money to pay the interest on what we had borrowed; then more to pay the interest on the interest; and when we could not borrow any more, we defaulted the interest.

Proposals for repudiation of debts.

Many, even statesmen, threw up their hands and said, "It is no use, we cannot pay; we will repudiate, and start afresh"; but that cannot be done. The Bolshevist régime in Russia cynically attempted such repudiation; but Russia can never take her place among the nations, until whatever government survives assumes the national mortgage, in taking the national farm. Of course, a nation, like an individual, may go through bankruptcy, to the ruin of its credit; but neither the one nor the other can merely repudiate honest debts.

Proposals for discrimination or partial repudiation.

Others, James Madison among them, urged discrimination. They said, where soldiers have kept their claims, we will pay them; but where they have got into the hands of gamblers and speculators, we will repudiate or pay a fraction of them. That caught the popular fancy. Everybody likes to kick a speculator, chiefly, perhaps, because nobody admits he is one. Once more, however, discrimination is impossible. If the debts are just, they must be paid, no matter into whose hands they may have passed. To repudiate them because of a change in ownership, is to destroy equally the credit of the debtor and the faith on which business relations rest. Further, how could they discriminate with regard to the indebtedness of the Revolution? Here was a claim sold by a soldier to a speculator: you would repudiate that. Here was a starving soldier, whose friend, to help him, bought his claim at a fair price: what would you do with that? Except in an occasional case, just discrimination was simply impossible.

Congress demanding a written report.

Hamilton had expected to report on the floor of the house, and prepared himself for it, assuming that heads of departments would have that natural relation to the legislative body. Congress established a precedent, subsequently harmful to the Nation's business, by refusing to hear him. Why? Because they were afraid of him: the man's dominating intellect, unerring grasp of moral principles, convincing power of logical statement, when he spoke by word of mouth. Understand, Hamilton was never an orator for the crowd; but when he addressed men of intellect, leaders, he dominated them with his convictions and carried them with him, with a sweeping power, unequalled by any other man in America, probably in the world, of his time.

Hamilton's power as an orator when addressing leaders.

So, fearing his personal power, Congress demanded a written report. Hamilton furnished it in five days: twenty thousand words of carefully reasoned argument, and more than that amount of figures and schedules, outlining his funding scheme for the colossal debts. How could he do it? Because he had it all thought out in his brain, ready for oral statement, and there was required merely the mechanical labor of writing it down.

The remarkable achievement of writing the great *Report* in five days' time.

That *Report,* of January 9th, 1790, is a master-

The basic thesis: to reestablish the public credit by paying every debt in full.

piece. Its initial thesis was, the first step in getting the Nation on its feet is to reestablish the public credit. That can be accomplished only by honestly assuming our obligations and paying every debt, internal and external, at face value. In his own words:

"To attempt to enumerate the complicated variety of mischiefs, in the whole system of the social economy, which proceed from a neglect of the maxims that uphold public credit, and justify the solicitude manifested by the House on this point, would be an improper obtrusion on their time and patience.

Hamilton's view that the future of the Nation depended upon the honest acceptance and just fulfillment of all obligations.

"In so strong a light, nevertheless, do they appear to the Secretary, that, on their due observance, at the present critical juncture, materially depends, in his judgment, the individual and aggregate prosperity of the citizens of the United States; their relief from the embarrassments they now experience; their character as a people; the cause of good government.

The only way of restoring the public credit.

"If the maintenance of public credit, then, be truly so important, the next inquiry which suggests itself is: By what means is it to be effected? The ready answer to which question is, by good faith; by a punctual performance of contracts. States, like individuals, who observe their engagements are respected and trusted, while the reverse is the fate of those who pursue an opposite conduct.

The ethics of organized society.

"To promote the increasing respectability of the the American name; to answer the calls of justice; to restore landed property to its due value; to furnish new resources, both to agriculture and commerce; to cement more closely the union of the States; to add to their security against foreign attack; to establish public order on the basis of an upright and liberal policy: these are the great and invaluable ends to be secured by

The ends Hamilton sought to achieve by establishing the public credit.

a proper and adequate provision, at the present period, for the support of public credit."*

Hamilton recognized that speculators would profit in some instances; but held that must be disregarded: to invalidate a debt, because its ownership had changed hands, would destroy the faith on which society and business proceed. The beauty of his plan was its honest simplicity. He merely applied to organized societies the principle of honesty and justice accepted for individuals: an application not yet universally made. Hamilton's enemies accused him of holding that a national debt was a blessing. That was not true. What he did argue was that the acceptance of common obligations tended to unify a people, and that the proper funding of the debt would furnish, in the stocks or bonds representing it, additional capital for business enterprise.

Significance in applying to society the morality prevailing among persons.

With the twenty thousand words of argument, Hamilton furnished, as has been stated, a still larger amount of figures and schedules for his funding plan, carrying the payment over a sufficiently long period, so that taxation would not be too burdensome in any one year. The Report was so admirable that Congress adopted it; and he had won the first round of the fight.

The funding plan.

Now came the problem of the practical functioning of the scheme. The next step was for the Federal Government to take over the debts, accumulated by

The assumption measure.

* Hamilton, in First Report on the Public Credit: *Works,* Vol. II, pp. 229-232.

the several States during the War for Independence, and pay them as the debt of the whole people.

Why assumption of state debts by the Federal Government was the key measure in Hamilton's great program.

Now see how this was the hinging element in Hamilton's plan. If the States retained their debts, and paid them severally, the State governments would have the superior taxing power. If the Federal Government assumed these debts, and paid them, as the debt of all the people in the land, then the Federal Government would have the superior taxing power. Now the government that has the supreme power of taxation is always the supreme government. One can go through all human history and find hardly an exception to that statement.

The selfishness of post-war thinking.

The post-war period, however, was, as always, one of selfish thinking. States that had suffered severely and accumulated a heavy war debt thought that, of course, the Federal Government should take over the state debts. States that had been outside the war zone and had sacrificed less argued: "What, the Federal Government assume our small debt, and tax us to pay the debts of other States? No, we will pay our own debts, and let them pay theirs!" The result was that Hamilton's key measure was in peril. If it failed, the whole plan to build an efficient government failed.

What the defeat of assumption would mean.

The States, retaining the taxing power, would be supreme in authority; while the new central government would be the weak Continental Congress over again, standing, cap in hand, to ask favors of the sovereign States. Incidentally, it would be practically impossible to get the debts accumulated by the

Continental Congress acceptably divided among the several States.

At this point, Hamilton took his first great step down, from statesman to politician. He took others, afterwards, far more reprehensible: this he could reasonably argue, was forced by the situation; but it was a step down, nevertheless. He went to Jefferson, and proposed that first great deal in American politics, the bargain already cited, that for the needed Virginia votes for assumption, Hamilton would furnish enough Federalist votes to have the new Capital placed in the South, where Jefferson and other Southern leaders wanted it. Hamilton was indifferent as to the location of the Capital: all he wanted was a strong, efficient government to function in it. Jefferson, as we have seen, at that time not opposed to the federal assumption of state debts, cheerfully agreed. In July, 1790, came the vote on the Capital; and Hamilton, true to the bargain, influenced enough votes to have it placed where it is today. The following month, came the final vote on assumption. Jefferson, fulfilling his part of the agreement, furnished the required Virginia votes; and Hamilton's great and hinging measure carried. The statement is so important that it must be repeated; and its significance should now be evident: that is why the Capital is at Washington; and *that is why* there was a government in it strong enough to survive the Civil War, and function efficiently to the present hour.

The political bargain with Jefferson.

This victory made a series of great measures pos-

Significance of establishing a National Bank.

sible. Hamilton's next step concerned the specific functioning of his plan. To carry out his funding scheme for the payment of the internal and external debt a national bank was needed. Unless you are intimately familiar with the history of finance, you can hardly imagine the meager banking facilities of those days. The first national bank was the stocking, or a hole in the woodshed floor; and that condition prevailed for a long time. Hamilton had previously established a state bank in New York, in 1784; and he now prepared a bill to establish the National Bank, necessary for the functioning of his plan. It passed the Congress; but here Washington drew back. He was not sure. He could find nothing in the Constitution warranting the President in signing a bill to establish such a corporation as a National Bank. He consulted Jefferson and Randolph, who both disapproved, holding the proposal unconstitutional. So he asked James Madison to prepare a veto message. Then, with his shrewd wisdom, Washington handed the opposed opinions to Hamilton, and asked him to answer them. Two days after Washington received Madison's draft of a veto message, Hamilton came back with eleven thousand words of carefully reasoned argument, completely convinced Washington, who signed the bill, and consistently supported, thereafter, every one of Hamilton's great measures for making the National Government a vital and growing reality. It was in this paper that Hamilton developed, for the first time, his theory of implied powers in the Consti-

Washington's doubt and handling of the problem.

Hamilton's view of the implied powers in the Constitution.

tution. His view was: in creating the Federal Government to fulfill certain ends, the Constitution grants, by implication, the powers necessary to achieve those ends. The Federal Government, once formed, moreover, is the government of all the people in the land. As such, it takes precedence over the governments of fractions or sections of the people in the land. All powers, therefore, not specifically reserved to the States in the Constitution, belong to the Federal Government, and may rightly be assumed by it, with the Supreme Court as the final arbiter and interpreter of the Constitution.

The fundamental opposition of Hamilton and Jefferson in political philosophy,

Now, if you wish, in clearest outline, the original cleavage in political philosophy, which was to divide the country ever after and culminate in the Civil War, remember that Jefferson held exactly the opposite. His view, as expressed in the Kentucky Resolutions and elsewhere, was: the State governments preceded the Federal Government as original sovereign authorities. They had united to form the Federal Government, as an instrument to perform certain limited functions; exactly as the nations have united and established the League of Nations to carry out certain defined functions, without compromising the sovereignty of the nations united in the League. The parallel is perfect. All powers, therefore, not specifically accorded to the Federal Government in the Constitution, belonged to the States; and each State might lawfully annul—nullify—any act of the Federal

Government not specifically authorized in the Constitution; with each State, as absolutely sovereign, its own final judge as to when its rights had been violated, thus denying the authority of the Supreme Court finally to interpret the Constitution.

The conflict that required a Civil War for its settlement.

There is the original conflict in the view of our government, held with equal sincerity on both sides, which was settled only through the horrors of a colossal fratricidal war, so far as such questions can be settled by warfare.

The great Report on Manufactures, of Dec. 5th, 1791.

Hamilton next established a mint and coinage system; and then wrote his great paper on manufactures, which, almost equally with the assumption and funding measures, produced a storm of controversy and attack. The naive thinking of the time is evident in the fact that he was compelled to argue that manufacturing industry is truly productive, as is agriculture, and that interest on capital is an economic factor equivalent to rent on land. A further evidence of the same state of thought is Hamilton's own error in holding that the employment of young children is an advantage in manufactures. One gasps at his statement, in the light of the tragic lessons experience has since taught us:

Evidences of the naive economic thinking of the time.

Hamilton's failure to see the evil of exploiting children in industry.

"It is worthy of particular remark that, in general, women and children are rendered more useful, and the latter more early useful, by manufacturing establishments, than they would otherwise be. Of the number of persons employed in the cotton manufactories of Great Britain, it is computed that four sevenths, nearly, are women and children, of whom the greatest proportion are children, and many of them of a tender age."*

How a great man may fall victim to the errors of his time.

This citing as an excellence, one of the saddest evils of the time, is only a painful illustration of how a great and wise man may fall victim to an error of his age.

Recognizing free trade and unhampered industry as the natural order.

In contrast to the opinions of many of those who profess to be his followers, Hamilton began his *Report* with a frank recognition of the natural advantages of free commerce, with no hampering interference by government; but argued of that policy:

> "If it had governed the conduct of nations more generally than it has done, there is room to suppose that it might have carried them faster to prosperity and greatness than they have attained by the pursuit of maxims too widely opposite."†

The European system of restraints on trade compelling the fostering of manufactures.

In place of that natural freedom of production and exchange, burdensome restraints had been established, especially against the exports of the United States. It was these restrictions on the part of European nations that convinced Hamilton of the necessity of fostering our own manufactures and developing greater domestic commerce.

The need for national self-sufficiency. Note the parallel argument in the disarmament program.

His supreme argument, however, was the need of national self-sufficiency, especially in war. Suppose the country were kept agricultural, and every knife and gun were bought from Britain; and then suddenly we were plunged into war with Britain: what would happen to us?

* Hamilton, from *Report on Manufactures: Works*, Vol. IV, p. 91.

† Hamilton, *Report on Manufactures: Works*, Vol. IV, p. 73.

"Not only the wealth but the independence and security of a country appear to be materially connected with the prosperity of manufactures. Every nation, with a view to those great objects, ought to endeavor to possess within itself, all the essentials of national supply. These comprise the means of subsistence, habitation, clothing, and defense.

Hamilton's view that making the Nation self-dependent was the next great step of progress.

"The possession of these is necessary to the perfection of the body politic; to the safety as well as to the welfare of the society. The want of either is the want of an important organ of political life and motion; and in the various crises which await a state, it must severely feel the effects of any such deficiency. The extreme embarrassments of the United States during the late war, from an incapacity of supplying themselves, are still matter of keen recollection; a future war might be expected again to exemplify the mischiefs and dangers of a situation to which that incapacity is still, in too great a degree, applicable, unless changed by timely and vigorous exertion. To effect this change, as fast as shall be prudent, merits all the attention and all the zeal of our public councils; 't is the next great work to be accomplished."*

The turn of the tide.

So far, Hamilton had been victorious in every round of the fight. Now the inevitable reaction came. The chief portfolio in the Cabinet is that of Secretary of State, held by Jefferson; but the chief figure in the Cabinet was Hamilton. Naturally, that was not pleasing to Jefferson. Then, as we have seen, Jefferson drew back in alarm from the rapidly growing power of the Federal Government under Hamilton's

* Hamilton, from *Report on Manufactures: Works*, Vol. IV, pp. 135, 136.

initiative and Washington's sanction. He came really to believe that Hamilton, and perhaps Washington, wished to develop an aristocracy and turn the government into a monarchy. That was not true; but Jefferson believed it. Moreover, he had some apparent warrant for his distrust in the fact that Hamilton had proposed, in the Constitutional Convention, a President and Senate elected on good behavior, which would be dangerously near monarchy. Hamilton's gravest limitation, moreover, was a lack of faith in the people, which Jefferson had in such abundant measure. From this lack sprang the errors in Hamilton's theory of government and the mistakes in his political career.

Reasons for Jefferson's growing opposition to Hamilton.

While strongly favoring republican government, Hamilton regarded it as an experiment, which must be proved in practice. His faith and doubt both are given frank statement in his long letter to Colonel Carrington, of Virginia, in 1792. After reviewing the, to him, puzzling growth of opposition and enmity to his work on the part of Jefferson and Madison, he said:

Letter to Colonel Carrington.

> "I am told that serious apprehensions are disseminated in your State as to the existence of a monarchical party meditating the destruction of State and republican government. If it is possible that so absurd an idea can gain ground, it is necessary that it should be combatted. I assure you, on my private faith and honor as a man, that there is not, in my judgment, a shadow of foundation for it. * * *
>
> "As to the destruction of State governments, the

Hamilton's view of republican government.

great and real anxiety is to be able to preserve the national from the too potent and counteracting influence of those governments. As to my own political creed, I give it to you with the utmost sincerity. I am affectionately attached to the republican theory. I desire above all things to see the equality of political rights, exclusive of all hereditary distinction, firmly established by a practical demonstration of its being consistent with the order and happiness of society. As to State governments, the prevailing bias of my judgment is that if they can be circumscribed within bounds, consistent with the preservation of the national government, they will prove useful and salutary. * * * As the thing now is, however, I acknowledge the most serious apprehensions, that the government of the United States will not be able to maintain itself against their influence. I see that influence already penetrating into the national councils and preventing their direction. Hence, a disposition on my part towards a liberal construction of the powers of the national government, and to erect every fence to guard it from depredations, which is, in my opinion, consistent with constitutional propriety. As to any combination to prostrate the State governments, I disavow and deny it. * * *

Fear lest the States should cripple the National government.

Why Hamilton desired a liberal construction of the Constitution.

"I said that I was affectionately attached to the republican theory. * * * I add that I have strong hopes of the success of that theory; but, in candor, I ought also to add that I am far from being without doubts. I consider its success as yet a problem. It is yet to be determined by experience whether it be consistent with that stability and order in government which are essential to public strength and private security and happiness."*

Frank expression of doubts as to the success of republican government.

* Hamilton, in Letter to Colonel Edward Carrington, Philadelphia, May 26, 1792: *Works*, Vol. IX, pp. 532-534.

Nothing could show better than this statement by the chief initiator and strongest leader of the Federal Government, how experimental our Republic was in its early phases. That the wise and temperate political philosophy, with the mingled faith and doubt, expressed in the above passage, was sincerely Hamilton's, his whole career attests. When one remembers, in contrast, Jefferson's enthusiastic and unquestioning faith in democracy and his distrust of centralized government, it is easy to understand his suspicions as to Hamilton's motives and his growing opposition to Hamilton's measures.

Evidence of the experimental character of our institutions in their early history.

Contrast between Hamilton's questioning and Jefferson's enthusiastic faith in democracy.

Jefferson, moreover, never understood Hamilton's funding plans, and was suspicious of them as merely an instrument of corruption. In his *Anas* Jefferson went so far as to say:

"Hamilton was not only a monarchist, but for a monarchy bottomed on corruption.

* * * * *

"Hamilton was, indeed, a singular character. Of acute understanding, disinterested, honest, and honorable in all private transactions, amiable in society, and duly valuing virtue in private life, yet so bewitched and perverted by the British example, as to be under thorough conviction that corruption was essential to the government of a nation."*

Injustice in Jefferson's matured estimate of Hamilton as statesman.

The fairness of Jefferson's personal estimate is only equalled by the injustice of his judgment of Hamilton as statesman and the almost childish re-

* Jefferson, *Anas: Writings*, Vol. I, pp. 278, 279.

sentment of Britain; but that was Jefferson's deep-seated conviction.

Madison's share in the controversy.

Himself disliking a controversy, Jefferson looked about for someone to answer Hamilton, and chose James Madison. Madison tried a time or two; and got his fingers burned. Nobody could answer Hamilton. He had the most trenchant pen, the most convincing logic, the clearest grasp of the infant nation's needs, the most dominating force of any man in America, at that time. So James Madison quit; and Jefferson tried less direct methods. He found a young literary man, Philip Freneau, and gave him a minor place in the State department, apparently on condition that Freneau should edit and publish an opposition newspaper in Philadelphia. The plan was carried out; and in Freneau's newspaper appeared attacks upon Hamilton, John Adams, other Federalist leaders and, finally, upon Washington.

Philip Freneau and the attacks in the opposition newspaper.

Afterwards, Freneau publicly testified that Jefferson never wrote nor inspired one of those attacks. Later, he stated privately that Jefferson wrote many of them and inspired them all. You may take your choice: one or the other time Philip Freneau lied.

The attack in Congress.

The attacks upon Hamilton got into Congress, where certain of the lesser leaders offered a resolution that Hamilton had broken the law, exceeded his authority and misused the funds of his department. A complete accounting was demanded. Consider the situation: Hamilton had had to build the Treasury department from nothing, while dealing with the complicated masses of internal and external debt, and fighting the incessant battle for government authority. A satisfactory accounting would have seemed almost a miracle. He had done his work so faithfully and kept his accounts so accurately that he was able in a brief time to furnish a complete report, accounting for every penny that had passed through the department, since its inauguration. He was completely exonerated. The next year an attempt was made to revive the charges; but it died in committee: there was no use: Hamilton's record was too entirely unimpeachable.

Hamilton's accurate accounting and complete exoneration.

In 1794, there came the only serious challenging by force, of the Federal Government, until the Civil War. One of the earliest taxes to be laid by the Federal Government was, rightly, the excise tax on intoxicating liquors. This caused bitter resentment, which came to a head in western Pennsylvania, where the Scotch Irish liked their liquor straight and untaxed. The resistance assumed the proportions of a rebellion. Instantly Hamilton saw the significance. It was not a matter of putting down some hundreds or thousands of recalcitrants in western Pennsylvania. The issue was: is the Federal Government to lay and collect taxes, carrying on the business of government, peaceably and with orderly authority, or is it not?

The Whiskey Rebellion: the first active resistance to the National government.

Hamilton therefore asked Washington if he might raise the army to put down the rebellion. Now he was not Secretary of War: Knox held that office; but, of course, the attack was on the Treasury department.

Hamilton's recognition of the issue and part in suppressing the rebellion.

Washington consented; and Hamilton raised 10,000 infantry and 2,000 cavalry; marching with Washington at the head of the troops into Pennsylvania. When the rebels saw the size of the force coming against them, they—well, they just evaporated. When the army got well into Pennsylvania, there were no rebels there. Thus Hamilton suppressed, practically bloodlessly, the only active challenging of the Federal Government till the Civil War.

Resignation from the Treasury.

The following year, 1795, feeling that his work in the Treasury was largely accomplished, he resigned to resume his law practice. With an expensive family, it was difficult to live on his secretarial salary. He could not escape politics, however. The members of the Cabinet and other leaders came continually to consult him, as the chief figure among those who had moulded the government; and thus, without wishing it, he was pushed into the position of boss of the Federalist party. This helps to explain the increase in the politician as compared with the statesman, in Hamilton's later years.

Circumstances making Hamilton boss of the Federalist party; thus increasingly the politician.

When Washington, in 1796, peremptorily refusing to consider a third term, wished to give a farewell message to the American people, he turned to his associate and old-time secretary for help. Before the close of his first term, he had asked similar assistance of James Madison. His mind now definitely made up, Washington jotted down the ideas he wanted to cover; but reluctant, as always, to take his pen in hand, he handed the paper, with probably Madison's sketch, to

Hamilton, and asked him to draft an address, on the basis of these points. Hamilton did so; and Washington was so pleased with the draft that he adopted it, and apparently, with a few changes, issued it as his *Farewell Address to the American People.* Do not forget, next time you read that classic, that it is the work of two minds: the ideas of the great chief, elaborated and expressed, as in the early years of the Revolution, by his life long co-worker and old-time secretary, Hamilton.

Drafting Washington's Farewell Address.

The worst attack of all, upon Hamilton, came in 1797, two years after his retirement from public office. Back in 1792, when he was in the thick of the fight in the Treasury department, two scoundrels, Clingman and Reynolds, were thrown into jail, accused of suborning perjury to obtain money on claims against the government. They let it be known that they had some hold on a high officer of the government; and Muhlenberg, speaker of the House, went to see them. They showed him certain letters from Hamilton, and told him Hamilton had conspired with them to defraud the government. While not believing the charge, Muhlenberg, being a Congressman, felt the matter must be investigated. He took two other congressmen, Venable and James Monroe; and the three called upon Hamilton, and informed him of the charges.

The attack upon Hamilton in 1797.

Hamilton frankly laid the whole private matter before them. He told them that, during one of the long periods in the country's service, a handsome, vulgar woman, Mrs. Reynolds, had called upon him, telling him she had been abandoned by her husband, was in dire need, and asked him for a little money. Hamilton told them he had gone to see her, had given her some money, and quickly discovered that, as he expressed it, she was open to other consolation as well. He explained that he had become involved in an unworthy relation with her; then an alleged husband had appeared on the scene, and they had blackmailed him. Yes, he had given them a thousand dollars, in two payments, and other small sums, disguised as loans. He turned over all the papers in the case to the three Congressmen, who took them for examination; and returning them, apologized to Hamilton for having bothered him.

Hamilton's publication of the Reynolds pamphlet.

After Washington's retirement, however, when party bitterness grew to an intense pitch, hardly equalled subsequently, except just before the Civil War, James Monroe, who had unfairly kept copies of certain of the papers, allowed them to get into print. The object, of course, was to destroy Hamilton's leadership of the Federalist party. Hamilton demanded a full statement from Monroe, who had completely exonerated him as a public servant; but Monroe temporized and evaded. Then Hamilton did the amazing thing, the thing his enemies never dreamed he would dare to do: he published the whole affair in the Reynolds pamphlet: all Mrs. Reynolds's passionate, misspelled letters, her husband's blackmailing letters, Hamilton's replies: there they were: fifty-two documents in all. Hamilton accompanied the documents with a statement, in the course of which he said, that he was sorry to have to do this, especially as it would give pain to one whom he dearly loved (of course, his wife, with whom he had long since made his peace); but his honor as a public man compelled it. The result was complete and permanent exoneration of his character as a public man and statesman, but grave private humiliation.

Significance of Hamilton's brief story of his life, in the letter to a relative in Scotland.

In 1797, the year of this most virulent attack, Hamilton wrote a long letter to a relative in Scotland, of the same name. His great achievement and fame had evidently aroused his Scotch relatives to claim the relationship! The letter is a brief, modest autobiography. As it gives, best of all surviving documents, Hamilton's view of his own life, answers many criticisms, and shows, at once, why he undertook the thankless task of the Treasury department and why he retired from public office, it is quoted entire:

"Albany, State of New York,
May the 2nd, 1797.

"My dear Sir: Some days since I received with great pleasure your letter of the 10th of March. The mark it affords of your kind attention, and the particular account it gives me of so many relatives in Scotland, are extremely gratifying to me. You no doubt have understood that my father's affairs at a very early day went to wreck; so as to have rendered his situation during the greatest part of his life far from eligible. This state of things occasioned a separation between him and me, when I was very young, and threw me upon the bounty of my mother's relatives, some of whom were then wealthy, though by vicissitudes to which human affairs are so liable, they have been since much reduced and broken up. Myself at about sixteen came to this country. Having always had a strong propensity to literary pursuits, by a course of study and laborious exertion I was able, by the age of nineteen, to qualify myself for the degree of Bachelor of Arts in the College of New York, and to lay the foundation for preparatory study for the future profession of the law.

"The American Revolution intervened. My principles led me to take part in it; at nineteen I entered into the American army as Captain of Artillery. Shortly after I became, by invitation, aid-de-camp to General Washington, in which station I served till the commencement of that campaign which ended with the siege of York in Virginia, and the capture of Cornwallis's army. The campaign I made at the head of a corps of light infantry, with which I was present at the siege of York, and engaged in some interesting operations.

Modest reference to his brilliant storming of the redoubt at Yorktown.

"At the period of the peace of Great Britain, I found myself a member of Congress by appointment of the Legislature of this State.

"After the peace, I settled in the city of New York, in the practice of the law, and was in a very lucrative course of practice, when the derangement of our public affairs, by the feebleness of the general confederation, drew me again reluctantly into public life. I became a member of the Convention which framed the present Constitution of the United States; and having taken part in this measure, I conceived myself to be under an obligation to lend my aid towards putting the machine in some regular motion. Hence, I did not hesitate to accept the offer of President Washington to undertake the office of Secretary of the Treasury.

Why Hamilton undertook the Treasury Secretaryship.

"In that office I met with many intrinsic difficulties, and many artificial ones, proceeding from passions, not very worthy, common to human nature, and which act with peculiar force in republics. The object, however, was effected of establishing public credit and introducing order in the finances.

The simple reference to his great achievement.

"Public office in this country has few attractions. The pecuniary emolument is so inconsiderable as to amount to a sacrifice to any man who can employ his time with advantage in any liberal profession. The opportunity of doing good, from the jealousy of power and the spirit of faction, is too small in any station to warrant a long continuance of private sacrifices. The enterprises of party had so far succeeded as materially to weaken the necessary influence and energy of the executive authority, and so far diminish the power of doing good in that department, as greatly to take away the motives which a virtuous man might have for making sacrifices. The prospect was even bad for gratifying in future the love of fame, if that passion was to be the spring of action.

The bitter lessons and mood of pessimism, resulting from Hamilton's experiences as statesman.

"The union of these motives, with the reflections of prudence in relation to a growing family, determined me as soon as my plan had attained a certain maturity, to withdraw from office. This I did by a resignation about two years since, when I resumed the profession of the law in the City of New York under every advantage I could desire.

Reasons for retiring from public office.

"It is a pleasant reflection to me, that since the commencement of my connection with General Washington to the present time, I have possessed a flattering share of his confidence and friendship.

Reverence and friendship for Washington.

"Having given you a brief sketch of my political career, I proceed to some further family details.

"In the year 1780 I married the second daughter of

Happiness of Hamilton's domestic life.

General Schuyler, a gentleman of one of the best families of this country, of large fortune, and no less personal and political consequence. It is impossible to be happier than I am in a wife; and I have five children, four sons and a daughter, the eldest a son somewhat past fifteen, who all promise as well as their years permit, and yield me much satisfaction. Though I have been too much in public life to be wealthy, my situation is extremely comfortable, and leaves me nothing to wish but a continuance of health. With this blessing, the profits of my profession and other prospects authorize an expectation of such addition to my resources as will render the eve of life easy and agreeable, so far as may depend on this consideration.

"It is now several months since I have heard from my father, who continued at the island of St. Vincent. My anxiety at this silence would be greater than it is, were it not for the considerable interruption and precariousness of intercourse which is produced by the war.

Evidence of Hamilton's later relations with his father.

"I have strongly pressed the old gentleman to come and reside with me, which would afford him every enjoyment of which his advanced age is capable; but he has declined it on the ground that the advice of his physicians leads him to fear that the change of climate would be fatal to him. The next thing for me is, in proportion to my means, to endeavor to increase his comforts where he is.

"It will give me the greatest pleasure to receive your son Robert at my house in New York, and still more to be of use to him; to which end, my recommendation and interest will not be wanting, and I hope not unavailing. It is my intention to embrace the opening which your letter affords me to extend my intercourse with my relatives in your country, which will be a new source of satisfaction to me."*

When John Adams succeeded Washington as president, he took over the existing Cabinet, whose members, as we have seen, went constantly to consult Hamilton. This greatly displeased Adams, who, forceful and opinionated, felt that he was quite able to run the government without outside help or interference. His consequent growing dislike of Hamilton was a case of one strong man resenting another. Then came the scare of war with France, over the *X Y Z Letters,* and Adams's appointment of Washington, as Commander-in-Chief, to raise an army. Washington accepted, on condition that he be privileged to appoint his subordinate generals; and named Hamilton, Pinckney and Knox. Adams, disliking Hamilton, wished to reverse the order, and commission Knox, Pinckney and Hamilton. Washington said No, Colonel Hamilton is the younger man, he has worked with me and understands my methods, I want him next under me. Well, even forceful John Adams could not oppose George Washington; so he gritted his teeth and issued the commissions, Hamilton, Pinckney and Knox; and hated Hamilton all the more. On one occasion Adams referred to Hamilton as "the bastard brat of a Scotch pedlar". That was unworthy and unfair; but he said it. Meantime, the

President Adams's resentment toward Hamilton.

The X Y Z Letters.

Appointment of Hamilton as first General under Washington.

* Hamilton, letter to his Scotch relative, Alexander Hamilton: *Works,* Vol. X, pp. 257-261.

war scare blew over, leaving Hamilton Inspector General of the army.

Then came the foolish enactment, against Hamilton's warning, of the vicious alien and sedition laws, with the consequent wrecking of the Federalist party. After Washington's death, President Adams, in a rage with Hamilton, got rid of Hamilton's remaining friends in the Cabinet.

Hamilton's reply to the accusation of leading a British faction.

During the last year of President Adams's administration Hamilton wrote him a letter, stating that Adams was reported to have declared Hamilton the leader of a British faction, and asking if the President had made such a charge. Receiving no reply, Hamilton waited exactly two months, and then wrote a second letter, in which he said:

> "This much I affirm, that by whomsoever a charge of the kind mentioned in my former letter, may, at any time, have been made or insinuated against me, it is a base, wicked and cruel calumny; destitute even of a plausible pretext, to excuse the folly, or mark the depravity which must have dictated it."*

Circumstances of the publication of Hamilton's pamphlet on *The Public Character and Conduct of John Adams.*

The result of all this was that, when the election of 1800 came, Hamilton prepared, for private circulation among the Federalist leaders, a pamphlet on *The Public Character and Conduct of John Adams.* Aaron Burr, his rival in New York politics, got hold of fragments of it and published them, compelling Hamilton to publish the whole, in self defense. Thus

* Hamilton, in letter to John Adams of Oct. 1st, 1800: *Works,* Vol. VII, p. 365.

Hamilton was in the anomalous position of supporting John Adams, as the most available candidate the Federalists had to succeed himself in the presidency; yet with this published pamphlet, severely criticising the candidate's public character and conduct. It was one of the several occasions where Hamilton allowed his passions to get the better of his judgment as statesman, always, of course, with bad consequences.

There was thus no chance for Adams to carry New York State; and there followed the equal number of votes for Jefferson and Burr, in the electoral college, throwing the election into the Federalist House. Hating Jefferson as the outstanding opposition leader, the House, as we have seen, was inclined to choose Burr, until Hamilton intervened to give the election to the one who, though his enemy, he recognized to be an earnest patriot, as against the man he had come to regard as an unprincipled adventurer. Let me repeat, it was one of the great and magnanimous achievements of Hamilton's career that his influence made Thomas Jefferson President of the United States.

Hamilton's part in making Jefferson President.

Naturally, Burr's hatred of Hamilton was increased. When they were both stripling young officers in the Revolution, Burr and Hamilton had been friends; but Burr's political methods aroused Hamilton's distrust, and he came to regard Burr as an unprincipled adventurer. When, in 1791, Burr was elected to the national Senate, in place of General Schuyler, the circumstances were such as to make

Burr's growing hatred of Hamilton.

Hamilton intensely bitter. As time went on, Hamilton attacked Burr, in letters to other statesmen, with increasing venom: a further example of the clouding of his statesmanship by his passions. Burr waited until the attacks became semi-public, and demanded an explanation. Hamilton gave one which Burr declared unsatisfactory; and challenged Hamilton to a duel.

The challenge to a duel.

Why did Hamilton accept? He hated the whole vicious duelling system. It is true, early in life, he had served as second to Laurens, in the duel with General Charles Lee, over the latter's scurrilous attack on Washington; but that was in military affairs, and the honor of their beloved chief was in question. Moreover, some years before Burr's challenge, Philip, Hamilton's eldest son, outraged by the vicious attacks upon his father, had challenged one of the detractors, and been killed in a duel at Weehawken, to his father's deep and lasting grief, and the mental breakdown of his sister. It is interesting that Hamilton's eighth and last child, born in 1802, was also named Philip (Little Philip, he was called) in memory of the favorite eldest son, who had gone the path his father shortly followed.

Reasons for Hamilton's acceptance of Burr's challenge.

Why then did Hamilton accept? The writings he left answer the question and show how his mind worked. He argued with himself: I am the head of the Federalist party, that is, of the group of men who have made our government. If I decline this challenge, public opinion being what is is, I shall be stigmatized as a coward, and my leadership destroyed. I would better be dead than have that happen. If I am to live, I must go on serving the cause, as leader of those who seek to foster the authority, efficiency and permanence of the nation's government. He accepted.

The intervening days. How Hamilton spent them.

An unusual number of days intervened between the acceptance and the duel. Hamilton spent the time setting his house in order, in the endeavor to leave his family in not too difficult circumstances, in the event of his death. He had earned liberally, but spent freely. His family had occupied several homes in New York; and then, wishing to live completely in the country, Hamilton had gone away beyond the city and built The Grange, far out in the wilderness—at 142nd Street and 10th Avenue. In the nights before the duel, Hamilton wrote two agonizingly tender love letters to his wife. Burr spent the intervening days in pistol practice on Long Island: he meant to kill.

Burr's intention to kill.

The duel occurred at morn, across the river at Weehawken, July 11th, 1804. Hamilton's pistol went off in the air: he had said that he would not fire upon his adversary. Burr shot to kill; and killed. Hamilton, mortally wounded, was carried across the river, and died the next day, July 12th, 1804: forty-seven and a half years old! He should have had another thirty years of service. O, maybe his work was done: the battle had been fought through and the great steps taken in establishing the government. In his last years, Hamilton had been increasingly the

The tragic end of a great career.

politician, as compared with the pure statesman of his great days: maybe his great work was done; but if he had gone on developing and serving, what might not the Hamilton of another thirty years of life have done for us!

Effect on the country.

The whole country was aroused by the murder, for as such it was regarded. That the Vice President of the United States should murder the greatest statesman in it, under the forms of a duel, so shocked the people, that it did more than anything else that ever happened to eliminate the infamous duelling system. Understand, it was a long time before it went; but the murder of Hamilton by Burr was a chief cause of its passing.

The long life-loyalty of Hamilton's wife.

Hamilton's wife survived him fifty years! She spent her active years, during that half century of widowhood, in seeking justice for her husband's memory. Hamilton's son grew up, and wrote the story of his father's life. The widow finally secured the purchase by Congress of Hamilton's papers, insuring their being kept intact. She won her fight! When she came to die, in 1854, at the age of ninety-seven, there was found upon her breast, enclosed in a little bag, tied about her neck with a piece of ribbon, the faded paper, containing the love verses Hamilton had written to her, as her fiancé, seventy-four years before.

V

LEE: THE AMERICAN WARRIOR

THE foregoing essays have dealt with the making of the Nation, the initiation of our institutions, their early progress, and the original cleavage in political philosophy, based on opposing views of the Constitution, and resulting in the political parties led by Hamilton and Jefferson. We come now to the culmination of that cleavage, in the terrible trial by fire, through which the Nation was reborn and present day America made possible; studying it through those two outstanding leaders, Lee and Lincoln, to whom the opposing sides turned in fratricidal conflict: both Nature's noblemen; each absolutely consecrated to his cause.

Culmination of the conflict in political philosophy.

The union of States was formed under the whip of necessity. During the Revolution, the Colonies were compelled to make common cause, establish the weak Continental Congress, and loosely confederate, in order to pull the struggle through to victorious independence. So, in those dark years following the Revolutionary War, the infant States were forced to get together, make a Constitution, unite under it and establish a central Federal government, to be able to stand on their feet and hold up a self-respecting face to a threatening and potentially hostile world.

The Union of the States compelled by circumstances.

Doubts of the Union's permanence.

Those who formed the Union doubtless hoped it would last permanently: that is proved by the fact that there is no provision for withdrawal in the Constitution; but it was hope rather than clear conviction. The view of the States as absolutely sovereign was universal; and even the strongest supporters of a union under a Federal government, such as Washington and Hamilton, had periods of depression when they questioned its continuance.

Growth in the power and authority of the Federal government.

Hamilton's far seeing fight had borne fruit, however, and the Federal government grew rapidly and steadily in power and authority. This resulted in part from the mere expansion of the country in territory and population. The larger the area over which a government functions, other things being equal, the more powerful it is apt to become.

Free trade among the States as fostering national unity.

The absence of trade restrictions among the States tended further to obliterate the older State attachments and make for national unity. Free, unhampered commerce is one of the most unifying forces known. With goods and persons moving freely across the State borders, those lines became increasingly mere convenient political divisions, with the Nation the unit on which patriotic feeling centered.

Effect of vast immigration on the nationalism of the North and West.

This process was accentuated, in the North and West, by the great tide of immigration that flowed across the Atlantic upon our shores, in multiplying volume. Those immigrants came, not to Massachusetts, Pennsylvania or Ohio: they came to America, which they regarded as the land of freedom and opportunity. They were scarcely more interested in State lines than in County and City divisions. Their patriotism, often intense in character, was focussed, not upon the State, but on the National government, as the government of all the people in the land.

A further cause, also affecting the North and West, was the rapid development of manufacturing industries. An industrial population is notoriously unstable, moving readily from place to place, as wages and conditions of employment vary. That growing population had no tradition of attachment to the State as sovereign: its loyalty also centered naturally on the government of the Nation.

Influence of manufacturing industries on the North.

Certain of these causes did not act, to the same extent upon the South. Little of that tide of immigration went south, during the first half of the nineteenth century. When the Civil War broke out, the majority of people living in the south Atlantic states had been born upon the soil where they lived. They had deeply the tradition of attachment to the sovereign State government, upon which patriotic feeling had originally centered. As the southwest territories were opened up, they were settled chiefly by people from the south Atlantic states, who carried with them this tradition of State affiliation.

Survival of the older tradition of State patriotism in the South.

The South, moreover, remained agricultural. An agricultural population is far more intensely attached to the soil than an industrial one. The World War gave an impressive illustration of that. The fervor of patriotism, marking the French people in the war,

Significance that the South remained agricultural.

came in no small measure from the French custom of dividing each farm among all the children of a family, so that each peasant has his little strip of land, which he regards as a bit better than any other land in France, and therefore in all the world. It was largely the attachment of the French peasant to the soil of France that gave the passionate loyalty France displayed in the war. Conditions of agriculture in the South, of course, differed widely from those in modern France; but there was a similar intense local type of patriotism, cherishing the tradition of State affiliation.

Reasons for the culmination of the Southern tradition in old Virginia.

Those differences, marking the South, received their supreme expression in old Virginia. Virginia had a great tradition. With Massachusetts, she had called for a union of the Colonies and initiated the Revolution. She had declared herself independent of Britain, and furnished the great commander-in-chief to lead the American forces to victory, returning him for two terms as first President of the infant Nation. Traditionally the "Mother of Presidents," she had sent, in turn, Jefferson, Madison and Monroe to follow Washington in leadership of the Nation.

Her population was largely of direct English descent, with a considerable fraction from the lesser British nobility. Virginia was the most impressive surviving example of the original sovereign State; and the devotion of her people to her was particularly fervid. All this was behind Robert E. Lee.

Lee was born at Stratford, Westmoreland County,

Virginia, a few miles from the birthplace of Washington, January 19th, 1807, of best Virginia families on both sides. His father was that Light Horse Harry Lee, Washington's beloved young comrade of the Revolution. You will remember his excellent service, at Paulus Hook and elsewhere. He was, indeed, the only officer, below the rank of general, to be voted a medal by the Continental Congress; and it was he whom the Congress invited to give the Memorial Address over Washington, in which he used those words, already quoted as still defining our view of Washington, that he was "First in war, first in peace, and first in the hearts of his countrymen." Moreover, some biographers identify that "Lowland Beauty," as Washington called her, of whom he was enamoured in his youth and to whom he wrote those tender but rather clumsy verses, as the same girl who afterwards married one of the Lees and became the mother of Light Horse Harry. If true, this would merely help to explain Washington's attachment for his young comrade in arms.

Lee's father, Light Horse Harry Lee.

Light Horse Harry Lee was twice married. His second wife was Anne Carter, of the eminent Carter family in Virginia; and her third son was Robert E. Lee.

Lee's mother.

When Lee was a child of four, the family moved to Alexandria, near Washington's Mount Vernon home, to secure better educational opportunities for the children. The following year, the War of 1812 broke out; and President Madison commissioned his

Circumstances of the injury and death of Lee's father.

friend, Light Horse Harry Lee, one of the generals to lead the army of invasion into Canada. He started North; stopped at Baltimore. There was a riot in that city; and in endeavoring to protect a friend, a Federalist editor, from the mob, Light Horse Harry Lee was injured. He went to the West Indies in search of health; did not get better; returned to an island off the Georgia coast, the home of General Nathanael Greene, his comrade of the Revolution; and died there in 1818, when his son Robert, was a boy of eleven. Thus Lee had the misfortune, at the age of eleven, to lose his father, exactly as had happened to Washington.

Parallel with Washington.

Lee was the main stay of his widowed and semi-invalid mother, treating her with beautiful courtesy and tender chivalry, taking upon himself the cares of the household, while continuing his studies. Lee differed from others of our great leaders in having excellent schooling. He was thoroughly prepared for West Point, having early decided to follow the footsteps of his father in a military career.

Lee's chivalry toward his mother.

Excellent early education.

One of Lee's cousins is authority for the statement that it was Mrs. Lewis, the Nellie Custis of Mount Vernon, Washington's favorite step-grandchild, and the aunt of the girl Lee afterwards married, who went with the young Lee to Washington, to intercede with General Andrew Jackson, then Senator from Tennessee, to get Lee admitted to West Point. In any case, he was admitted at the age of eighteen. Then, as now, the discipline was strict and the cur-

Entering West Point at eighteen.

riculum hard. Lee went through his four years without a single demerit mark. He was early cadet officer; then adjutant of the entire batallion, the most coveted honor at West Point; and he was graduated second in a class of forty-six. Taking those facts together, they make an almost unequalled record for the whole history of West Point.

Remarkable record at West Point.

Then, as today, the engineers were the aristocracy of the army. Lee entered that corps; and his first service was at Hampton Roads, where he was employed in improving the fortifications of the harbor. While on this service, Lee made frequent visits to Arlington, the beautiful home of George Washington Parke Custis, Washington's step-grandchild, adopted, with his sister, as Washington's own children, after the death of the father, Jack Custis, when Washington became convinced he was not to have a direct heir.

First service at Hampton Roads

Here at Arlington, Lee resumed what had been a boy and girl friendship with Mary Parke Custis, daughter of the family. A warm love affair quickly developed. There seems to have been some opposition to an engagement, on the part of the young woman's parents, owing to Lee's limited financial circumstances; but the young persons succeeded quickly in overcoming this opposition; and the year that Lee was twenty-four, he and Mary Parke Custis were married.

Lee's engagement and marriage to Mary Parke Custis.

Thus Lee's marriage added a further bond, to the many already existing, between his family and that

Bonds between Lee's family and that of Washington.

of Washington. Very early in life, Lee had deliberately chosen Washington as his hero and model. His whole conduct and career were consciously moulded on the example of Washington; and it is interesting to note how many characteristics were the same in both men. Lee had Washington's absolute integrity, his devotion to duty. Lee said repeatedly that "duty is the noblest word in our language"; and he made it the guiding principle in his conduct of life. He had Washington's courage and patient endurance, Washington's modesty and selflessness. Moreover in the crisis of his career, Lee dreamed of achieving, for his State and section, what Washington had won for the whole group of Colonies, namely, complete independence from what he had come to regard as external tyranny.

Washington as Lee's hero and model.

Identity of character in Lee and Washington.

Lee's marriage, resulting from the warm and tender love affair, was lived with entire loyalty through his whole life. No breath of scandal ever touched the personal character and conduct of Robert E. Lee. Seven children were born of the union, all growing up to maturity. Three of Lee's sons became officers in the Confederate army, and two of them reached the rank of Major General. Lee's letters to his wife and children are beautiful combinations of tenderness and affection with that reserve, that marked him as it did Washington. Lee had more introspection than Washington; otherwise their characteristics seem the same.

Domestic life.

A few months after Lee's marriage, a terrible series

of events occurred in the southeastern corner of Virginia. A certain Nat Turner, negro slave and half-crazed religious fanatic, believing himself called of God to redeem and revenge his people, and seeing in the heavens signs that the hour had struck, started on a murdering expedition. He associated other negroes with him, and others were forced to join the band; in the end it numbered fifty-three. Five of the family of Turner's master were murdered in their beds. The only white persons in the neighborhood who escaped were those protected by faithful slaves. In all, fifty-seven whites were murdered, including all the children in a school. Bands of white men gathered together, troops were sent from Fortress Monroe, the negroes were hunted down; and the leaders were, not lynched, but tried, convicted and legally hanged.

The Nat Turner rebellion.

This rebellion produced a terrible impression all over the South. It wakened the southern people to a realization of the slumbering volcano on which they were living, and to what would happen were that volcano suddenly to explode. The result was severer laws regarding freed negroes, stricter treatment of slaves and a general stopping of the wide spread movement for gradually emancipating the slaves, then on all over the South.

Far reaching effects of the Turner rebellion on the South.

This series of events produced a deep impression on Lee. His letters to his wife, at the time, show how profoundly he was affected by them. Please remember this series of events: it had much to do with what followed.

After Hampton Roads, Lee's next important work was at St. Louis. The channel of the Mississippi was changing, threatening a part of the city; and St. Louis appealed for help to General Scott, head of the United States army. General Scott responded that he knew but one man capable of meeting the problem. He said, "He is young, but if the work can be done, he can do it"; and recommended Robert E. Lee.

Lee's work at St. Louis.

Lee went to St. Louis. The work went forward thoroughly, but slowly. The people of St. Louis became impatient. It is said that a cannon was even placed where it could be fired upon Lee and his men, if desired. Lee said, "They can do as they like with their own, but I was sent here to do certain work, and I shall do it;" and he did it, so efficiently, that the present channel of the Mississippi river, at St. Louis, is determined by the great existing bulwarks, erected by Robert E. Lee.

Earlier, Lee had surveyed the upper Mississippi, and opened it to navigation; and his report to the government really determined our present national policy on inland water ways.

The years of service in New York harbor.

At thirty-five, Lee was sent to New York, to improve the harbor defenses. He lived for several years at Fort Hamilton. He issued from this work with the rank of captain, and was appointed one of the visiting inspectors of West Point.

Lee's great training for his later career, however, came through the war with Mexico. It is aside from our purpose to go into the causes of that war; but you will recall it broke out in 1846, when Lee was thirty nine. The list of officers of the United States army in the war with Mexico reads like a roster of the generals on both sides in the Civil War. There were McClellan, Hancock, Thomas and Grant. There were Jefferson Davis, Stonewall Jackson, Beauregard, Longstreet, Joseph Johnston, Jubal Early and Lee.

The war with Mexico.

Officers in the war with Mexico who became generals in the Civil War.

Lee did admirable service in the war with Mexico. He was honorably mentioned for his work at the taking of Vera Cruz. He was then attached to General Scott's personal staff, and given much of the difficult work of advance. For instance, at Cerro Gordo, General Santa Anna was posted in an apparently impregnable pass in the mountains. Lee discovered a by-path around the summit; led a portion of the army over it to a position in front; posted batteries by night; and in the morning, executed a turning movement that drove Santa Anna out.

Lee's brilliant service and training for his later career, in the war with Mexico.

In his report on Cerro Gordo, General Scott said:

> "I am compelled to make special mention of the services of Captain R. E. Lee, Engineer. This officer, greatly distinguished at the siege of Vera Cruz, was again indefatigable, during these operations, in reconnaissances as daring as laborious, and of the utmost value. Nor was he less conspicuous in planting batteries, and in conducting columns to their stations under the heavy fire of the enemy."*

General Scott's report on Lee's service at Cerro Gordo.

Still more important was Lee's work at Contreras,

* Scott, Gen. Winfield, in Supplemental Report on Cerro Gordo, Apr. 23rd, 1847: *Memoirs*, Vol. II, p. 450.

on the road to the City of Mexico. Here, the road lay between impassable swamps, rivers and lakes, on one side, and on the other, a tangled mass of twisted lava rock, called the Pedrigal. Lee discovered a mule track through the Pedrigal; widened it with his engineers; led two divisions over it to the front. Then it was discovered that they were out of touch with headquarters, and General Scott must be notified. So alone, at night, in a drenching storm, Lee made his way back across that desolate twisted mass of lava rock; reported to General Scott; and again returned alone, arriving in time for the assault, the following morning.

Lee's remarkable feat at Contreras.

Referring to this feat, General Scott said:

General Scott's repeated praise of Lee.

> "Of the seven officers * * * not one has succeeded in getting through these difficulties, increased by darkness. They have all returned. But the gallant and indefatigable Captain Lee, of the Engineers, who has been constantly with the operating forces, is (eleven o'clock p. m.) just in * * * to ask that a powerful diversion be made against the center of the entrenched camp toward morning."*

In his summary of the campaign, General Scott mentioned "Captain R. E. Lee, as distinguished for felicitous execution as for science and daring." † Those are authentic words. General Scott is further reported to have said that Lee was the greatest military genius in America. Whether he said it or not, it was true. Thus Lee issued from the war with

Lee at the conclusion of the war with Mexico.

* Scott, Gen. Winfield, *Memoirs*, Vol. II, p. 475.
† Ibid., pp. 500, 501.

Mexico, brevetted Colonel, with the warm approbation of all his superiors, and without the jealousy of his associates: a signal illustration of his modesty and generosity, as well as nobility of spirit.

Lee was now made Superintendent of West Point; and served in that capacity from the age of forty five to forty nine. His discipline was strict, but his attitude fatherly; and the students all loved him devotedly. His own son, Custis, was a cadet at West Point, during these years.

Four years as Superintendent of West Point.

Then in 1856, Jefferson Davis, United States Secretary of War, commissioned Lee Lieutenant Colonel of a regiment of cavalry, and ordered him to Texas, to protect the Texans against the Indians. Lee regretted leaving his beloved engineers corps, and disliked the assignment because of the necessary long periods of absence from home; but, of course, obeyed orders. He went to Texas for several years of desultory Indian fighting, still further equipping him for his later career.

Service in Texas.

In 1859, he was called home to Arlington by the death of his father-in-law, G. W. Parke Custis. He adjusted his father-in-law's estate. In the will, it was provided that all the slaves should be freed at a certain date. Lee had long since let go the few slaves he had inherited; and he freed these others on the assigned date, which, strange to say, fell one week after Lincoln issued the Emancipation Proclamation.

Called home in 1859.

While Lee was at home on furlough, the John

Brown raid occurred; and the Secretary of War telegraphed Lee to take a detachment of marines, proceed to Harper's Ferry and arrest the raiders. Singular, that this service should have fallen to Lee's lot, owing to the accident of his being on furlough at Arlington. Lee took his marines; went to Harper's Ferry; stormed the engine house, in which John Brown and his associates were barricaded; arrested the raiders, and turned them over to the civil authorities. It was all done quietly and effectively, as Lee fulfilled every task assigned him.

The John Brown raid, and Lee's part in suppressing it.

Lee returned to Texas, for another period of Indian fighting; and then, in the spring of 1861, he was suddenly ordered to Washington. He arrived to find seven states already seceded; their representatives having met in Montgomery, Alabama, and in early February, weeks before Lincoln took office as President, formed the Southern Confederacy, with Jefferson Davis, ex-United States Secretary of War, as President, and Alexander H. Stephens as Vice President. Lee thus returned to Washington to find the Southern Confederacy an accomplished fact, already formed and functioning.

Lee ordered to Washington in the spring of 1861; arriving to find the Southern Confederacy already established.

The Civil War was simply the culmination of that cleavage of political philosophy, which began in the Constitution itself, and took shape immediately after in the divisions of opinion led by Jefferson and Hamilton. The makers of our Constitution, after the months of wrangling, established a dual system of government. We are unique among the nations

The Civil War as the culmination of the original conflict of opinion concerning our Constitution and Government.

in living under that dual system of government. Certain rights and powers were reserved, in the Constitution, to the State Governments. Others were specifically assigned to the new Federal Government; but, of course, the delegates could not cover the ground. New problems have arisen in every decade of our history. Immediately the question arose as to which government was entitled to exercise the powers unassigned in the Constitution. Here came the cleavage; and it is so important for our whole history, that it must be repeated.

Our dual system of government.

Jefferson held that the State governments were the original sovereign governments. Their representatives had met and formed the Federal Government to execute certain limited functions. Therefore, the Federal Government could not lawfully exercise any power, not specifically granted to it in the Constitution; and each State could rightly annul (nullify) any act of the Federal Government, not specifically warranted in the Constitution; with each State, since absolutely sovereign, its own final judge, as to when its rights had been violated; thus denying the authority of the Supreme Court finally to interpret the Constitution.

The political philosophy of Jefferson and his followers.

Hamilton held just the opposite. His view was, you remember, that the Federal Government, once formed, was the government of all the people in the nation. As such, it was superior to the government of any fraction or section of the population. Thus all powers not specifically reserved to the subordinate

The view of Hamilton and his party.

State governments, in the Constitution, belonged to the government of the whole nation, and might rightfully be assumed by the Federal Government, with the Supreme Court as the final judge and interpreter of the Constitution.

The original conflict of opinion.

There, in the simplest possible statement of it, is the original conflict of opinion, held with equal sincerity on both sides, which divided our country for more than a half-century, and was settled, or suppressed, only by the terrible arbitrament of fratricidal war.

Attitude of the founders of our government toward the question in dispute.

It seems almost as if the founders of our government meant to leave the question of this conflict open for later solution; for Article X of the Constitution (one of the first series of Amendments, declared in force December 15th, 1791) reads:

Article X of the Constitution.

> "The powers not delegated to the United States by the Constitution, nor prohibited by it to the States, are reserved to the States respectively, or to the people."

If the unassigned powers were reserved to the States, then Jefferson's view was right; if they were reserved to the people, Hamilton's interpretation was justified.

The Civil War a conflict of loyalties.

The Civil War was thus a conflict of loyalties; and we Americans may well be proud of the fact that all our great wars have been wars of ideas and not primarily of interests. The War for Independence, the Civil War and the World War were all dominantly wars of ideas.

The original conflict of opinion, regarding State

and Nation, was in no degree sectional: it ran through all the States, dividing the citizenship everywhere. The first vigorous opposition to the Federal government, moreover, and affirmation of the rights of the States over against it, came, not from the South: it came from New England; and the statement is made by one of Plymouth Rock ancestry on both sides.

The original cleavage as not sectional.

In the war of 1812, for instance, certain New England States were incensed at measures taken by the National government; and Daniel Webster, then Representative in Congress, made a speech, in December, 1814, on the Conscription bill in which he said:

New England as first challenging the Federal government and affirming State rights.

> "No law professedly passed for the purpose of compelling a service in the regular army, nor any law which, under color of military draft, shall compel men to serve in the army, not for the emergencies mentioned in the Constitution, but for long periods, and for the general objects of war, can be carried into effect. In my opinion it ought not to be carried into effect. The operation of measures thus unconstitutional and illegal ought to be prevented by a resort to other measures which are both constitutional and legal. It will be the solemn duty of the State governments to protect their own authority over their own militia, and to interpose between their citizens and arbitrary power. These are among the objects for which the State governments exist; and their highest obligations bind them to the preservation of their own rights, and the liberties of their people. I express these sentiments here, Sir, because I shall express them to my constituents."*

Daniel Webster's speech in the House of Representatives, Dec. 9th, 1814.

Had Webster's opinion prevailed, men could not have been drafted in the World War and sent across the ocean to fight in France.

The "arbitrary power" of the Federal government.

* Daniel Webster, from Speech on the Conscription Bill, House of Representatives, December 9, 1814: *Writings,* Supplem. Vol. II, p. 68.

We think of Daniel Webster as the great defender of the Union and its government: he became that in the later conflict; but this is what he said in 1814. He may have regretted it, afterwards, but he said it.

Significance of the Hartford Convention and its resolutions.

Massachusetts and Connecticut had acted, moreover, on the view Webster's speech expresses, refusing to turn over their militia to the Federal Government in the war of 1812. The Government, in consequence refused to pay the war expenses of those States. As a result, the same month of Webster's speech, representatives of Massachusetts, Connecticut, New Hampshire, Vermont and Rhode Island met at Hartford, Connecticut, and passed resolutions bitterly attacking actions of the Federal Government —resolutions regarded in many quarters as treasonable. The original cleavage of opinion was in no sense sectional.

The doctrine of State sovereignty in William Rawle's *View of the Constitution.*

An eminent northern lawyer, William Rawle, Chancellor of the Philadelphia Law Association, and author of a Manual of Cases, still quoted by lawyers when they wish particularly to impress a judge with authority, wrote a book on the Constitution, published in 1825. We are told it was used at West Point, during the following fifteen years, as an official text book for the education of the cadets, thus through the period in which Lee was a student there. In the course of that text-book, William Rawle says (quoted from the edition of 1829, with identical wording):

"The States, then, may wholly withdraw from the

Union; but while they continue they must retain the character of representative republics.

* * * * *

"The secession of a State from the Union depends on the will of the people of such State."*

No southern leader in the Civil War ever claimed more; yet that is the view of a most eminent northern legal mind, in the second quarter of the nineteenth century. The original division of opinion was in no degree sectional.

Andrew Jackson and the Union.

During Jackson's administration, South Carolina, you remember, wanted to nullify and possibly secede; and it was a President, not from Massachusetts, New York or Pennsylvania: it was Andrew Jackson of Tennessee, who said, *"The Union must and shall be preserved"*; and it was preserved, indeed, while Andrew Jackson was President.

The Haverhill petition.

Again, in 1842, John Quincy Adams, then Representative from Massachusetts, presented on the floor of Congress, a petition from the people of Haverhill, Massachusetts, asking a dissolution of the Union. The original cleavage of political conviction was not sectional.

Reasons why the conflict in opinion finally became sectional.

As time went on, it did tend, however, to become sectional, placing in opposition the North and the South. Certain causes of this have already been cited: the vast immigration, with the development of manufacturing industries in the North, obliterating

* William Rawle, *A View of the Constitution of the United States of America*, pp. 297, 302, Philadelphia, 1829.

State lines and producing attachment to the National Government; while the South, remaining agricultural, little changed by immigration, perpetuated the original tradition of devotion to the sovereign State.

Effect of the discrepancy in population, North and South.

The same causes, immigration and manufactures, produced a preponderant increase in population, in the North and West as compared with the South. When the Civil War broke, there were nearly four whites to one, in the States remaining in the Union compared to those seceding from it. This discrepancy was partly alleviated by allowing five slaves to count as three white votes, in determining national representation; but this did not overcome the difference.

The influence of a protective tariff policy on the South.

The North, with its developing industries, wanted protection for them; and with its larger population could vote it, while the South could not help herself. Thus she had to buy her manufactured articles from the North and from Europe at protection prices; and sell her agricultural staples, cotton, tobacco and corn, to the North and to Europe at free trade prices. That was unfair; but with hardly more than one vote to four, the South could not protect herself. This situation tended further to make the Southern people draw away and cherish the older State affiliation.

The supreme cause of a sectional cleavage.

The great cause, however, of the sectional cleavage was the dark blot of negro slavery. Originally prevailing throughout the land, it had died out in the North, chiefly because it was too uneconomic for the conditions of northern production. It had been stopped by law, in the Northwest, at the beginning of 1800, through the bill fathered, you recall, by Thomas Jefferson. It survived for a longer period in the South, because, though an utterly uneconomic institution, it was better adapted to the conditions of southern agricultural production, particularly in the Cotton States. The result was a wide difference in the manners and customs of the people, North and South, leading to a jealous cherishing of the State rights on the part of the South.

The survival of slavery as dividing the Nation.

The North, moreover, no longer afflicted with the incubus of slavery, took increasingly a moral view of it. You know it is easy to take high moral ground with reference to a problem a long way off: if you do not know it, you should; for it is a factor influencing our views, today as yesterday. The South compelled to live with slavery, knowing the problem at first hand, took naturally the political and economic view of it.

Growth of abolition sentiment in the North.

The people of the North, moreover, seeing the slaves from a long distance, often viewed them through rose-colored glasses. So intelligent a man as Wendell Phillips went about publicly proclaiming that in one generation after emancipation, the slaves would be intellectually and morally superior to their masters. In his lecture on *Toussaint L'Ouverture,* given in New York and Boston, in December, 1861, Wendell Phillips said:

Abolitionist views of the negro.

Wendell Phillips in 1861.

"In the hour you lend me tonight, I attempt the Quixotic effort to convince you that the negro blood, instead of standing at the bottom of the list, is entitled, if judged either by its great men or its masses, either by its courage, its purpose, or its endurance, to a place as near ours as any other blood known in history."*

To us who come after the event, North and South, such views seem strange; but they were widely held among the northern Abolitionists. The Southern people, living with the slaves, knew well what a long road the negro has still to travel, before even approximately catching up with the advanced races in civilization.

Contrasting view in the South.

Under this situation, think what the disproportion in population, already cited, meant to the South. Suppose the rapidly growing abolition sentiment should get the upper hand in Northern politics, what would happen? The South remembered the Nat Turner rebellion. That had been followed by the Charleston, South Carolina, conspiracy. In October, 1859, came the John Brown raid at Harper's Ferry: a frank attempt to lead the negro slaves to rise in rebellion against their masters, exultantly applauded by the Abolitionists. Wendell Phillips, their outstanding spokesman, said in a speech in Plymouth Church, Brooklyn, two weeks after the raid and three days after John Brown's conviction:

Significance for the South of the disproportion of voting population.

What the John Brown raid meant to the South.

"Virginia, the Commonwealth of Virginia! She is only a chronic insurrection. I mean exactly what I say. I am weighing my words now. She is a pirate ship, and John Brown sails the sea a Lord High Ad-

The Abolitionist view of the raid.

* Phillips, Wendell, in lecture on *Toussaint L'Ouverture: Speeches, Lectures and Letters,* Series I, p. 469.

miral of the Almighty, with his commission to sink every pirate he meets on God's ocean of the nineteenth century."*

Imagine what the public expression of such sentiments did to the South! Suppose the John Brown raid had achieved its purpose: of course, there was not a chance in a million: the slaves were too loyal to their masters; but suppose it had succeeded. What would have happened to the South: to the children of the South, to the women of the South, to the beautiful culture of the South, elaborated through a hundred and fifty years? That was the terror in the heart of every thoughtful Southerner; and the demand for the extension of slave territory, on the part of the people of the South, did not mean that they were permanently committed to the institution of slavery. Suppose all the new territories came in as free States: the vote was already nearly four to one: suppose it became six to one, eight to one? Then let the intense and growing abolition sentiment of the North get the upper hand in Northern politics; with the result suddenly of eliminating slavery, either by legislation or a Constitutional amendment? Think what disaster this would mean to the South. Thus, *the demand for the extension of slave territory, on the part of the people of the South, was a struggle for self-preservation, not to be completely out-weighed*

The Southern fear of a negro uprising.

Significance of the demand for the extension of slave territory by the people of the South.

* Phillips, Wendell, in speech on *The Lesson of the Hour,* delivered in Plymouth Church, Brooklyn, New York, Nov. 1st, 1859: *Speeches, Lectures and Letters,* Series I, p. 272.

and out-voted in the national councils. Every person, born and reared north of Mason and Dixon's line, should realize that, to understand the conflict of loyalties in the Civil War.

One compromise after another was attempted, the Missouri Compromise being the most lasting and important; but none worked, except for a time. Hate and bitterness grew rapidly on both sides, obscuring the vision and clouding the judgment of men. The South took the election of Lincoln as a direct challenge. Four days after his election, the South Carolina Senators resigned and went home; and six weeks after the election, months before Lincoln took office as President, South Carolina seceded from the Union. Her example was followed by the five "Cotton" States, and shortly afterwards by Texas. In early February the representatives of these States established the Confederacy, still weeks in advance, as has been shown, of Lincoln's inauguration. This was the situation Lee came home to face.

Immediate results of the election of Lincoln.

The situation Lee faced on arriving at Washington.

His feeling on returning is expressed in a letter to his son, Custis, written in December, 1860:

"Feeling the aggressions of the North, resenting their denial of the equal rights of our citizens to the common territory of the commonwealth, etc., I am not pleased with the course of the 'Cotton States', as they term themselves. In addition to their selfish, dictatorial bearing, the threats they throw out against the 'Border States', as they call them, if they will not join them, argues little for the benefit or peace of Virginia should she determine to coalesce with them. While I wish to do what is right, I am unwilling to do what is wrong, either at the bidding of the South or the North. One of their plans seems to be the renewal of the slave trade. That I am opposed to on every ground."*

Lee was as earnestly opposed to the institution of slavery as was Washington. The following passage gives his view: taken from a letter written home from Texas, intended, not for the public, but for his wife:

Lee's view of the institution of slavery.

"In this enlightened age there are few, I believe, but will acknowledge that slavery as an institution is a moral and political evil in any country. It is useless to expatiate on its disadvantages. I think it, however, a greater evil to the white than to the black race, and while my feelings are strongly interested in behalf of the latter, my sympathies are stronger for the former. The blacks are immeasurably better off here than in Africa, morally, socially and physically. * * * Their emancipation will sooner result from a mild and melting influence than the storms and contests of fiery controversy. * * *

"Is it not strange that the descendants of those Pilgrim Fathers who crossed the Atlantic to preserve the freedom of their opinion have always proved themselves intolerant of the spiritual liberty of others."†

A comment instructive to some of us, because it was not written for us!

During the Civil War, Lee proposed that the Confederacy should free all the slaves in its domain, and give a bond to each slave owner for the value of his slaves; such bond to be a first claim on the Con-

* Lee, in letter to his son, Custis, of Dec. 14th, 1860, from San Antonio, Texas: Jones, *Life and Letters of Lee,* p. 119.

† Lee, in letter to Mrs. Lee, Fort Brown, Texas, Dec. 27th, 1856: Jones, *Life and Letters of Lee,* pp. 82, 83.

federacy after independence had been achieved. That gives sufficiently Lee's views of slavery.

Lee's view of the Nation and devotion to the Union.

Lee was, moreover, devoted to the Union, regarding its possible disruption as the greatest of catastrophes. In another letter home from Texas, he wrote:

> "I can anticipate no greater calamity for the country than a dissolution of the Union. It would be an accumulation of all the evils we complain of, and I am willing to sacrifice everything but honor for its preservation. * * * Secession is nothing but revolution."

Revolution as the last right of liberty.

That is just what it was. Of course, revolution is the last right of liberty: when everything else fails, men may turn to revolution, if they dare and are willing to pay the price. The only difference History makes, between a revolution and a rebellion, is that one succeeded and the other failed. Every revolution in history that failed goes down as a rebellion; every rebellion that succeeded goes down as a revolution: History does not go behind the returns.

Lee continues:

Deep-seated conviction against coercion by the Nation toward the State.

> "The framers of our Constitution never exhausted so much labor, wisdom and forbearance in its formation, and surrounded it with so many guards and securities, if it was intended to be broken by every member of the Confederation at will. * * * Still, a Union that can only be maintained by swords and bayonets, and in which strife and civil war are to take the place of brotherly love and kindness, has no charm for me. I shall mourn for my country and for the welfare and progress of mankind. If the Union is dissolved, and the Government disrupted, I shall return to my native State and

share the miseries of my people, and save in defense will draw my sword on none."*

Lee had been, moreover, for more than thirty years in honorable service in the United States army: its commanders were his approving superiors, its officers, his affectionate friends and comrades.

Lee's thirty-two years of service in the United States army.

When Lee reached Washington, President Lincoln, through Blair, offered him the command-in-chief of the Union armies. Lee declined, of course: he could not imagine leading an army of invasion into his own State, against his own people. Had he been able to accept, the war could scarcely have lasted a year: with Lee's incomparable military genius transferred from the one side to the other, it would have been quickly over. He declined. He went into General Scott's office, told of the offer that had been made him, and explained the reasons for his declination. Then he went home to Arlington.

Lee offered and declining the command in chief of the Union armies.

What Lee's acceptance of President Lincoln's offer would have meant.

The next night Lee spent walking to and fro in an up-stairs room, while his wife waited anxiously in the room below. The sound of his footfalls ceased only when he knelt in prayer. Toward morning he came down, and said quietly to the anxiously waiting wife: "Well, Mary, the question is settled. Here is my resignation, and a letter I have written General Scott." The letter said:

The night of struggle with the problem.

Lee's letter to General Scott accompanying his resignation from the United States army.

"Since my interview with you on the 18th inst., I have felt that I ought no longer to retain my commission in

* Lee, Letter home from Fort Mason, Texas, January 23, 1861: Jones, *Life and Letters of Lee,* p. 121.

the army. I therefore tender my resignation, which I request you will recommend for acceptance. It would have been presented at once but for the struggle it has cost me to separate myself from a service to which I have devoted all the best years of my life and all the ability I possessed.

"During the whole of that time—more than a quarter of a century—I have experienced nothing but kindness from my superiors, and the most cordial friendship from my comrades. To no one, General, have I been as much indebted as to yourself for uniform kindness and consideration, and it has always been my ardent desire to meet your approbation. I shall carry to the grave the most grateful recollections of your kind consideration, and your name and fame will always be dear to me.

"Save in defense of my native State, I never desire again to draw my sword. Be pleased to accept my most earnest wishes for the continuance of your happiness and prosperity, and believe me,

"Most truly yours,

"R. E. Lee."*

The letter to his sister on the day of his resignation.

On the same day with this letter to General Scott, Lee wrote his sister, Mrs. Marshall, at Baltimore:

"My dear Sister: I am grieved at my inability to see you. I have been waiting for a more convenient season, which has brought to many before me deep and lasting regret. Now we are in a state of war which will yield to nothing. The whole South is in a state of revolution into which Virginia, after a long struggle, has been drawn; and, though I recognize no necessity for this state of things, and would have forborne and pleaded to the end for redress of grievances, real or supposed,

* Lee, letter to General Scott, Arlington, Va., April 20th, 1861: Jones, *Life and Letters of Lee*, pp. 132, 133.

yet in my own person I had to meet the question whether I should take part against my native State. With all my devotion to the Union, and the feeling of loyalty and duty of an American citizen, I have not been able to make up my mind to raise my hand against my relatives, my children, my home. I have therefore resigned my commission in the army, and save in defense of my native State, with the sincere hope that my poor services may never be needed, I hope I may never be called on to draw my sword.

"I know you will blame me, but you must think as kindly of me as you can, and believe that I have endeavored to do what I thought right."*

The explanation in a letter to his brother.

Also on the same date, Lee wrote to his brother:

"After the most anxious inquiry as to the correct course for me to pursue, I concluded to resign, and sent in my resignation this morning. I wished to wait until the Ordinance of Secession should be acted on by the people of Virginia; but war seems to have commenced, and I am liable at any time to be ordered on duty which I could not conscientiously perform. To save me from such a position, and to prevent the necessity of resigning under orders, I had to act at once, and before I could see you again on the subject, as I had wished. I am now a private citizen, and have no other ambition than to remain at home. Save in defense of my native State, I have no desire ever again to draw my sword."†

Significance of the one reiterated reservation.

April 13th, a week before Lee's resignation from the United States army, Sumter had fallen. April 15th, Lincoln called for seventy-five thousand volun-

* Lee, in letter to his sister, April 20th, 1861: Long, *Memoirs of Robert E. Lee*, p. 95.

† Lee, in a letter to his brother, Arlington, Va., April 20th, 1861: Captain Lee's *Recollections and Letters*, pp. 26, 27.

teers. April 17th, Virginia, whose Legislature had voted not to secede, and then, by a larger majority, had voted that the Union had no right to use force to coerce a State to remain in it, purely on the State versus Nation issue, seceded; followed by North Carolina, Tennessee and Arkansas. April 23rd, three days after his resignation, Lee was summoned to Richmond, and offered the command of the Virginia forces for defense: he accepted; and the great, the crucial decision was made.

Circumstances of the great decision.

Accepting command of the Virginia forces for defense.

The reasons for it? If you have followed the preceding argument, those reasons are evident: Lee's inheritance, his early environment, the great tradition of Virginia; his education, the interpretation of the Constitution he had studied under government sanction at West Point; his deep-seated conviction that the Union had no right to use force to compel a sovereign State to remain in it; his utter devotion to duty, as the guiding principle of his life, without regard to his interests or career; the impossibility of going against his own people: if they went, he must go with them, share their miseries and help to bear their burdens. The decision was the only one Robert E. Lee could make, being who he was; and it was the decision you or I would have made, with Lee's inheritance, environment, education and his utter devotion to duty as the guiding principle of life.

Reasons why the crucial decision was inevitable to Lee's conscience.

The decision once made, there was no return to questioning: Lee was the military leader to the end of the war. He had no illusions regarding the conflict however. North and South, with the arrogance of hate, men were boasting of easy victory. All over the North, they were saying the war would be a picnic: well, war is never that! Everywhere South, they were boasting that one Southerner could whip four Yankees any day; which is just about what they would have had to achieve to win the war. Not so Lee: he wrote his wife, "Make your preparations for several years of war." Moreover, he did not wish his decision to influence others, even his own son. He wrote to his wife regarding his son, Custis, who had been a cadet at West Point, while his father was Superintendent, and who was now an officer in the United States army:

Lee's high magnanimity.

> "Tell Custis he must consult his own judgment, reason, and conscience as to the course he may take. I do not wish him to be guided by my wishes or example. If I have done wrong, let him do better. The present is a momentous question which every man must settle for himself and upon principle."*

Letter of Lee regarding his son's decision.

Could loving father say more? Of course, Custis went with his father, as did Lee's other sons. Let it be said, further, for Robert E. Lee, that no word of hate or abuse of the North, or of the people of the North, ever came from his lips, to the end of his life. Nature's nobleman, indeed, he was!

Nature's nobleman.

When the war began, there were twenty-two million people living in the States remaining in the

---

* Lee, in letter to his wife, May 13, 1861: Jones, *Life and Letters of Lee*, p. 140.

Union. There were five and a half million whites and three and a half million blacks in the seceding States: nearly four white citizens to one, in the North as compared with the South. The Union had a government, long established and efficiently functioning, with an army and plans for immediate war mobilization. The South had the newly formed Confederate Government, with everything to be done from the ground up. The Union had a navy: the Confederacy had none. The North was rich in manufactures; the South had practically none. During the war, the Union enlisted two and one-half million men. The Confederacy, calling every stripling and graybeard, who could move about and carry a gun, enlisted nine hundred thousand. The mountain population of the South, moreover, gave the Union armies a hundred and eighty thousand men. When the war closed, there were nine hundred and eighty thousand Union soldiers in the field, and about a hundred and seventy-five thousand Confederates.

Contrasting situation and equipment of the Union and the Confederacy in the great conflict.

It looked hopeless for the South from the start, did it not? There were two chances. First, foreign intervention: that was the hope of President Davis and of many others, to the end of the war; and not without reason. It had happened in the Revolution, when France entered at the critical moment and turned the scale; why might it not happen again? Britain looked across the ocean at the great lion cub, sprung from her loins, that had grown so swiftly powerful. Many of her statesmen would have been glad to see us

The two chances the South had in the struggle.

The first hope: foreign intervention.

divided, and no longer so strong. Other nations felt much the same. If the South could carry on the war successfully for a considerable period of time, it was not unreasonable to hope that some power might intervene in her favor. Lee did not cheat himself with that illusion. Moreover he saw, as did Washington in the Revolution, that if victory were to be worth while, the South must win it for herself.

There was another chance for the South, however. Barring the mountain population, the people of the South were solidly behind the war, as is usually true of an invaded land: the people of the North were not. All over the North was a large body of citizens, believing with sincere conviction in the very political philosophy on which the Southern States had seceded from the Union. Deploring the rift in the Union, these men held that the seceding States had the constitutional right to go, if they chose to do so. Those citizens, therefore, regarded the war as unjust, and were actively opposed to it.

Northern citizens opposed on conviction to the war.

Besides these, was another large group negatively opposed to the war; indeed, the Abolitionists were generally in that camp during the first year and a half of the war. They saw only their own issue. They were willing to fight through a war to free the slaves; but President Lincoln told them that was not this war, that it was a war to preserve the Union; and many were unwilling to fight for that. Their spokesman, Wendell Phillips, in those desperately dark days of January, 1861, gave a speech in Music Hall,

The group negatively opposed to the war.

The Abolitionists as pacifists.

Boston, on *Disunion,* in which he exulted in the breaking of the Union, saying:

> "Why do I set so little value on the Union? Because I consider it a failure."*

On February 17th, speaking in the same hall on *Progress,* he said:

> "We do not want the Border States. Let them go, be welcome to the Forts, take the Capital with them."†

The view of these extremists was: We do not want slaves in the Union; the South wants slaves: let her take her slaves and go, and stew in her own juice.

The second hope for the South.

With this large party in the North, actively or negatively opposed to the war, if the South could make a successful showing on the battle field, and carry the war well into the North, was there not reason to hope that the opposition in the North might get the upper hand, and the South win peace with independence? That was the hope Lee cherished till near the end of the war.

Lee's amazing military achievement.

That, in the face of the seemingly insuperable odds, Lee carried through three years of brilliant warfare, winning a series of victories unequalled except in the career of Napoleon, makes him one of the great military captains of all history; and it was possible, further, because of the utter devotion of the South behind him.

---

* Phillips, Wendell, in speech on *Disunion,* Music Hall, Boston, Jan. 20th, 1861: *Speeches, Lectures and Letters,* Series I, p. 356.

† Phillips, Wendell, in speech on *Progress,* Feb. 17th, 1861: *Speeches, Lectures and Letters,* Series I, p. 387.

When Virginia, a short time after seceding, entered the Confederacy, Lee was automatically reduced in rank, as he was in command merely of the Virginia forces for defense. He went to Richmond, and spent the first months of the war raising and equipping an army. Thus he was not at Bull Run; but it was his work and plans which made the Confederate victory at Bull Run possible.

Service during the first year of the war.

Then he was sent into West Virginia. Owing to a series of accidents, the West Virginia campaign was a failure; but the President of the Confederacy did not lose faith in Lee. He was sent south to improve the coast defenses; and he made Georgia and the Carolinas impregnable by sea till the end of the war. In March, 1862, he was recalled to Richmond, and made Chief of Staff under President Davis. To understand that one must remember that the President of the Confederacy regarded himself as the active head of its military forces. Lincoln did not take that attitude in the Union. Of course, as President, he was absolute authority over the armed forces of the Nation; but always he wanted an active commander-in-chief, in the field under him. President Davis, however, who was a graduate of West Point, had risen to the rank of Colonel in the army, and had experienced active service in the Black Hawk war and the war with Mexico, besides serving as United States Secretary of War, regarded himself as actively in command of the Confederate armed forces. Lee, therefore, did not have, as chief of staff, the authority

Lee, Chief of Staff from March, 1862.

President Davis as active military head of the Confederate forces.

to order the concentration of armies, as Grant for instance, could do. It was not until February, 1865, two months before the war closed, when the Confederacy, at its last gasp, was grasping at any straw, that Lee was finally made Commander-in-Chief: singular that it came so late! Had that appointment been made earlier, certain events of the war would have been different, though the final outcome could hardly have been changed.

Consequences of Lee's limited authority.

Nothing, moreover, better shows Lee's magnanimity and generosity than his whole relation to the President of the Confederacy. President Davis was whole-souled in devotion to his cause. He gave it the best wisdom and service he had in him; but he was strong in his opinions and something of a martinet in discipline. He quarreled with certain of his generals; and some of them were dismissed in consequence. Lee was in closer relation to him than any other Southern general; and there was never a word of misunderstanding to the end of the war. This was to Lee's credit. His attitude was, I am not a politician, but a military man, concerned solely with carrying out orders in the field. When his opinion was asked, he gave it frankly and fully; but never intruded. Thus he maintained entirely friendly relations with President Davis to the end.

Significance of Lee's relations with President Davis.

In the Spring of 1862, McClellan, urged on by Lincoln, who had yielded to the popular cry, "On to Richmond," invaded Virginia with a splendidly equipped and now well trained army of 115,000 men.

McClellan's campaign: "On to Richmond!"

For the protection of Richmond, now the Capital, Lee had some 53,000; and there were perhaps 17,000 more elsewhere in the State. Against the advice of his generals, Lee decided on a frontal attack. He summoned Jackson to him; and with his united army of 70,000 men, at Malvern Hill, rolled McClellan's army back upon itself; completely outgeneralled McClellan; won victory after victory; and at the end of the seven days' fighting, McClellan barely succeeded in getting what was left of his shattered army across the Potomac to temporary safety.

Malvern Hill and the seven days' victories of Lee.

The point is, Lee was able to think all around McClellan: indeed he could *go* all around him; for Stuart, the "Light Horse Harry" of Lee's army, with 1,200 cavalrymen, rode completely around the Union armies, getting every position, and returning unscathed; which seriously shook the confidence of Lincoln and the North in McClellan's leadership.

You see Lee had served with McClellan in the war with Mexico, and he knew McClellan's psychology. McClellan was an admirable drill-master. Few men have been so able to whip an army into shape and prepare it for battle as was McClellan; but he lacked the audacity and the imagination necessary to brilliant work in the field; and then he was obsessed with the idea that there were about three times as many Southern troops as really were in Lee's army opposed to him. Lee, knowing his mental processes, was able to anticipate his every move and so completely to outgeneral him.

Reasons for Lee's outgeneraling of McClellan.

The result was, Lincoln issued an order creating a second army, for the protection of Washington, placing Pope in command; and a little later, called Halleck to the chief command at Washington.

Lee, with Napoleonic audacity, divided his little army of 50,000 men; placed half, under Jackson, behind Pope, the other half in front; came through Thoroughfare Gap; and Pope's incompetence in meeting Lee's strategy resulted in the second Bull Run, of August, 1862. From now on Lee was the hero of the Confederacy, with the burden of its fortunes upon his shoulders.

Pope and the second Bull Run.

At this point, Lee decided to carry the war into the North. He had to do it, to strengthen the morale of the South, in the hope of bringing about foreign intervention, in the expectation of Maryland rising and joining the South, in the further hope that the party opposed to the war in the North might get the upper hand and grant the South peace with independence, and finally, he had to do it to subsist his army. It is one of the amazing features of Lee's career that he carried through those three years of war largely with arms and supplies captured from the enemy armies: it seems incredible; but he did it.

The situation compelling Lee's compaign into Maryland.

In early September, 1862, Lee crossed into Maryland, and issued his proclamation to the people of the State. That document is so characteristic in its dignified restraint, widely differing from the usual military proclamation, and expresses so clearly the view

Lee had come to take of the great conflict, that it is quoted entire:

"Headquarters, Army of Northern Virginia,
"Sept. 8th, 1862.

"To the People of Maryland:

"It is right that you should know the purpose that has brought the army under my command within the limits of your State, so far as that purpose concerns yourselves.

Lee's Proclamation to the people of Maryland, giving his view of the conflict.

"The people of the confederate States have long watched with the deepest sympathy the wrongs and outrages that have been inflicted upon the citizens of a commonwealth, allied to the States of the South by the strongest social, political and commercial ties, and reduced to the condition of a conquered province.

"Under the pretence of supporting the Constitution, but in violation of its most valuable provisions, your citizens have been arrested and imprisoned upon no charge, and contrary to all the forms of law.

"A faithful and manly protest against this outrage, made by a venerable and illustrious Marylander, to whom in better days no citizen appealed for right in vain, was treated with scorn and contempt.

Significance that Lee's appeal was wholly in the name of freedom and justice.

"The government of your chief city has been usurped by armed strangers—your Legislature has been dissolved by the unlawful arrest of its members—freedom of the press and of speech has been suppressed—words have been declared offences by an arbitrary decree of the Federal Executive—and citizens ordered to be tried by military commissions for what they may dare to speak.

"Believing that the people of Maryland possess a spirit too lofty to submit to such a government, the people of the South have long wished to aid you in throwing off this foreign yoke, to enable you again to enjoy the inalienable rights of freemen, and restore the independence and sovereignty of your State.

"In obedience to this wish our army has come among you, and is prepared to assist you with the power of its arms in regaining the rights of which you have been so unjustly despoiled.

"This, citizens of Maryland, is our mission, so far as you are concerned. No restraint upon your free will is intended—no intimidation will be allowed within the limits of this army at least.

"Marylanders shall once more enjoy their ancient freedom of thought and speech. We know no enemies among you, and will protect all of you in every opinion.

"It is for you to decide your destiny, freely, and without constraint. This army will respect your choice, whatever it may be; and while the Southern people will rejoice to welcome you to your natural position among them, they will only welcome you when you come of your own free will."

"R. E. Lee,
"General Commanding."*

Maryland did not rise in answer to this appeal. McClellan withdrew to Frederick, and Lee followed. By some mischance, Lee's whole plan of battle was found, wrapped around some tobacco and carried to McClellan. Fortunately for Lee, he apparently discovered in time that McClellan knew his plans; changed swiftly and completely his order of battle; and brought the engagement at Antietam: one of the

Antietam.

* Lee, *Proclamation to the People of Maryland,* Sept. 8th, 1862: *The Rebellion Record,* edited by Frank Moore, New York, 1865, Supplement, Vol. I, Documents, p. 755.

bloodiest battles of the war, excepting Gettysburg. One fourth of the men engaged on each side fell. Again Lee's superior generalship made up for lesser numbers; and after Antietam, Lee withdrew his shattered army across the Potomac unmolested.

Stuart's second ride around McClellan's army.

Once more Stuart, with 1,800 cavalrymen, rode completely around McClellan's army, going as far north as Chambersburg, Pennsylvania; riding 126 miles in two days and eight hours, and returning without the loss of a man. The result was, President Lincoln dismissed McClellan, and called Burnside to the chief command.

Burnside's campaign.

Burnside moved on Richmond with 113,000 men. Lee had some 78,000. The culminating engagement came at Fredericksburg, Dec. 11th, 1862, where Burnside's folly resulted in the slaughter of 12,500 Union soldiers; and Burnside withdrew. There was deep depression throughout the North. The South believed the war was over; but Lee knew better.

Hooker's campaign in the Spring of 1863.

In the Spring of 1863, Lincoln called Hooker, "Fighting Joe Hooker", to the chief command. Hooker had all the qualities McClellan lacked; and lacked all the qualities McClellan had. He was audacious, brilliant; but he was without McClellan's caution and drill-mastery. He moved south in April, with an admirably equipped army, more than twice the size of Lee's opposing army; and as he did so, he made a rather profane boast. He said he had the Confederate army exactly where he wanted it, and God Almighty couldn't snatch a victory from him now. He was to be sadly punished for his boast. Lee waited with his little army, and brought the culminating engagement at Chancellorsville, May 1st and 2nd, 1863; where Lee's generalship, with Stonewall Jackson's fulfillment, won a brilliant victory. These two men worked together with a perfect harmony one finds in no other two military captains in history. Lee was the greater strategist, with more brilliant military imagination; but Jackson could carry out his great captain's plans, not only with entire fidelity, but with clock-like accuracy. Thus, the two working together, in a flank attack, rolled Hooker's army upon itself, drove a portion of it to wild panic rout; and after the two days' battle, Hooker, bewildered, was glad to get his defeated forces back across the Rappahannock to safety.

Chancellorsville.

Lee and Stonewall Jackson.

At Chancellorsville, however, Lee lost what he called his "right arm"; for Stonewall Jackson, in the confusion fired upon by his own men, was mortally wounded, and died a little time after. It was indeed the loss of Lee's right arm, worse for his cause than the loss of many battles.

The loss of Lee's "right arm."

Again the North was in sackcloth and ashes, and the South exultant; but Lee saw the situation truly. The North could replace her losses; the South could not. She was already using what Lee called her "seed corn": those splendid young striplings, who ought to have been the fathers of tomorrow, and who were going down to their death with a smile on their lips, in utter devotion to their beloved leader and their

Lee's wise view of the situation after the brilliant victory at Chancellorsville.

cause. Thus, unless Lee could destroy the army of the Potomac, his victories were sterile. No matter how many brilliant victories he might win, if the Union did not yield to discouragement and continued to replace its losses, the end could be only one way. Recognizing this, Lee appealed to the President of the Confederacy to concentrate all forces at two points: such troops as were needed at Vicksburg, on the Mississippi, and all the rest in Virginia, letting everything else go for the time being. Had he been Commander-in-Chief he could have ordered that; but as Chief of Staff under the President, he could only appeal. The President and Cabinet only partly responded. Lee took such reinforcements as they gave him, and planned his second campaign into the North.

His plan and appeal to President Davis.

At this time Lee's wife was ill, his daughter dying. One of his sons was wounded and in a Union prison. That son's wife was dying. Another son offered to take his brother's place; and the Union authorities refused! Lee buried these personal sorrows heroically in his heart, and went forward with his campaign.

Personal sorrows.

His aim was to maneuver Hooker out of his position on the Rappahannock, take a wide sweep around into Pennsylvania, and bring a culminating engagement at York, Gettysburg or Chambersburg, with the hope of destroying the army of the Potomac, subsisting his own army, causing the evacuation of Washington and the recall of the troops before Vicksburg, and so bringing the Union to yield the Confederacy peace with independence.

Plan and purpose of Lee's second campaign into the North.

He easily maneuvered Hooker out of his position; and then a quarrel between Hooker and Halleck resulted in Meade's being given the command in the field. Lee executed his wide sweep into Pennsylvania; a part of his army going nearly to Harrisburg: in fact, would have taken Harrisburg, had it not mistaken the road. The culminating engagement came, as everyone knows, at Gettysburg, July 1st to 3rd, 1863: one of the most terrible and bloody battles, not only of the Civil War, but of all history. Moreover, we Americans, North and South, have every reason to be proud of the splendid courage shown on both sides. Those Union soldiers went into that holocaust of destruction with unfaltering courage. Those Southern troops, gravely outnumbered, but with Lee's generalship compensating for this, went down to their death with dauntless heroism. The battle raged through those three terrible days, until both sides were exhausted and neither could attack again. That should be called a drawn battle, should it not? It was a Union victory only in the sense that Lee had failed of the object of his campaign: he had not destroyed the army of the Potomac; and was forced to withdraw the shattered remnants of his own army again to Virginia soil. Meade was too exhausted to follow, at least failed to pursue, in spite of Lincoln's urging; and Lee had three months' breathing space to reorganize his army.

The significance of the battle of Gettysburg.

Concerning Gettysburg, as other great battles, military history is filled with fruitless discussions as to what would have happened if supporting generals had more accurately obeyed orders and carried out the plans of their chief. It is characteristic of Lee's spirit that he never placed on a subordinate, blame for a failure, but always assumed it himself. Some days after Gettysburg, a Charleston, South Carolina, newspaper published an article, blaming one of Lee's officers for the failure and indirectly attacking the Confederate administration. President Davis sent the article to Lee, who replied with one of his noblest letters. In the course of it he said:

Lee's attitude in defeat.

> "No blame can be attached to the army for its failure to accomplish what was projected by me, nor should it be censured for the unreasonable expectations of the public—I am alone to blame, in perhaps expecting too much of its prowess and valor. It however in my opinion achieved under the guidance of the Most High a general success, though it did not win a victory. I thought at the time that the latter was practicable. I still think if all things could have worked together it would have been accomplished. But with the knowledge I then had, and in the circumstances I was then placed, I do not know what better course I could have pursued."*

Lee's letter to President Davis assuming full responsibility for Gettysburg.

A few days later he wrote, saying that when a military leader failed, usually the best course was to remove him, and offered to resign; but President Davis wisely would not hear of it.

There followed some months of desultory fighting;

---

* Lee, in letter to Pres. Davis, Camp Culpepper, July 31st, 1863: Freeman, *Lee's Dispatches*, p. 108.

and in the Spring of 1864, the tide definitely turned, with the emergence of Grant. The day following Gettysburg, July 4th, 1863, Vicksburg surrendered to Grant. This was followed by his successes at Lookout Mountain and Missionary Ridge. Lincoln had been eagerly watching, praying for a general who could stand up a month against Robert E. Lee. So in March, 1864, Lincoln called Grant to Washington, and made him Commander-in-Chief; and Grant began the campaign that ended the war.

The tide turning with Grant's appointment as Commander in Chief, in March, 1864.

The comparison of the two great military leaders is interesting. Grant was at that time forty-two years old; Lee, fifty-seven. Lee was the highly cultivated Southern aristocrat and Virginia gentleman; Grant, rather rough in exterior, somewhat Western in type. Both were men of great military genius: Lee, far the greater strategist, with far more brilliant imagination; Grant, with dogged determination and indomitable will. Grant had a splendidly equipped and provisioned army of 120,000 men; Lee, perhaps 65,000, ragged, shoeless, half-starved, but dauntless. Behind Grant were the inexhaustible resources of the North, in men, money and manufactures; behind Lee, an exhausted Southland. So the final campaign began.

Grant and Lee compared.

Grant formulated a comprehensive plan. There were to be no more maneuvers, only a steady drive. Early in May, 1864, Grant moved south. There followed those terrible days of battle in the Wilderness. Lee knew every country road and by-path. He

Grant's plan.

completely outgeneralled Grant. The Union losses were enormous. There was a wail all over the North; but now a strange thing happened. Hitherto, a Union general, defeated by Lee, moved back, in retreat; Grant, defeated, moved *forward*: that is what ended the war. You remember his famous word of May 11th, 1864: *"I propose to fight it out on this line, if it takes all summer."* Well, it took all summer, all autumn, all winter and the next spring; but he fought it out on that line, and won the war.

The terrible days in the Wilderness.

Grant's word of May 11th, 1864, as defining the will and action that, with the overwhelming Union resources, won the war.

Grant blundered repeatedly. At Cold Harbor, he unnecessarily sacrificed thousands of men. He mistakenly attempted to storm Petersburg, and wasted another 10,000. Grant's losses during the whole campaign were greater than Lee's entire army opposed to him. There was growing bitterness and resentment throughout the North; Greeley was shrieking in the New York Tribune to end the hopeless war and horrible butchery; but Grant, with Lincoln steadfast behind him, pushed on. Lee sent Early, in a last attempt to take Washington; but Lew Wallace saved Washington, till Grant could send reinforcements.

Grant's frightful losses.

Steady hammering gradually wore away the granite rock of Lee's resistance. By the Spring of 1865, Lee's army had dwindled to 30,000 men; and there were no more to be called to fill the broken ranks. Grant was closing in with 100,000 troops. Lee made a last desperate stand at Five Forks, and failed. April 1st, Petersburg fell. April 2nd, Richmond was abandoned. April 3rd, it was occupied by Union troops.

Constant hammering depleting Lee's forces to 30,000, by the Spring of 1865, with no more men to be called.

Lee attempted to retreat on Danville, and was blocked. He changed his route toward Lynchburg, and was stopped; and he made his humane decision.

Last days of the war.

Now see: Lee's army was unbroken in spirit, still dauntless in courage. Lee could have divided his little army, and carried on guerrilla warfare for months, perhaps years of time; and gone down to history, unbeaten and unsurrendered as a military captain; but he said, *No!* the final issue is the same anyway, and I will not sacrifice a single unnecessary man. So he made his overtures in response to Grant's appeal. Grant gave generous terms: the Southern soldiers were to keep their side arms and their horses, and go home; only giving their word that they would not take arms against the Union, during the remainder of the war, or until exchanged.

Lee's humane decision.

So, on April 9th, 1865, at Appomattox Court House, Virginia, Lee surrendered his ragged, dauntless army; and walked away, head up, silent, erect, military bearing unchanged. Only God and General Lee knew what thoughts were in his heart at that hour.

Circumstances of Lee's surrender.

Those half-starved Confederate soldiers instantly fraternized with the Union troops, and ate the first good meal they had had for months, on the ample Union rations. Soldiers do not hate; big men do not hate: it is little men, who stay at home and elaborate their hooded viper poison, who hate.

Five days after the surrender, occurred the assassination of Lincoln. Lee bitterly deplored and condemned the act. He knew what it meant for the South: the removal of that great, kindly, merciful figure, whose chief aim, during the last two years of the war, had been to forestall the hate of little men and the revenge he knew they would seek upon the South, once the Union had achieved victory.

Lee's bitter regret over the assassination of Lincoln.

Lee went to Richmond, where he was greeted as a conquering hero, as indeed he was. Then, if you please, a couple of months later, a grand jury at Norfolk, Virginia, composed of negroes and white trash, indicted Lee for treason! When Grant heard the news, he was indignant. He said it was directly against the terms of surrender he had given Lee; and through Grant's influence, the indictment was quashed. To the astonishment of many in the South, in June, Lee applied for pardon, under the Amnesty proclamation. His Southern friends could not understand that; but Lee's attitude was: if I surrender, I surrender completely; if we are going into the Union, we will go whole heartedly, and seek to heal the scars and close the wounds. So he applied for pardon, sending his application papers through Grant. Grant laid them before our government; and *no notice was taken of them;* and, to the shame of the North, be it said, Lee died five years later, a prisoner on parole!

The indictment at Norfolk and Grant's just conduct.

Lee's attitude in the application for pardon.

Numerous offers of employment were made to him. One corporation is said to have offered him a large sum per year, just for the use of his name. Lee's response is said to have been: "Well, if my name is so valuable, I would better be careful how it is used";

Offers of employment.

and he refused. Would there were more like him in the land! He declined the Rectorship of the University of Virginia; he declined the Presidency of the University of the South, at Sewanee, Tennessee; he refused to stand for the Governorship of Virginia: he would have been elected unanimously. Finally, the trustees of little Washington College, at Lexington, Virginia, now appropriately, Washington and Lee University, asked him if he would not please be their President.

Lee's purpose in accepting the Presidency of Washington College.

It was a small, struggling college, paying its President perhaps fifteen hundred dollars a year. It looked humble enough even for Lee's beautiful modesty; but Lee was not sure. In his letter to the trustees, he said:

> "I think it is the duty of every citizen in the present condition of the country, to do all in his power to aid in the restoration of peace and harmony, and in no way to oppose the policy of the State or General Governments, directed to that object."*

Lee's magnanimous efforts to cultivate harmony.

If he could further that aim, he would serve; so Lee accepted, and spent the last five years of his life educating citizens for our America. His whole consecrated effort was to overcome the hate and bitterness, the war had left, and cultivate union and harmony. His generous attitude is well expressed in a letter, written in August, 1865:

---

* Lee, letter to the Trustees of Washington College, when offered the Presidency: Jones, *Life and Letters of Lee*, pp. 408, 409.

"The questions which for years were in dispute between the State and General Government, and which unhappily were not decided by the dictates of reason, but referred to the decision of war, having been decided against us, it is the part of wisdom to acquiesce in the result, and of candor to recognize the fact.

Statement of Lee's view of reconstruction in the letter to John Letcher.

"The interests of the State are therefore the same as those of the United States. Its prosperity will rise or fall with the welfare of the country. The duty of its citizens, then, appears to me too plain to admit of doubt. All should unite in honest efforts to obliterate the effects of war, and to restore the blessings of peace. They should remain, if possible, in the country; promote harmony and good feeling; qualify themselves to vote; and elect to the State and general Legislatures wise and patriotic men, who will devote their abilities to the interests of the country, and the healing of all dissensions. I have invariably recommended this course since the cessation of hostilities, and have endeavored to practise it myself."*

In 1866, to a Union officer, living in Lincoln's state, who had been a friend in earlier years, Lee wrote:

"I must give you my special thanks for doing me the justice to believe that my conduct during the last five eventful years has been governed by my sense of duty. I had no other guide, nor had I any other object than the defense of those principles of American liberty upon which the constitutions of the several States were originally founded; and, unless they are strictly observed, I fear there will be an end to Republican government in this country. I have endeavored to pursue this

The letter to Captain May, of Illinois, giving Lee's fundamental conviction.

* Lee, in letter to Hon. John Letcher, Near Cartersville, Va., August 28th, 1865; *Jones, Personal Reminiscences,* p. 203.

course myself since the cessation of hostilities, and have recommended it to others."*

The last chapter.

In the Spring of 1870, Lee was ill and broken. He went away, on vacation, in search of health. He went to visit the grave of his daughter, who had died during the war, while her father was at the front. He stopped at Virginia Hot Springs; did not get better; came home, and grew rapidly worse. During the last hours, his mind wandered, evidently going over his old battles; for almost his last words were, "Tell Hill he must come up!" So October 12th, 1870, Lee died, sixty-three years old.

Summary of Lee in character and conduct.

Nature's nobleman, he was, of high and spotless personal life; with absolute integrity of character, unvarying in obedience to duty as the guiding principle of life; the greatest military genius the Anglo-Saxon race has produced, not excepting George Washington and the Duke of Wellington; so fine and lofty in character and conduct, as to furnish an example for imitation by the youth of America, North, South, East and West; loved by his own people with an enthusiastic devotion given to no other American, not excepting Washington; incarnating all that is noblest and best in that beautiful, passionate and loyal Southland, which is today so precious a part in our united America.

---

* Lee, in letter to Captain James May, of Rock Island, Ills., Lexington, Va., July 9th, 1866: Jones, *Personal Reminiscences*, p. 218.

VI

LINCOLN: THE PROPHETIC AMERICAN

FOR our closing study, we come to that great man, to whom the nation turned in its hour of sorest trial, on whom it laid its heaviest burden, through whom the Union was reborn and present day America made possible, and who, in character and leadership, represents all that we hope democracy will some day be.

There could scarcely be a greater contrast, in background and early experience of life, than between Lee and Lincoln: The one, a fine flower of that beautiful Southern aristocracy, with a rich cultural environment, and excellent preparation for the business of life; the other, of the poorest of poor wandering nomads, at the very bottom of the pioneer ladder, with no material equipment for life at all: the one, incarnating all that was best and most beautiful in the past; the other, prophetic, of the future that is to be.

Contrast in family background and early environment of Lee and Lincoln.

Lincoln was born at Hodgenville, Kentucky, February 12th, 1809. He was thus two years younger than Lee. Lincoln, throughout his life, regarded his family as of common stock on both sides. The admirers among his biographers have done their best to rehabilitate his family tree; and they have discovered, and established beyond question, that Lincoln's father, Thomas Lincoln, was of the sixth generation, in direct line of descent, from certain sturdy English yeoman Lincolns, who came over and settled at Salem, Massachusetts in 1637, and at Hingham in 1640.

The Lincoln family history.

The Lincolns, however, were from the beginning wandering stock. It is true, they loved land; and wherever they went, bought it or took it up; but they wandered across Massachusetts, through New York into New Jersey; over into Pennsylvania; down into southern Pennsylvania; thence into Virginia; and the immediate grandfather of Lincoln, also named Abraham, took his wife and children, and moved still further west into Kentucky, then, of course, Virginia territory.

The grandfather, Abraham Lincoln.

The grandfather was working in the field one day, when an Indian killed him; seized the little six year old Thomas, and was about to kill him, when an elder brother, from the house, shot the Indian. This Thomas was to be Lincoln's father. The incident is mentioned merely to indicate how all the hardship and adventure of frontier life were behind Lincoln.

The biographers have similarly tried to rehabilitate the family of Nancy Hanks, Lincoln's mother; but with less success. Certainly, at the time she married Thomas Lincoln, Nancy Hanks and her relatives were of those "poor whites", pushed ever out or moving out, to the newer frontier, to escape the degrading competition with slave labor. Nancy Hanks herself, however, was a rare flower of the forest; sensitive,

Lincoln's mother, Nancy Hanks, and her family.

highly emotional, there are stories of her intense response to those wild religious revivals, that furnished one of the few emotional outlets for the frontier. She had obtained a little education. Why she married the rather shiftless Thomas Lincoln, is a question: possibly, as one story tells, as a result of the excitement of one of those same religious revivals. In any case, she did marry him, when she was twenty-two and he was twenty-eight years old.* Three children were born of the union: a daughter, two years older, who grew up to womanhood, married, and died without leaving children, Lincoln, and a boy who did not survive infancy.

Thomas Lincoln, carpenter and farmer.

The father had largely abandoned his carpenter's trade, and taken a poor farm at Hodgenville. When Lincoln was a child of three, Thomas Lincoln gave up this farm and moved a dozen miles to another somewhat better farm. When Lincoln was a child of seven, Thomas Lincoln decided to abandon Kentucky altogether. He sold his farm for twenty dollars and four hundred gallons of whiskey; loaded the stuff; crossed to the Ohio, and over the river; and filed a claim for a forest farm in Spencer County, southern Indiana, returning to bring over his family and belongings. On his new claim, he built a "half-

The settlement in Spencer County, Indiana.

* William E. Barton has established the fact, which Lincoln himself believed, that Nancy Hanks was the daughter of Lucy Hanks, born seven years before the latter's marriage to Henry Sparrow. The tradition that Nancy Hanks's father was a well-to-do Virginia planter has never been authenticated.

See Barton, *Life of Abraham Lincoln*, Vol. I, Chapter IV.

faced camp," that is, a shack with three sides and an open front, in which the family lived for a year. The next year, Thomas Lincoln rose to the dignity of a one-room, four-walled cabin, with a loft over it.

Death of Lincoln's mother.

The hardships of pioneer life were, however, too much for the sensitive mother; and the year that Lincoln approached the age of ten, Nancy Hanks Lincoln died, of one of those epidemics that scourge the frontier, called in this instance milk sickness, and was buried in a lonely grave in the forest. For the following months the family was in the care of the girl of twelve. The next year, Thomas Lincoln went back to Kentucky, and wooed successfully a widow with three children, whom he had unsuccessfully courted before her first marriage; and brought her back, as his second wife. She seems to have been of rather forceful character; she had something more in the way of household utensils, and she set about, as she expressed it, trying to make Thomas Lincoln's children a little more human.

Circumstances of Thomas Lincoln's second marriage.

Lincoln's relation to his step-mother.

Lincoln's relation to his second mother was very warm and tender. She seems to have had for him, not only deepening affection, but steadily growing respect, because of his utter integrity of character: that was what distinguished him from the beginning.

The boy Lincoln's tenderness for animals.

The chief fact that stands out from Lincoln's earliest years is his tenderness for animals. He was repeatedly whipped for releasing trapped animals. He would never carry a gun. One traditional story is especially significant: Lincoln had frightened away a fawn just as the hunter was about to fire at it; and a boy comrade remembered, later in life, his puzzled bewilderment when the lad, Lincoln, remarked, "God might think as much of that fawn as of some people."

Lincoln's schooling was extremely meager, more so than in the case of any of the statesmen previously studied. He had learned his letters from his own mother; and he had a few sporadic months of irregular schooling from wandering masters, who came by, set up a frontier school for a month or two, then closed it and moved on.

Lincoln's extremely meager schooling.

Lincoln was, however, a natural student, from the beginning, with a passion for reading and knowing. He never read rapidly or very widely, but he read thoughtfully, and he had a most tenacious mind, so that whatever he did read was his for life. We know that during his earliest years he had: the *Bible, Pilgrim's Progress, Aesop's Fables, Robinson Crusoe,* a short *History of the United States,* Weems's eulogistic *Life of Washington* and, probably, Franklin's *Autobiography*: few, but all great books; and Lincoln absorbed them, made them part of the very fibre of his character, as well as of his mind. Then, in the Indiana days, he early came upon a copy of the *Indiana Statutes.* That does not seem like very inspiring reading; but it was Lincoln's first introduction to the Law, and he was at once interested in it, as giving the foundation principles of government and of human society. The book contained, moreover, a complete copy of the *Declaration of Independence,* the

The first books that moulded Lincoln's character.

Value of the copy of the *Indiana Statutes* in Lincoln's development.

Influence of the Declaration of Independence on Lincoln's permanent program of Ideas.

nation's birth charter, as written by Thomas Jefferson. It fascinated Lincoln, and he made it part of himself. Indeed, this document had more influence than any other literary production on Lincoln's permanent convictions and on his entire career.

Early developed abundant humor.

Lincoln's abundant sense of humor early developed. This, in contrast to his temperamental melancholy, was the balancing grace in his character, perhaps saving him from insanity in certain crises of his life. It showed at first, and for long, in retelling those conventional country-store stories, which furnished the staple of frontier humor, and alas! are still a large element in our boasted American humor. Lincoln's forte, however, lay in the literary skill with which he retold these stories, so that they caught the imagination of his audience, frequently giving him credit for inventing what he had merely borrowed and skillfully redressed.

Education by hard manual labor.

Until he was twenty-one, his labor was, of course, his father's. At sixteen he was working out at six dollars a month, and turning the money over to his father. We hear of him slaughtering hogs at thirty-one cents a day: that must have been particularly trying labor for one with his instinctive tenderness for animals. He developed great physical strength, and was regarded as an unusually skillful rail splitter.

The youthful Lincoln.

Moreover, in a society much given to drink and immorality, he was marked by entire sobriety and personal purity. By the age of nineteen, he had already reached his full height of six feet, four inches. So

Lincoln grew up, a tall, gaunt, awkward backwoodsman, welcomed everywhere in the neighborhood for his good comradeship, abundant humor and story telling, but a solitary, brooding soul within: a kind of feminine soul in a masculine body.

First contact with the larger world.

The year that Lincoln was nineteen, he had his first opportunity for a look out on the big world: he floated down the Ohio and Mississippi rivers to New Orleans, as a hand on a flat boat. New Orleans was an active, important port city, in constant intercourse with Europe, largely French and Spanish in population. It was Lincoln's first contact with cosmopolitan civilization. He saw it wholly from the under side; but he saw it, and it must deeply have affected him, though he apparently had little to say about it on his return.

Circumstances of the move to central Illinois.

The year that Lincoln was twenty-one, the wandering mood again seized his father; and spurred on by another of those frontier epidemics, Thomas Lincoln loaded his family and belongings into a wagon, trekked across Indiana into Illinois, on into central Illinois, and stopped about ten miles west of Decatur, on the banks of the Sangamon. Here Lincoln helped his father clear another piece of land; and now twenty-two, he felt that he had done his part for his family, and struck out for himself. Understand, he did not desert his family; all through the years he recurringly responded to their appeals and needs, even when his own circumstances were straitened. One shiftless step-brother, in particular, was continually appealing to him for money, and usually getting it, no matter

Lincoln's independent start at twenty-two.

how hard it was to send; but from the age of twenty-two, Lincoln never lived in his father's home again.

Odd jobs in the neighborhood.

He did all sorts of odd jobs in the neighborhood. One contract has come down, in which he agrees to "split four hundred rails, for each yard of brown jeans for trousers"; rather expensive trousers, one would think, in terms of hard manual labor. Then, the same year he left his father's house, came his second opportunity for a brief contact with the larger world. Again he went to New Orleans; this time in charge of a shipment of freight a local merchant wanted to dispose of in that port city. It was on this second visit that Lincoln saw the New Orleans slave market; and although the remark attributed to him was doubtless invented by his admirers afterwards, the experience must deeply have impressed him.

The second trip to New Orleans.

He returned, and the merchant who had sent him South made Lincoln "Manager" of his store in New Salem, which means that he was the one clerk in the store. The business failed shortly after, however, and Lincoln was again out of a job. He decided to offer himself as a candidate for the State Legislature, issuing a quaintly characteristic announcement; but was not elected. During this period, Lincoln had his one brief chapter of active military experience, though with no actual fighting, in the Black Hawk Indian war. His standing with his young comrades was shown, much to his gratification, by his election as captain of the voluntary company; his own simple modesty by his immediate re-enlistment, as private, on its disbandment.

Then he and a young friend, named Berry, decided to start out in business for themselves. They opened a store in New Salem as "General Merchants," purchasing the stock almost entirely on credit; but Berry was rather idle and given to drink, and Lincoln wanted to read all the time; so the business languished. At this time, Lincoln would walk twenty miles to Springfield to borrow a book. It was now that he came to know Burns and Shakespeare; and they became his life companions, to whom he turned, all through the years, for personal solace and spiritual companionship.

Berry and Lincoln as general merchants.

Lincoln's reading.

One incident of Lincoln's brief business career is worth retelling: a traveller came by with a barrel of rubbish he wished to dispose of, and offered it to Lincoln for a half dollar. Lincoln took a chance and bought it; and upending the barrel, out of the bottom dropped Blackstone's *Commentaries!* A singular place to find that classic on the Law; but if the story is true, that was where Lincoln found it. This was his second and greater introduction to the Law, as giving the foundation principles of society and government. Lincoln was fascinated by the book and absorbed it.

Circumstances of finding *Blackstone's Commentaries,* and the effect of the volume on Lincoln.

The business soon failed; and although Lincoln was neither legally nor morally bound to do so, he took the whole partnership debt upon himself, and paid it off with scrupulous fidelity. It took him fifteen years to do it. He used to refer to it, jestingly, as the "National Debt"; but it burdened him until he was forty. At that age, when Representative in Congress, he sent back part of his salary to pay items of that old partnership debt: a further signal illustration of that utter integrity of character that was Lincoln.

Business failure and scrupulous honesty in paying the partnership debt.

He served for a time as assistant to the County Surveyor and as Postmaster. He was, for the second time, a candidate for the State Legislature; was elected; went to Vandalia and served his term, making no impression whatever. Returning to New Salem, he continued as local Postmaster, carrying the mail around in his hat, but delivering it with great carefulness. Indeed, Lincoln's hat, afterwards the famous high silk hat, was always his favorite place for carrying memoranda and letters, even as President in the White House.

Early political services.

Lincoln as Postmaster at New Salem.

At this period, occurred the one deep love affair of Lincoln's life. Sweet, lovely, sensitive Ann Rutledge, who must in some ways have reminded Lincoln of his own mother, was the daughter of the family in the house where Lincoln boarded. She had engaged herself to a young man from the East. He had gone back home; his letters stopped. It was even rumored in the neighborhood that he had been married at the time he courted Ann Rutledge; and the poor girl was in deep distress, not knowing whether she was bound or free. Lincoln was deeply drawn to her, and came to love her very tenderly. Finally, she felt

The one deep love affair of Lincoln's life.

sufficiently free to engage herself to marry Lincoln; but whether the cause was her mental and spiritual distress or another of those scourging epidemics, sweet Ann Rutledge died, the year that Lincoln was twenty-six.

Effect of his first spiritual crisis on Lincoln.

It was Lincoln's first great spiritual crisis, shocking his solitary, brooding soul into consciousness of the transiency of human life, of the frail foundation on which our happiness must ever rest. He went away, for a time, in deep distress and melancholy. His friends even feared for his sanity. It was perhaps at this time Lincoln came to love the poem that remained his favorite, and its recurring refrain was his favorite and most often quoted line: "O why should the spirit of mortal be proud!"

Lincoln again in the State Legislature.

Lincoln returned to New Salem, and stood again for the State Legislature, was elected, and served his term. During it, he and his associates, by the conventional "log-rolling" methods of politics of those days, and alas! of these days, succeeded in getting the Capital removed from Vandalia to Springfield. It was a wise step to move it, but that was not why they did it; they wanted it near by.

Lincoln's admission to the Bar and removal to Springfield.

During these years, Lincoln had been assiduously studying law, in every spare moment; and at twenty-eight he felt ready to take his examinations; which he passed successfully and was admitted to the Bar. So he decided to remove to Springfield, which he and his friends had recently made the State Capital, to begin the practice of the Law.

Joshua Speed tells the story of how Lincoln came into Speed's store in Springfield, threw down his saddle bags, and asked something about a lodging. Speed glanced up; and says that he thought he had never looked into so sad a face in all his life. Moved by a sudden impulse, he said, to the effect, "O, I have a room with a double bed in it; if you want to share that, till you get on your feet and find out what you are going to do, it's all right with me." Lincoln gladly accepted, and it was the beginning of the closest friendship of Lincoln's life. Please note that Lincoln did not have intimate friends. He never got on well in polite society, so there was no chance there. True, the men everywhere liked him, for his good comradeship and admirable story telling; but they were never admitted to the inner sanctuary. Lincoln's personal and spiritual life was singularly and tragically solitary. Even Herndon, for so many years Lincoln's law partner, who thought he knew everything about Lincoln, was never admitted to the Holy of Holies; his book on Lincoln sufficiently proves that. Joshua Speed was the nearest to an intimate friend Lincoln had; perhaps because he was associated with Lincoln's later love affair and marriage.

Occasion of forming Lincoln's most intimate friendship.

Mary Todd, a little woman, of high Kentucky and Virginia family, excellent finishing school education, with keen social ambitions and a quick, not always controlled temper, was the sister-in-law of one of the leading Springfield citizens. Why did she turn to Lincoln? During the same period she was being

Engagement and marriage to Mary Todd.

courted by the affable and socially cultivated Stephen A. Douglas. Was it that, through the awkward and forbidding shell of the man, she was drawn to the deep soul within, and divined something of his coming greatness? Why did Lincoln turn to her? Was it his longing for feminine society, his sense that she was all that he was not in the way of social cultivation? In any case, they were engaged to be married; and then, on New Year's Day of the following year, the engagement was suddenly broken, under quite mysterious circumstances. Lincoln was in great distress of mind, not knowing whether he had behaved disgracefully and forfeited his own best life, or whether he should be thankful for his release from an impossible situation.

Significance of the Hamlet element in Lincoln.

Note that there was much of the Hamlet tendency in Lincoln. As his ideas developed, they became settled convictions, the basis of his life; but in conduct he was for long uncertain, apt to respond to the nearest counsel, vacillating, subject to alternating moods of profound depression and relative self-confidence. It was only in the terrible crucible of war, that the man of inflexible ideas finally became the man of equally inflexible action.

At this crisis, Speed took him away to Kentucky. Speed's mother helped to nurse him back to mental and moral health. He returned to Springfield; and under almost equally peculiar circumstances, the engagement was renewed; and in November of the year that Lincoln was thirty-three, he and Mary Todd were married.

Lincoln as husband and father.

Lincoln was an entirely loyal husband to the end of his life, and a beautiful father to his children. He never disciplined them; possibly Mary Todd Lincoln may have done enough of that for both; but affectionate tenderness and companionship he gave, in fullest measure. When the little boy, Willie, died, in the darkest period of the Civil War, it helped to plunge Lincoln into one of those long periods of depression.

His wife loved him with real and lasting affection. She helped him in various ways. She tried hard to improve his social etiquette, but with limited success. He would come into the living room in his shirt sleeves, when fashionable ladies were calling. One instance will illustrate: a number of such ladies called, and Lincoln went in and told them Mrs. Lincoln would be down "as soon as she got her trotting harness on." You can imagine what such behavior did to the socially ambitious Mary Todd Lincoln. Understand, Lincoln was a natural gentleman, with that instinctive courtesy of Nature's nobleman, especially toward the hurt and broken, that springs from a tender and kindly heart, but he never got on well in polite society.

Effect of his domestic life on Lincoln.

His wife had excellent practical judgment: she saved Lincoln from certain mistakes. For instance, when Lincoln, returning from his term in Congress with a sense of failure and a mood of profound depression, was inclined to accept the offered governorship of Oregon as the best way out, his wife put her little foot down hard and said, No, she wouldn't go to Oregon and he shouldn't go either; and so saved him for a national career. Had he gone to Oregon, he would have been removed from the national theater just at the critical time. Mrs. Lincoln was entirely loyal to her husband's and the Union's cause, while suffering the tragedy of her own relatives fighting with the Confederate forces. It must be frankly recognized, nevertheless, that Lincoln's married life in no degree answered the deeper needs of his heart and spirit; and possibly his domestic setting served only to accentuate the brooding solitariness of the soul within.

After a period of miscellaneous practice in Springfield, with two more terms in the Legislature, Lincoln was offered a partnership by Judge Logan, one of the leaders of the Illinois Bar; which means that Judge Logan must have seen, through Lincoln's awkward immaturity, something of his coming greatness. So Lincoln had, with Judge Logan, several years of admirable training in the Law. His interest, as we have seen, was in the Law as giving the basic principles of human society and government. He was not interested in legal technicalities and the tricks for winning cases. His colleagues sometimes thought him lazy, in consequence. He was not lazy, though there was a certain inertia in his giant frame and brooding spirit; it was merely that the petty legal devices did not interest him.

The law partnership with Judge Logan.

Lincoln's interest and training in the Law.

Lincoln and Herndon.

After the years with Judge Logan, Lincoln left that partnership, and formed another, with Herndon as junior partner; and the shingle, Lincoln and Herndon, was out in Springfield till Lincoln's death; that partnership was never broken.

Standing for Congress at 37.

In 1846, Lincoln stood for Congress as a "personal" candidate. His opponent, Peter Cartwright, was a somewhat bigoted religionist. During the campaign he attacked Lincoln as an "aristocrat" and an "infidel." Lincoln answered the first charge, jocularly; it was easy to answer; and remained silent on the second. Why? Well, during the forties of the nineteenth century a wave of liberal thinking had gone across the country. Emerson, six years older than Lincoln, was writing his early books and giving his lectures. Lincoln was deeply influenced by the movement. He had read the religious writings of Thomas Paine, and had come about to the point of view of Channing and Theodore Parker. While naturally a religious man, and deepeningly so under the terrible burden of war, he was never able to express his faith in the conventional orthodox forms or accept the ordinary creedal statements. Rather than attempt to answer his opponent, he thus remained silent: a further illustration of the absolute moral integrity that was Lincoln.

Lincoln's religious views.

Relative failure in Congress, and Lincoln's resulting depression.

In spite of this situation, he was elected, served his term in Congress, and made no impression. True, the men liked him, as always, in committee rooms and hotel lobbies, for his story telling and good comradeship, but as a statesman he was unrecognized. He voted as a strict party man. His only independent action was to propose a bill for the elimination of slavery in the District of Columbia; and it died painlessly in Committee, never reaching the floor of the House. At forty, Lincoln came home to Springfield, feeling that he had failed completely, wondering whether he was fit for public life anyway, inclined to take the offered governorship of Oregon as the easiest way out; a step from which, we have seen, his wife's decision saved him.

The years of circuit riding.

He threw himself into his law practice with a new fervor. There follows a series of years of circuit riding; Lincoln going from court to court, in what is described as "a ramshackle buggy, with a poky old horse." He got on well with everybody, opposing as well as friendly counsel; but where the other lawyers went home for week-ends, Lincoln usually remained on circuit. There may have been partly a domestic reason to account for this; but mainly it was due to Lincoln's feverish desire to make up the deficiencies of his early schooling. While the others slept, or rested at home, he would read until two o'clock in the morning. At this time he mastered Euclid. Now what did Lincoln want with Euclid at forty! There is something pathetic about it all. Of course, Franklin went through similar struggles; but Franklin had a genial, buoyant temperament Lincoln was without, and then Lincoln had nothing of that personal vanity which, as we saw, helped Franklin over many a hard

Struggles to make up for meager educational opportunities.

place in the road. Thus Lincoln's double life went forward: outwardly, the companionable humorist and story teller; inwardly, the brooding thinker and earnest student, sombre and solitary.

Characteristics determining Lincoln's success as a lawyer.

Lincoln's strength with a jury came, first of all, from his profound ethical grasp. He would frequently state his opponent's case, better than the opposing counsel could state it; and then sheer down to the very heart of the matter, basing his appeal on the fundamental moral principles involved. With this, it was his warm humanity, the quick turns of humor that frequently won a case, and his growing power of simple, direct, logical statement that made him successful as a lawyer.

Lincoln's behavior toward lying and guilty clients.

Lincoln did not get on well where he was not sure of the justice of his cause; indeed, we are told he would refuse criminal cases when not convinced of his client's innocence. He would even abandon a case in court, upon discovering that his client had lied to him. One instance will illustrate: in this case, the testimony suddenly revealed that his client was guilty, after assuring Lincoln of his entire innocence. Without a word to anyone, Lincoln turned and left the courtroom. It came time for him to take his part in the trial; the judge looked around; where was Mr. Lincoln? No one knew. The judge sent a messenger to the hotel. He found Lincoln in the wash room, washing his hands. Lincoln sent back word to the judge that he was trying to clean his client's dirt off of him; and he never went back into court with that

The utter moral integrity that was Lincoln.

case; he left it right there. It was this moral integrity that made everyone trust him: clients, judges, counsel on both sides.

The gathering storm over the nation.

Meantime the clouds were gathering for the titanic conflict that had to come. It has already been shown that the original cleavage of political philosophy, on the State versus Nation issue, was for decades not sectional, that it became sectional as a result of the differences in population and production, North and South, and especially because slavery survived in the South, while dying out in the North and abolished in the Northwest. Further, it has been made clear that the fight for the extension of slave territory, on the part of the people of the South, did not mean that the South was permanently committed to the institution of slavery: that it was a struggle for self-preservation, to prevent the South being completely outvoted and outweighed in the national councils.

The anomalous combination of interests in the party founded by Jefferson.

Besides this, however, there was, in the fourth, fifth and sixth decades of the nineteenth century, a curious combination of vested interests within the party, founded by Thomas Jefferson to fight such interests. The great slave owners were constantly demanding new territory to exploit with the uneconomic slave labor. These large operators were financed, not in the South, but from the moneyed interests of the North and East, especially of New York. The party, within which these interests combined, was led from Illinois by Stephen A. Douglas. Originally from Vermont, he had gained national prominence in Illinois politics; and was now a leader of his party at Washington, as Senator from Illinois. Yielding to the pressure from within his party, he helped to engineer the repeal of the Missouri Compromise, early in 1854, on the ground that the people of a territory should have the right to decide for themselves whether it should enter as a slave or free state; which was a popular and apparently democratic policy. His Kansas-Nebraska Bill further divided all the territory west of Missouri and north of 36° 30′, into two parts, with the aim of making it easier to vote the southern half slave territory.

Douglas, national democratic leader from Illinois, engineering the repeal of the Missouri Compromise.

There was thus a curious reversal of party positions toward the eternal problem of powerful vested interests. Lincoln referred to this, in that letter to the Boston Committee inviting him to the celebration of Jefferson's birthday, from which has already been quoted the passage on the Declaration of Independence. Lincoln said:

Lincoln's humorous statement of the reversal of party attitudes, in his letter to the Boston Committee.

> "Bearing in mind that about seventy years ago two great political parties were first formed in this country, that Thomas Jefferson was the head of one of them and Boston the headquarters of the other, it is both curious and interesting that those supposed to descend politically from the party opposed to Jefferson should now be celebrating his birthday in their own original seat of empire, while those claiming political descent from him have nearly ceased to breathe his name everywhere. * * *
>
> "I remember being once much amused at seeing two partially intoxicated men engaged in a fight with their

great-coats on, which fight, after a long and rather harmless contest, ended in each having fought himself out of his own coat and into that of the other. If the two leading parties of this day are really identical with the two in the days of Jefferson and Adams, they have performed the same feat as the two drunken men."*

In further application of Lincoln's story, it may be added that the above is not the only instance of the exchange of overcoats by our political parties. It might seem invidious to cite later illustrations; but if you have a keen mind and are interested in crossword puzzles, you might figure out for yourself who's wearing whose overcoat now.

Lincoln's political principles based wholly on those of Thomas Jefferson, as enunciated in the Declaration of Independence.

Lincoln was a Whig, but he based himself wholly on the principles of Thomas Jefferson, especially as formulated in the Declaration of Independence, "the white man's charter of freedom." His ideas, moreover, were clarifying and becoming the steadfast basis on which his life was to rest. In his own family background, he knew all the evils, to the poor whites, of competition with slave labor. Wherever slavery existed, it was, of course, degrading to a free man to work at the same task as a slave. Those whites, therefore, too poor to own slaves or be trained for skilled labor, had to move out, ever further on the frontier, to escape the degrading competition with the labor of negro slaves. Lincoln had come to the settled conviction that the new territories were needed to give

* Lincoln, from letter to the Boston Committee, Springfield, Ills., April 6, 1859: *Writings*, Vol. V, pp. 24-26.

opportunity for poor white people to take up the land, till the farms, build their homes, rear their children, and by hard toil develop into self-respecting, prosperous American citizens, without suffering the degrading competition with slave labor, or, later, the evil effects of using such labor.

Reasons for Lincoln's settled "free soil" convictions.

In the campaign of 1854, there were three candidates for the Senate from Illinois: Douglas's candidate, representing the regular Democratic party; the candidate of the bolting Democrats, who had broken with the party because of the repeal of the Missouri Compromise, and Lincoln. Twice during the campaign, Lincoln publicly answered a speech by Douglas. In his second reply, at Peoria, Lincoln laid down the first half of his life-program, in the following words:

The Peoria speech, answering Douglas, in 1854.

> "Whether slavery shall go into Nebraska or other new Territories, is not a matter of exclusive concern to the people who may go there. The whole nation is interested that the best use shall be made of these Territories. We want them for homes for free white people. * * * Slave states are places for poor white people to remove from, not remove to. New Free States are the places for poor people to go to and better their condition. For this use the nation needs these Territories."*

The first half of Lincoln's life program.

No further extension of slave territory, no more new slave states: this, Lincoln had come to see as the first element in the solution of the nation's overshadowing problem. At the same time, he insisted on the

---

* Lincoln, in speech at Peoria, Illinois, in reply to Senator Douglas, October 16, 1854: *Writings*, Vol. II, pp. 212, 213.

enforcement of the Fugitive Slave Law, enacted in 1793, revised and made more stringent in 1850. That law so offended abolition sentiment that all the New England States and several others in the North enacted personal liberty laws, practically nullifying the Federal statute. Nullification, like the affirmation of State sovereignty was, in our history, not originally a sectional matter. Lincoln's view was that, since the Fugitive Slave Law was a national statute, it must be enforced. He was attacked for standing with the slaveholders on that issue, and with the Abolitionists on the free soil question. He replied in the Peoria speech:

Lincoln's insistence on the enforcement of the Fugitive Slave Law, in spite of nullification by numerous Northern States.

> "Some men, mostly Whigs, who condemn the repeal of the Missouri Compromise, nevertheless hesitate to go for its restoration, lest they be thrown in company with the abolitionists. Will they allow me, as an old Whig, to tell them, good-humoredly, that I think this is very silly? Stand with anybody that stands right. Stand with him while he is right, and part with him when he goes wrong. Stand with the abolitionist in restoring the Missouri Compromise, and stand against him when he attempts to repeal the Fugitive Slave law. In the latter case you stand with the Southern disunionist. What of that? You are still right. In both cases you are right."*

"Stand with anybody that stands right." Any politician who can say that and consistently act upon it becomes a statesman.

"Stand with anybody that stands right."

* Lincoln, in speech at Peoria, Illinois, in reply to Senator Douglas, October 16, 1854: *Writings*, Vol. II. p. 221.

To defeat Douglas, Lincoln threw the election to the candidate of the bolting Democrats; and from 1854, on, the Illinois battle was between Lincoln and Douglas.

Results of repealing the Missouri Compromise.

The repeal of the Missouri Compromise had thrown the whole question of the new territories open again, and multiplied the bitterness on both sides. There followed the rush into Kansas, with the sack of Lawrence by the pro-slavery party, and the massacre by John Brown and his associates at Pottawatomie: "Bleeding Kansas," indeed it was! Then came the Dred Scott decision. Everyone knows what that was; but not all realize its implications. Dred Scott was a negro slave, taken by his master into free territory, and into a free State, and then back into a slave State. The slave held that, inasmuch as he had been taken into territory where slavery was forbidden by law and could not exist, he was a free man; and the Missouri Supreme Court decided he was still a slave. There was an appeal to the Supreme Court of the United States. Its decision, withheld until after the election of 1856, delivered March 6, 1857, denied the right of any slave or descendant of a slave to sue in a United States Court, declaring that "A negro whose ancestors were imported into this country and sold as slaves cannot become a member of the political community formed and brought into existence by the Constitution of the United States." Besides thus denying any rights of citizenship to freed negroes, the Court further gratuitously stated that neither Con-

"Bleeding Kansas!"

The Dred Scott decision and its consequences.

gress nor the State Legislatures had any right to restrict the spread of slavery, thus making unconstitutional the law forbidding slavery in the Northwest Territory, the Missouri Compromise and all similar enactments.

Now see what that did: if one owner could take a slave into free territory, and still hold him a slave, why not a thousand owners, a thousand slaves each? The decision seemed to throw the whole nation open to slavery. That was what the opponents of slavery feared, and the advocates of it believed. Indeed, one pro-slavery leader boasted that he would yet call the roll of his slaves on Bunker Hill: imagine what that did to the Abolitionists!

Douglas's situation in the campaign of 1858.

When it was proposed to admit Kansas as a state, with a constitution permitting slavery, against the wish of the majority of the inhabitants of Kansas, Douglas voted his convictions, against the measure; and thus broke with his party leaders at Washington. In the campaign of 1858, he was up for reelection as senator; and his problem was to hold his constituency in Illinois, for if he lost that, he was out completely politically.

Why Lincoln joined the recently formed Republican party and accepted its nomination for the National Senate.

Lincoln did not join the Republican party when it was formed. He waited a year and a half: he wanted to see whose overcoat it was going to wear! When he became convinced, however, that it was wearing, at that time, the overcoat of Thomas Jefferson, that it was formed to secure justice for the common people and protect them against the combination of powerful interests, then in the opposing party, Lincoln joined it, and accepted its nomination for the senate in 1858, against Douglas, the Democratic candidate.

Lincoln's acceptance speech at Springfield, laying down the second half of his life program.

In his speech at Springfield, accepting the nomination of the Republican Convention, Lincoln laid down the second half of his life-program in these words:

> "I believe this government cannot endure permanently half slave and half free. I do not expect the Union to be dissolved; I do not expect the house to fall; but I do expect that it will cease to be divided. It will become all one thing, or all the other. Either the opponents of slavery will arrest the further spread of it, and place it where the public mind shall rest in the belief that it is in the course of ultimate extinction, or its advocates will push it forward till it shall become alike lawful in all the States, old as well as new, North as well as South."*

This speech displeased the party politicians. They held that Lincoln had unnecessarily invited trouble and damaged his chances of election. Lincoln replied that he was "after bigger game," meaning, not that he aspired to a higher office, but that his own election or defeat was unimportant, compared to the great problem the nation faced and had to solve. He never took the abolitionist view of that problem, recognizing that the South had inherited slavery, and the existing generation was in no degree responsible for it. He held, therefore, that slavery should be let alone where

* Lincoln, from the speech delivered at Springfield, Ills., June 17, 1858, at the close of the Republican State Convention which had nominated Lincoln for U. S. Senator: *Writings*, Vol. III, p. 2.

it was, but confined within its existing limits, with the hope that the southern people would voluntarily work out a constructive solution through gradual emancipation. Such was the now clearly defined program of settled ideas on which his life work was to rest.

Lincoln's challenge to Douglas, and the partial acceptance.

Early in the campaign, Lincoln challenged Douglas to debate the issues publicly all over Illinois; and Douglas somewhat reluctantly partly accepted: for one important place in each of seven Congressional districts of Illinois. There followed that great series of debates, the greatest ever held, not only in our country, but anywhere in the world at any time. Lincoln began that series of debates, a frontier lawyer and local politician, hardly known outside central Illinois; he closed it, a national figure, talked of all over the northern half of the country as available for the presidency.

The great Debates.

Contrast between Lincoln and Douglas.

The contrast between the two men is impressive: Lincoln, the awkward, six-foot-four giant; Douglas, called "The Little Giant," short, rotund, polished in manner. Lincoln usually began his speeches in a shrill, unpleasing voice, with hands tightly clenched behind his back or used in awkward gestures, until he forgot himself; then his voice would deepen, his head would begin bobbing, his gestures grow forceful, while with direct, logical statement and whimsical turns of humor, he drove home his ideas. Douglas was smooth, ponderous, with a flow of language and flights of rhetoric, able to cover up an issue with a torrent of words, when he desired. Lincoln, with a program of deep, inflexible ethical ideas; Douglas, rather an opportunist, but with certain tenacious convictions. Lincoln, slow and deep; Douglas, facile and brilliant: the one, with profound faith in the people; the other allied with wealth and aristocracy.

The significant contrast in the two ways of touring the State.

The contrast extended to the way the two men toured the state. George B. McClellan, then an official of the Illinois Central Railroad, whom Lincoln was afterwards to call to the command of the Union armies, offered Douglas his private car; and in this Douglas toured the state in luxurious fashion. Lincoln went about in any possible way: in the caboose of a freight train, the smoker of a local, on horseback, on foot: any way he could get around. Enthusiastic crowds gathered; families drove in from the countryside, bringing luncheon, supper and breakfast, sleeping out all night on the ground: it was a wonderful series of debates.

Douglas's misuse of Lincoln's Springfield speech.

In practically every debate, Douglas sarcastically quoted Lincoln's "House divided against itself" speech, ridiculing its Scriptural language and claiming that Lincoln wished to plunge the Nation into civil war. Regularly and patiently Lincoln explained that war was the thing he most of all wished to avoid, and then reiterated his view of the moral issue. In the final debate, at Alton, he summed it up:

"Although Henry Clay could say he wished every slave in the United States was in the country of his ancestors, I am denounced by those pretending to respect Henry Clay for uttering a wish that it (slavery) might sometime, in some peaceful way, come to an end. The Democratic policy in regard to that institution will not tolerate the merest breath, the slightest hint, of the least degree of wrong about it. Try it by some of Judge Douglas's arguments. * * * He contends that whatever community wants slaves has a right to have them. So they have, if it is not a wrong. But if it is a wrong, he cannot say people have a right to do wrong. He says that upon the score of equality slaves should be allowed to go in a new Territory, like other property. This is strictly logical if there is no difference between it and other property. * * * But if you insist that one is wrong and the other right, there is no use to institute a comparison between right and wrong. You may turn over everything in the Democratic policy from beginning to end, whether in the shape it takes on the statute book, in the shape it takes in the Dred Scott decision, in the shape it takes in conversation, * * * it everywhere carefully excludes the idea that there is anything wrong in it.

Summary of Lincoln's program of ideas in the closing debate at Alton.

"That is the real issue. That is the issue that will continue in this country when these poor tongues of Judge Douglas and myself shall be silent. It is the eternal struggle between these two principles—right and wrong—throughout the world. They are the two principles that have stood face to face from the beginning of time, and will ever continue to struggle. The one is the common right of humanity, and the other the divine right of kings. It is the same principle in whatever shape it develops itself. It is the same spirit that says, "You work and toil and earn bread, and I'll eat it." No matter in what shape it comes, whether from the mouth of a king who seeks to bestride the people of his own nation and live by the fruit of their labor,

Lincoln's grasp of the eternal issue.

Universal application of the ethical issue.

or from one race of men as an apology for enslaving another race, it is the same tyrannical principle."*

Significance of Lincoln's thought for the problems of our time.

It was this inflexible grasp of the fundamental moral issue that made Lincoln the great leader; and how his words ring out in application to the same problem, more subtly clothed in the injustices of our current society. Chattel slavery is gone; but "the eternal struggle between these two principles—right and wrong"—goes on.

Lincoln's crucial questions.

In the debate at Freeport, the second of the campaign, Lincoln deliberately imperilled his chance of election, by asking Douglas a number of questions, of which the most important was this: "Can the people of a United States Territory, in any lawful way, against the wish of any citizen of the United States, exclude slavery from its limits prior to the formation of a State Constitution?" Do you see the significance of the question? It concerned the whole range of consequences of the Dred Scott decision. It put Douglas in a quandary. If he answered, "Yes, they can," he expressed his conviction, but went against the leaders of his party. If he said, "No, they cannot," he sided with his party leaders, but violated his own publicly reiterated convictions and offended his constituency in Illinois. So he hedged, argued on both sides, covered up the issue with a torrent of words, shouted that, of course, while the people have a police force, they can keep out anyone they wish to keep out

Douglas's dilemma.

* Lincoln, in last debate with Douglas, Alton, Ills., Oct. 15th, 1858: *Writings*, Vol. IV, pp. 266-268.

can't they?; caught the fancy of the crowd; was elected; but Lincoln had split his party and practically destroyed his national leadership, thus proving himself a great political strategist.

Douglas elected, but Lincoln's measure of victory for his cause.

Had Lincoln possessed that strategy, without his inflexible moral convictions, he would have been a scheming politician; with those profound convictions, his skill in political strategy made him a great and successful statesman.

Following the election, Lincoln went into one of those long periods of depression, to which he was recurringly subject. He had earnestly desired to be elected; and was, indeed, strongly ambitious for place and political recognition. His sacrifice of the election had been for duty's sake, in the interest of his cause. The period of depression lasted well into 1859. It was not until near the close of that year that he began to take seriously the widespread movement for nominating him for the presidency.

The year of depression.

In the winter, a literary club of young men, in Plymouth Church, Brooklyn, wrote Lincoln, asking if he would not come on and give a lecture in Plymouth Church, offering him the then large fee of two hundred dollars. Lincoln had been neglecting his law practice, spending much of his time in unpaid political service. He needed the money: others have since, even vice presidents, we are told; so he accepted.

The invitation to lecture in Brooklyn.

He evidently prepared with extreme care a lecture giving the complete historical data regarding the views of the signers of the Constitution, on the power

Lincoln's careful preparation for his Brooklyn lecture.

and authority of Congress to prohibit slavery in the national territories. He had done this work so thoroughly that no unfriendly critic was able afterwards to find any misstatement of historical fact. It is quite possible that if the Brooklyn lecture had been given as originally planned, it would have been limited to the historical argument and its application; thus giving the authority for his stand in the debates with Douglas, and justifying his view that the Dred Scott decision was unconstitutional, and that slavery could and should be restricted to its existing limits.

The embarrassing change of plan.

When he reached New York, however, he found the situation entirely changed from the original plan: instead of speaking in Plymouth Church, Brooklyn, under the auspices of a literary club, he was to address a metropolitan audience, composed largely of statesmen and politicians, in the great hall of Cooper Union, New York. The point is, the East was profoundly curious to see and hear Lincoln. Everybody had read the debates with Douglas; Lincoln had been caricatured in the opposition press all over the country: the favorite later cartoon representing him as a great, gaunt gorilla, with hideous, ape-like face, and long, hairy arms. The East wanted to see what kind of man this backwoods lawyer, who had suddenly sprung into national prominence, was anyway.

Attitude of the East toward Lincoln.

Lincoln was greatly disturbed by the change of plan. He isolated himself in his hotel room on lower Broadway, tried to whip his address into shape for the altered occasion. The meeting came the evening of February 27th, 1860. It was a great gathering. William Cullen Bryant presided; Horace Greeley and Dudley Field escorted Lincoln to the platform; nearly every important statesman from the neighborhood was in the audience. It was a tolerantly respectful audience: they wished to hear what he could say for himself. Lincoln, much embarrassed, began, as usual, with unpleasing voice and awkward gestures; then soon forgot himself and gave a great speech. There was none of the buffoonery many had been led to expect; there was even nothing of the quaint and sparkling humor, characteristic of his less formal campaign speeches. He must have seemed puzzlingly sombre, in his commanding native dignity, to his distinguished audience, once his awkwardness was forgotten.

Circumstances of the Cooper Union address.

He gave in full his sedulously prepared historical argument on the views and purpose of the "fathers": it reads a little dry, without the vivid intensity of the speaker's personality and the tension of absorbed interest when the great conflict was on. He spoke generously conciliatory words to the Southern people. He deprecated the John Brown raid, denying any connection with it or sanction of it on the part of the Republican party and its members, saying:

Argument of the Cooper Union speech.

> "That affair, in its philosophy, corresponds with the many attempts, related in history, at the assassination of kings and emperors. An enthusiast broods over the oppression of a people till he fancies himself commis-

View of the John Brown raid.

sioned by Heaven to liberate them. He ventures the attempt, which ends in little else than his own execution."*

Then, in the concluding paragraphs of the address, he sheered down to those now clear and changeless convictions, that made him the Lincoln he was and whom we reverence. He described the conflict as fundamentally between those "holding that slavery is morally right and socially elevating" and those "thinking it wrong." With all his temperate conciliation, he never wavered from the conviction that slavery was eternally wrong, and therefore must be confined to its existing area, with a reasonable hope of its ultimate extinction. He closed with these characteristic ringing words:

Conclusion of the speech that made Lincoln President.

"Wrong as we think slavery is, we can yet afford to let it alone where it is, because that much is due to the necessity arising from its actual presence in the nation; but can we, while our votes will prevent it, allow it to spread into the national Territories, and to overrun us here in these free States? If our sense of duty forbids this, then let us stand by our duty, fearlessly and effectively. Let us be diverted by none of those sophistical contrivances wherewith we are so industriously plied and belabored—contrivances such as groping for some middle ground between the right and the wrong, vain as the search for a man who should be neither a living man nor a dead man. * * *

"*Let us have faith that Right makes Might, and in*

---

* Lincoln, in speech at Cooper Union, New York, Feb. 27, 1860: *Writings*, Vol. V, p. 142.

*that faith let us, to the end, dare to do our duty as we understand it."**

That speech put Lincoln in the White House. There is an interesting story connected with it. Lincoln left the hall depressed, as usual not knowing whether he had done well or not. A New York statesman happened to walk out beside Lincoln. They crossed to Broadway; it began to rain; and they got into a street car, going down towards Lincoln's hotel. When the car reached the corner of the street on which the statesman lived, he got out and went home. When he sat down at home, he says that he could not help thinking of Lincoln's face: he thought he had never seen so lonely and sorrowful a face in all his life; and he wished he had gone on to Lincoln's hotel with him. It is worth remembering that, after the speech that put Lincoln in the White House, he was allowed to go back to his lower Broadway hotel room alone.

Lincoln nominated.

Lincoln made a few speeches in New England, and went home to Springfield. When the Republican party Convention was held in Chicago, in June, the fight between Seward and Greely threw the nomination to Lincoln on the third ballot. When the election came in the autumn there were four candidates: Breckenridge, representing the extreme pro-slavery group; Douglas, standing for those who wished to put the slavery issue aside, indifferent whether it was "voted up or down"; Bell of Tennes-

The election of 1860.

* Lincoln, from his speech at Cooper Union, New York, Feb. 27, 1860: *Writings*, Vol. V, p. 149.

see, the candidate of all who would not join the Republicans because of the Abolitionists, but who feared Douglas and slavery; and Lincoln.

Significance that Lincoln was elected by a distinct minority of the popular vote.

Four and a half million votes were cast in the election. Lincoln received less than two million, but was elected. Please note that Lincoln was one of our several presidents who have been elected by a minority of the popular vote: that has much to do with what followed. The most important fact of the election, however, was that Breckenridge, the frank pro-slavery candidate, did not receive a majority of the vote in the slave states; which proves the contention that the demand for the extension of slave territory did not mean that the South was permanently committed to the institution of slavery. Seward and other leaders thought the trouble was now over; but bitterness and hate had increased on both sides, blinding men's eyes. The South took the election of a Republican President as a direct challenge; and, as we have seen, four days after the election, the South Carolina senators resigned and went home; and six weeks after the election, months before Lincoln took office as President, South Carolina seceded from the Union. President Buchanan, a good man, did nothing to restrain South Carolina, and sent in a weak and frightened message to Congress. Back home in Springfield, Lincoln said to his law partner, Herndon, "Billy, you know you sometimes have a case in court, and before you get there, your fellow lawyer goes into court and gives away the case. Well, President Buchanan is

Significance in the fact that the pro-slavery candidate did not receive the majority vote of the slave States.

The immediate consequences of Lincoln's election.

President Buchanan as "giving away the case."

giving away the case"; and he was. In consequence, by February, 1861, Mississippi, Florida, Alabama, Georgia, Louisiana, and, shortly afterwards, Texas followed the example of South Carolina; and the representatives of these seceding states met at Montgomery, Alabama; and on February 9th, weeks before Lincoln's inauguration, established the Southern Confederacy.

Secession of seven States, and formation of the Southern Confederacy, the month before Lincoln's inauguration.

Lincoln thus came to Washington to be inaugurated President, with the Southern Confederacy an accomplished fact, already formed and functioning. His Inaugural Address had been awaited with feverish interest. It was temperate but frank. Certain expressions had been softened to please Seward; and Seward feeling the Address ended too bluntly, had written a sounding imaginative paragraph. Lincoln, realizing its value, translated it into his own simple diction, and used it as the concluding paragraph of his Address. He was generous and conciliatory toward the South; but he stated firmly that the Union of States was perpetual and must be preserved, and that the Federal posts in seceding states would be held. That, of course, was the initial question; and the storm centered on Fort Sumter. That post being in South Carolina waters, and South Carolina having first seceded, the State authorities demanded that the Federal government withdraw its garrison and turn the fort over to them. Now see what that involved: if the Federal government acceded, it was practically sanc-

The situation Lincoln faced on becoming President.

Seward's part in the Inaugural Address.

The firm but conciliatory Inaugural Address.

Reasons why Fort Sumter was the storm center.

tioning secession, saying, "Go, you have our blessing"; if it refused, it meant *war*.

Seward and Lincoln.

Lincoln was not yet certain in action; but Seward was. Seward was sure he should have been president; and a large part of the Republican party thought so too. Seward regarded Lincoln, with his social handicaps, awkward behavior and vacillating action, as a mere figurehead anyway; and considered himself, as Secretary of State, the real head of the administration. He was audacious, where Lincoln was slow and cautious, brilliant where Lincoln was deep, rather a cynical opportunist in politics, in contrast to Lincoln's inflexible convictions. Thus Lincoln learned from Seward; and afterwards Seward learned from Lincoln.

Seward's *"Thoughts for the President's Consideration."*

Not yet sure of himself, Lincoln ordered an expedition fitted out for the relief of Fort Sumter, but ordered it not to sail. On April 1st (note the significant date) Seward handed Lincoln a paper, headed *"Some Thoughts for the President's Consideration."* Lincoln never told: he put the paper away in his desk, and not until twenty-five years later, when his secretaries issued their great *Life* of him, did the public know what had happened. In that remarkable document, Seward somewhat impertinently declared that the Administration was still without a policy. For a domestic policy, he would change the question before the public from Slavery to Union or Disunion; and to that end terminate the Fort Sumter incident, but hold the other Federal posts in the South.

For foreign nations, he would demand explanations from Spain and France, and if satisfactory ones were not received, would convene Congress and declare war against them. He would further seek explanations from Britain and Russia, sending agents into all American countries to arouse a vigorous spirit of independence against European intervention.

Seward's plan for a foreign war to reunite the nation.

The policy adopted must be energetically pursued and incessantly directed, either by the President or some member of the Cabinet. Seward closed the amazing document with the words, "I neither seek to evade nor assume responsibility." *

Seward was, of course, right on what was the fundamental domestic issue, which Lincoln already recognized, as evidenced in his Inaugural Address; but note the cynicism of the proposed foreign policy! Seward deliberately schemed to bring on a foreign war, which would rouse the spirit of national patriotism in all the States, make people everywhere forget the domestic issues, and bring the seceding States quickly back into the Union. He anticipated that the uncertain Lincoln would turn the conduct of the war over to the assured Seward; he would carry the country through brilliantly, and be the great man of America.

He was, obviously, astute in recognizing that nothing else temporarily so unites a nation as a foreign war. Any people will fight, under any government, as long as there are foreign invaders on the soil: that

* Nicolay and Hay, *Abraham Lincoln,* Vol. III, pp. 445, 446.

is what gave the Bolshevist régime its initial strong hold upon Russia. How cynical a scheme, however, and how costly a price to pay for clouding and postponing, instead of solving domestic problems!

Lincoln's answer to the "Thoughts."

Lincoln, the same day, wrote a brief, dignified reply to Seward, with no trace of personal resentment in it, quietly re-stating his policy and affirming that he would carry it out, with the advice of his Cabinet. He then put Seward's paper away, telling no one of the incident. Seward, however, still believing Lincoln would agree, sent in some orders for the President's signature. Lincoln signed them without reading them. That was bad, but that was Lincoln: careless in business details. A little later, Welles, Secretary of the Navy, came into the office in intense indignation: "Look what you signed": an order giving the Powhatan, the only powerful warship in the expedition to relieve Fort Sumter, over to the Commander of the Fort Pickens, Florida, expedition. Lincoln acknowledged signing it, but said he had not read it; and he gave Welles instructions to recall the ship. At a later meeting Seward was called in. He argued for his policy that Fort Sumter should be given up, but the other posts, about which there was no immediate controversy, should be held. Lincoln said "No"; Seward fumed; Lincoln was inflexible, and ordered Seward to recall the ship, and told Welles to order the Fort Sumter expedition to sail. Seward left the office in a huff; and wrote a telegram to the Commander of the Fort Pickens expedition reading, "Give up the

The Powhatan affair.

Powhatan"; and signed it "Seward." The recipient had thus two orders in his hands: a prior one signed by the President, giving him the ship, a later one signed by the Secretary of State, taking it away. Well, he wanted the ship and argued, "I will obey the President," which was right; and sailed away. April 12th, Fort Sumter was fired upon. April 13th, the expedition for its relief arrived, without the only warship strong enough to pass the South Carolina batteries: Fort Sumter fell. April 15th, Lincoln called for 75,000 volunteers. Virginia, purely on the State versus Nation issue, seceded; followed by North Carolina, Tennessee and Arkansas. These four joined the other seven States in the Southern Confederacy; and the war was on.

The war begun.

The four additional seceding states.

Lincoln's ideas, meantime, were clarifying; and on July 4th, he sent in a great message to Congress, defining the purpose of the war. There was not a word in it on slavery: the war was to preserve the Union. Lincoln had come to see the Government of the United States as the translation into a vital organism, of the Declaration of Independence as written by Thomas Jefferson. He saw that Government as the hope of the liberal party throughout the world, and the attempt to destroy it as anarchy, which, if successful, would defeat the progress of mankind. He said:

Lincoln's great message of July 4th, 1861, defining the purpose of the war.

> "This issue embraces more than the fate of these United States. It presents to the whole family of man the question whether a constitutional republic or democ-

Lincoln's view of the issue.

racy—a government of the people by the same people—can or cannot maintain its territorial integrity against its own domestic foes."*

Bull Run and its consequences.

The message fell cold upon Congress; but Lincoln, yielding to the pressure of the politicians and the people, against the opinion of the military leaders, ordered McDowell to strike at Manassas Junction; and Bull Run followed on July 21st. This disaster sobered the nation; it even sobered Congress, which passed the Crittenden Resolution, accepting Lincoln's view of the war.

Enmity and obstruction to Lincoln in his own party.

It was long before Lincoln came, in action, out from under the cloud; and, meantime, his worst enemies were those of his own household. First, there were members of his own party in Congress, led by Trumbull, Chandler and Wade. They regarded Lincoln as a weakling, anyway, and unfit for his job. Strong in sectional hatred, they viewed the war as a war of the Republican party (others have made the same mistake since!) to be fought through for the glory of the Republican party; and bitterly resented Lincoln's ceaseless efforts to unite the whole country behind the war. They formed investigating committees, the favorite device of the legislative body to embarrass the executive, and embarrassed and hampered Lincoln at every turn.

Then, as has been shown, the Abolitionists were largely pacifists during the early period of the war.

---

* Lincoln, in Message to Congress, July 4, 1861: *Writings*, Vol. V, p. 323.

They were willing to fight a war to eliminate slavery; but Lincoln told them that was not this war; it was to preserve the Union. He further offended them by holding to the enforcement of the Fugitive Slave Law for border states remaining in the Union. When General Fremont issued his proclamation at St. Louis, freeing slaves of all who had taken active part against the United States, and setting up a "Bureau of Abolition," Lincoln wrote, warning him. Fremont, sharing the contemptuous opinion of Lincoln, paid no attention; and Lincoln abolished his Bureau. The Abolitionists, unable to see anything but their one issue, were intensely indignant. So prominent a leader as Wendell Phillips went about publicly attacking Lincoln.

Why many Abolitionists were pacifists the first year of the war.

Lincoln's measures which incensed the Abolitionists.

It is hard for us today to understand how such attacks were possible from those who should have been the President's most loyal supporters. After passionately advocating, in the winter of 1861, "disunion," license to the seceding States to go and take the Border States and the National Capital with them, Wendell Phillips, said, in his speech on *The Cabinet,* so late as August 1st, 1862:

Wendell Phillips's bitter attack on the President, expressing the view of many Abolitionists.

> "I believe Mr. Lincoln is conducting this war, at present, with the purpose of saving slavery. * * * If Mr. Lincoln believed in the North and in Liberty, he would let our army act on the principles of Liberty. He does not.
>
> * * * * *
>
> "I do not say that McClellan is a traitor, but I say this, that if he had been a traitor from the crown of

his head to the sole of his foot, he could not have served the South better than he has done since he was Commander-in-Chief. * * * And almost the same thing may be said of Mr. Lincoln—that if he had been a traitor, he could not have worked better to strengthen one side, and hazard the success of the other.

* * * * *

"The President, judged by both proclamations that have followed the late confiscation Act of Congress, has no mind whatever."*

Paradox in these attacks, when the Emancipation Proclamation was already planned.

When these venomous words were spoken, Lincoln had already proposed the Emancipation Proclamation to his Cabinet; and was waiting only for a Union victory to issue it. As late as January 21st, 1863, in his address on *The State of the Country,* Phillips could say:

"Your President sat in Washington, doubtful what he ought to do, how far he might go. Month after month, stumbling, faithless, uncertain, he ventured now a little step, and now another."†

With this attitude on the part of those the President might naturally have expected to be his friends, there was ceaseless harassment, from the opposing political party. Strong Democratic leaders, such as Douglas, had rallied to the war. Douglas came to see Lincoln, and asked whether he could serve better at Washington or in Illinois. Lincoln replied, "Illinois." So Douglas went home, and made a flaming

Douglas's attitude.

* Phillips, Wendell, in speech on *The Cabinet,* Aug. 1st, 1862: *Speeches, Lectures and Letters,* Series I, pp. 448-454.

† Phillips, Wendell, in speech on *The State of the Country: Speeches, Lectures and Letters,* Series I, p. 529.

war speech before the Legislature at Springfield, April 25th, 1861. It is a pity he died a little time later, June 3rd, 1861: he would have been a great asset to Lincoln had he lived. The Democratic party was thus left to the leadership of lesser men, who temporized, equivocated, and thwarted Lincoln in many ways.

Conduct of the opposing political party.

Finally, a new constitutional question had arisen. Our Constitution is very specific in prescribing powers and functions; but allows a wide latitude of war powers, without specifically assigning them. The leaders in Congress argued: we are a people ruled by law; Congress is the Supreme legislative body; the Constitution intends that Congress should exercise the war powers. Lincoln held rightly: all the war powers are executive functions; the President is the supreme executive, responsible to the people of the nation; the Constitution means that the President shall exercise the war powers. He solved the controversy by assuming the war powers and exercising them, while attacks multiplied and the cabal in Congress howled against him. That Woodrow Wilson could exercise those powers in the World War was due to the fact that Lincoln took them over and fought the issue through.

The new Constitutional question and Lincoln's solution of it.

Under the shock of the war, Lincoln was wakened to recognize that the same eternal issue, he had characterized in his debates with Douglas, applied to the relation of social groups in economic production. It is typical of his mind that he saw the universality of the problem, and gropingly stated it in his Message to Congress in 1861:

Application of Lincoln's fundamental ideas to the labor problem.

"Labor is prior to and independent of capital. Capital is only the fruit of labor, and could never have existed if labor had not first existed. Labor is the superior of capital, and deserves much the higher consideration. Capital has its rights, which are as worthy of protection as any other rights. * * * There is not of necessity any such thing as the free hired laborer being fixed to that condition for life. Many independent men everywhere in these States a few years back in their lives were hired laborers. * * * No men living are more worthy to be trusted than those who toil up from poverty. * * * The struggle *of* today is not altogether *for* today; it is for a vast future also."*

The passage is only another expression of Lincoln's changeless conviction that the struggle to save the Union was the battle for the future of mankind.

The winter of 1861 and 62 and the spring of 1862 were a period of low tide for Lincoln. He allowed wheels within wheels of war councils, partly accepting, partly rejecting their decisions. He neither fully supported McClellan nor definitely overruled him. Gradually, however, Lincoln emerged, and by the summer of 1862, the inner and outer Lincoln had become one; the man of inflexible ideas had become the man of equally inflexible action; Hamlet, at last, was Prospero. There were no more war councils: Lincoln issued an order, creating a new army for the protec-

Emergence of the final Lincoln.

* Lincoln in Annual Message to Congress, Dec. 3rd, 1861: *Writings*, Vol. V, pp. 407-409.

tion of Washington, placing Pope at its head; and a few weeks later, called Halleck to Washington, to the supreme command.

These appointments, too, were partly mistakes. Lincoln did not have that absolute judgment of men that marked Washington, perhaps because he was so much more introspective, tending to estimate them by what he knew within himself; and of course, they did not rise to that. In estimating this aspect of Lincoln, however, and judging these generals, one must remember that he was sending them out against the greatest military captain of the Anglo-Saxon race, who broke more military reputations than any other leader in history, except Napoleon, Robert E. Lee.

Lincoln's judgment of men.

With slavery subordinated in Lincoln's mind to the problem of saving the Union, he was, nevertheless, watching for opportunities to further the gradual extinction of the institution, according to his long cherished hope. He repeatedly urged upon Congress and the border States plans for emancipation of the slaves, with generous Federal compensation; but there was little response.

Meantime, as the months went by, Lincoln became increasingly impressed that he must take some decisive step to unite the whole country behind the war. On July 22nd, 1862, he quietly announced, at a Cabinet meeting, his intention to issue the Emancipation Proclamation. The members of the Cabinet were surprised, but favorable. Seward suggested, however, that the time was not right, that they should wait for a

Proposal of the Emancipation Proclamation.

Union victory. Lincoln agreed with this, and put the paper away in his desk. In the interim, Horace Greeley attacked him bitterly, in the New York Tribune, on the slavery issue. Lincoln replied in an open letter to the press, in which he said:

Lincoln's open letter in answer to the attack of Horace Greeley.

"I would save the Union. I would save it the shortest way under the Constitution. * * * If there be those who would not save the Union unless they could at the same time save slavery, I do not agree with them. My paramount object in this struggle is to save the Union, and is not either to save or destroy slavery. If I could save the Union without freeing any slave, I would do it; and if I could save it by freeing all the slaves, I would do it; and if I could do it by freeing some and leaving others alone, I would also do that. What I do about slavery and the colored race, I do because I believe it helps to save this Union; and what I forbear, I forbear because I do not believe it would help to save the Union. * * * I have here stated my purpose according to my view of official duty, and I intend no modification of my oft-expressed personal wish that all men, everywhere, could be free."*

At the time, Lincoln had the Emancipation Proclamation prepared, and was waiting only for a Union victory, to issue it: which proves that he regarded the proclamation as a necessary war measure. Lee's first campaign into the North closed with the carnage at Antietam, followed by Lee's retreat. Lincoln interpreted this as a Union victory; and a few days later, on September 23, 1862, issued the proclamation.

* Lincoln, in open letter to Horace Greeley, Executive Mansion, Washington, August 22, 1862: *Writings*, Vol. VI, pp. 123, 124.

The proclamation is usually taken to be one freeing all slaves. Actually, it contained four items:

The first Emancipation Proclamation and the significance of its four items.

First: All slaves in States or parts of States, in rebellion against the United States, were to be free on January 1, 1863. That did not free all slaves: it declared free the slaves in just those territories where the Federal government could not, at the time, enforce the declaration, except in conquered territory.

Second: Loyal slave owners were to receive compensation.

Third: Lincoln promised to urge pecuniary aid to slave States within the Union, adopting a plan of gradually freeing their slaves.

Fourth: The war was being fought to preserve the Union.

The Proclamation issued as a needed war measure, and as such, a masterpiece.

That was the first Emancipation Proclamation: issued as a needed war measure; and while it aroused some immediate antagonism, as such, it was a masterstroke. It won the Abolitionists to the war to the end. It brought to the Union the support of the liberal party throughout the world. It cut the ground from under the cabal in Congress, left it hanging in the air, and pushed the leaders of the opposition party into the position the cabal had occupied. Finally, it was a supreme assumption of war powers by the President.

Further disasters in the field.

Meantime, in the field, Burnside had followed McClellan to defeat at the hands of Lee, with the culminating holocaust at Fredericksburg, well on the road to Richmond.

The cheering message from the cotton workers of Manchester.

Under the multiplying burden and disappointments, Lincoln was greatly cheered by the whole-hearted expression of support on the part of the suffering workers at Manchester, England, long out of employment through the cutting off of cotton supplies by the war. He wrote them:

Lincoln's reply, again expressing his conviction that the war was for humanity.

"I know and deeply deplore the sufferings which the workingmen at Manchester, and in all Europe, are called to endure in this crisis. It has been often and studiously represented that the attempt to overthrow this government, which was built upon the foundation of human rights, and to substitute for it one which should rest exclusively on the basis of human slavery, was likely to obtain the favor of Europe. * * * Under the circumstances, I cannot but regard your decisive utterances upon the question as an instance of sublime Christian heroism which has not been surpassed in any age or in any country. It is indeed an energetic and reinspiring assurance of the inherent power of truth and of the ultimate and universal triumph of justice, humanity and freedom."*

Lincoln calling Hooker to the chief command.

Early in 1863, Lincoln called Hooker to the chief command. Hooker had been talking rashly about the need for a dictator, evidently implying that he would make a good one. In appointing him, Lincoln wrote Hooker a characteristic letter:

"*Major General Hooker.*

General:—I have placed you at the head of the Army of the Potomac. Of course I have done this upon what

* Lincoln in letter to the Working Men of Manchester, England, Executive Mansion, Washington, Jan. 19, 1863: *Writings*, Vol. VI, p. 250.

appear to me to be sufficient reasons, and yet I think it best for you to know that there are some things in regard to which I am not quite satisfied with you. I believe you to be a brave and skilful soldier, which of course I like. I also believe you do not mix politics with your profession, in which you are right. You have confidence in yourself, which is a valuable if not an indispensable quality. You are ambitious, which within reasonable bounds does good rather than harm; but I think that during General Burnside's command of the army you have taken counsel of your ambition and thwarted him as much as you could, in which you did a great wrong to the country and to a most meritorious and honorable brother officer. I have heard, in such a way as to believe it, of your recently saying that both the army and the government needed a dictator. Of course it was not for this, but in spite of it, that I have given you the command. Only those generals who gain successes can set up dictators. What I now ask of you is military success, and I will risk the dictatorship. The government will support you to the utmost of its ability, which is neither more nor less than it has done and will do for all commanders. I much fear that the spirit that you have aided to infuse into the army, of criticising their commander and withholding confidence from him, will now turn upon you. I shall assist you as far as I can to put it down. Neither you nor Napoleon, if he were alive again, could get any good out of an army while such a spirit prevails in it. And now beware of rashness. Beware of rashness, but with energy and sleepless vigilance go forward and give us victories."*

The characteristic letter to Hooker.

---

* Lincoln, letter to General Hooker, Executive Mansion, Washington, D. C., Jan. 26th, 1863: *Writings*, Vol. VI, pp. 254, 255.

Defeat in place of hoped-for victory.

In place of the begged-for victory, came the overwhelming defeat of Chancellorsville, with Hooker's bewildered retreat, followed by Lee's second campaign into the North, culminating in the critical battle of the war, Gettysburg.

Gettysburg the turning point of the war.

After Gettysburg and the failure of Lee's campaign, Lincoln was sure that the Union would win the war. If only he could hold the people together, and he was convinced now he could do that, the war could end but in one way. His thoughts thus turned away from the war to what would follow after; and he began planning to forestall the hate of little men, which he saw victory would free for vengeance upon the stricken South. In his Gettysburg Address, November 19, 1863, he achieved perhaps his highest spiritual interpretation of the war; and showed he had added to his old power of simple, direct statement, an ability to lift the common mind with a sweep of imaginative vision, proving that he had finally become a literary master.

Significance of the Gettysburg Address as showing Lincoln's final literary mastership.

The greatest classic in our American literature.

> "Four score and seven years ago our fathers brought forth on this continent, a new nation, conceived in Liberty, and dedicated to the proposition that all men are created equal.
>
> "Now we are engaged in a great civil war, testing whether that nation or any nation so conceived and so dedicated, can long endure. We are met on a great battlefield of that war. We have come to dedicate a portion of that field, as a final resting place for those who here gave their lives that that nation might live.

It is altogether fitting and proper that we should do this.

"But, in a larger sense, we can not dedicate—we can not consecrate—we can not hallow—this ground. The brave men, living and dead, who struggled here, have consecrated it, far above our poor power to add or detract. The world will little note, nor long remember what we say here, but it can never forget what they did here. It is for us the living, rather, to be dedicated here to the unfinished work which they who fought here have thus far so nobly advanced. It is rather for us to be here dedicated to the great task remaining before us—that from these honored dead we take increased devotion to that cause for which they gave the last full measure of devotion—that we here highly resolve that these dead shall not have died in vain—that this nation, under God, shall have a new birth of freedom—and that government of the people, by the people, for the people, shall not perish from the earth."*

Why the Gettysburg Address is the highest expression of Lincoln's soul in literature.

It is no accident that the world has come to regard this Address as the purest classic in our literature. In utter sincerity of feeling, elevation of spiritual vision, noble restraint and compact brevity of style, with that lofty simplicity that is the utterance of the heart, it is the supreme literary expression of Lincoln's soul.

Congress not in session from March to December, 1863.

During some nine months of 1863, Congress was not in session; and its members were all over the country, getting the reaction of their constituents. To their surprise and often chagrin, they found that Lincoln had become the people's hero. Why? First

* Lincoln, Address at Gettysburg, November 19, 1863: *Writings*, Vol. 7, p. 20.

of all, it was the growing recognition of his absolute integrity of character. He made mistakes, many of them; but he was utterly honest, he meant always the highest, and could be wholly trusted. With this, it was his warm humanity, his mercy, humor and tenderness. The military men would come to him and say that he must not let off those who had seriously broken their regulations, that it destroyed military discipline. Lincoln would reply, "O, I am their father. I have to consider their mothers and fathers. I am not a military man. I can't let a simple minded boy be shot for running away, and not touch the man who induced him to desert"; and he went right on pardoning them. The military men fumed; but the people loved him.

Why Lincoln had finally become the people's hero.

There was Mrs. Bixby, who was supposed to have lost five sons in the war. Lincoln heard this report, and wrote her that beautiful letter: so tender in humanity, so spiritually exalted, so noble in patriotism: it caught the imagination of the people all over the land.

The letter to Mrs. Bixby.

The response of the people to Abraham Lincoln is one of the supreme justifications of our faith in democracy; for it proves that there is in the breast of common humanity, a power finally to recognize the highest when it appears.

Significance for the future of democracy in the response of the people to Lincoln.

Before the close of 1863, in his effort to thwart the hate of little men, Lincoln issued his Amnesty Proclamation, a year and a half before the war closed. It offered full pardon, with restoration of all rights of citizenship and property (except slaves), to all but a few at the top, on taking the oath of allegiance to the United States. It further provided that where ten per cent of the voters in a seceded State would establish a new state government in allegiance to the Union, Lincoln would recognize that government.

Lincoln's purpose in the Amnesty Proclamation of 1863.

The cabal in Congress was furious. Efforts were made to transfer the action to Congress, and later to thwart Lincoln's carrying out of the Proclamation; but Lincoln pressed steadily on, in this final assumption and execution of war powers.

It was in the spring of 1864 that Lincoln called Grant, from his victories in Tennessee, to the command in chief of the Union armies; and Grant began that ceaseless driving campaign that ended the war. After the terrible losses of those frightful days in the Wilderness, Lincoln was in deepening misery; but two days after Grant uttered those famous words, "I propose to fight it out on this line if it takes all summer," Lincoln quoted Grant in a speech at Philadelphia, and added, "We are going through on this line if it takes three years more." Thus Grant, with Lincoln inflexible behind him, pushed on. The cumulative Union losses, equalling in the end Lee's entire opposing army, widely increased the pacifist sentiment in the North, which expressed itself in blundering efforts for premature peace. Lincoln handled these attempts with consummate wisdom, enabling Grant to continue his relentless hammering. Lincoln generously conceded everything else; but stood, un-

Calling Grant in March, 1864.

Lincoln's steady support of Grant, in spite of the terrible losses and against the growing opposition.

Futile efforts for peace.

alterable, on the preservation of the Union. The Southern leaders would accept nothing but complete and separate independence. Every negotiation reached that impasse; and the war dragged on.

Lincoln renominated.

At the Union convention in June, Lincoln was renominated. When he heard the news, he said, "I suppose they didn't want to swap horses crossing a stream." During the last hours of Congress, Lincoln urged through the bill drafting men without monetary commutation. Up to that time, a man drafted could pay a limited amount of money, and get off. Under this bill, every man drafted would have to serve. His party leaders warned Lincoln that, if he signed that bill, he would not be re-elected. Lincoln told them that this law was necessary to save the Union; and he signed the bill.

The worst attack upon Lincoln, between the nomination and election.

The result was wide resentment over the approaching draft. This, with the furious opposition to Lincoln's assumption of war powers, and the exasperation of the growing pacifist sentiment over the failure of the embarrassing negotiations for peace led to the worst attack of all upon Lincoln, in the summer between the nomination and election. Leaders of his own party issued a public Manifesto, declaring him a usurper of the constitutional rights of Congress. There was a strong movement to nominate another candidate, acceptable to Lincoln's enemies in Congress, in place of the one they regarded as a failure and unfit for his task. Lincoln's friends, frightened, took to cover; his enemies were jubilant.

The Wade-Davis Manifesto.

Lincoln was imperturbable. In utter disregard of his personal fortunes, he pressed forward in his task of saving the Union, through winning the war. He wrote out his view of his duty, sealed the paper in an envelope, and asked the Cabinet members to initial it, at a meeting on August 23rd. At a Cabinet meeting, following his election, he asked the members to open and read the paper. It was:

Lincoln's consecration to his cause and disregard of his own interests.

> "This morning, as for some days past, it seems exceedingly probable that this Administration will not be re-elected. Then it will be my duty to so cooperate with the President elect, as to save the Union between the election and the inauguration; as he will have secured his election on such ground that he cannot possibly save it afterward."*

Significance of the sealed paper.

Could there be a higher example of his utter selflessness, in consecration to his cause? It was his task to win the war and save the Union; all else lay with God.

Again it was the fresh discovery that the people were with him that saved him. Stimulated by a succession of Union victories, public opinion rallied to him. New England came out for him. Even Greeley came over to him. He was re-elected, carrying all the States, except New Jersey, Delaware and Kentucky, with a considerable majority, this time, of the popular vote. It was his utter sincerity, integrity and selfless devotion that proved supreme statesmanship.

The triumphant reelection.

Lincoln's second inauguration came when the war

---

* Lincoln, *Writings,* Vol. VII, pp. 196, 197.

The second Inaugural Address.

was clearly drawing into its last phase. His brief address attempted no prophesy, but clearly expressed the hope in his heart for speedy and permanent peace, and stated the idea achieved. It closed with those noble words, familiar to every school boy, but which cannot be too often repeated:

Closing words of the Address.

> "With malice toward none, with charity for all, with firmness in the right as God gives us to see the right, let us strive on to finish the work we are in, to bind up the nation's wounds, to care for him who shall have borne the battle and for his widow and his orphan, to do all which may achieve and cherish a just and lasting peace among ourselves and with all nations."*

Those words are the soul of Abraham Lincoln.

Last days of the war.

He spent some days at the front, with Grant, at Petersburg and Richmond; and returned to urge that *all* the States should vote on the Thirteenth Amendment. April 9th, came the news of Lee's surrender. Two days later, Lincoln made a speech, in whch he urged that the Southern States should be treated as if they had never left the Union. That is a magnanimity and generosity, unequalled and unexampled in any other victor in history. At his last Cabinet meeting, he urged his associates to put aside all thoughts of hatred and revenge: only if resentment were extinguished, could there be hope of unity and harmony.

Lincoln's magnanimity toward the South.

Lincoln had aged terribly during the last years of

---

* Lincoln, concluding passage from his second Inaugural Address, March 4, 1865: *Writings*, Vol. VII, p. 331.

the war: it seemed as if he felt the death of every man, as if it had been his own son; but now, with the end at hand, the burden was eased from his long-troubled heart. With a lighter spirit than he had known for years, he went out, on April 14th, for a long drive with Mrs. Lincoln. She reports him as talking very freely with her on that day, as saying, in effect, "Well, Mary, we have had a hard time of it since we came to Washington, but better days are in sight now. We will get through these next four years somehow, and go back to Illinois. I have saved a little money. I can earn some more with my law practice back there. There are some quiet, peaceful years ahead of us now."

The drive with Mrs. Lincoln on April 14th.

That evening, in this happier mood, he went to Ford's theater to see Laura Keene in *Our American Cousin.* Mrs. Lincoln had planned the theater party, and invited the Grants. At the last minute, they could not go; which saved Grant's life, for he, too, was marked as victim; but Mrs. Lincoln said she would not have her theater party spoiled; so they went. You know the last chapter: John Wilkes Booth, ex-actor, half crazed with the sufferings of his people, and seeing in Lincoln the symbol and head of what he regarded as the tyranny that had caused those sufferings, knowing every alley way of the theater, laid all his plans, crept behind the presidential box; and shortly after the play started, shot Lincoln through the head from behind. Lincoln never regained consciousness, and died the next morning,

The theater party.

The last tragic chapter.

April 15, 1865, fifty-six years old: *centuries* old, with the burden of the nation's suffering he had borne so long on heart and brain!

Disaster to the South in Lincoln's assassination.

That shot, fired by John Wilkes Booth, was the most terrible blow the South ever received. It was worse than any invading campaign; it was worse even than Sherman's merciless march to the sea. It put the little men in the saddle, the little men who hate. The result was the horrors and wickedness of the reconstruction period in the South: horrors and wickedness that would have been avoided, had Lincoln lived; for the major effort of the last two years of his life had been to forestall the revenge, he knew would be attempted upon the South when the war closed. In the end, however, Lincoln's ideas conquered: better men came into power; more just and generous counsels prevailed; and the result is the *one united Nation,* we love and cherish today.

Significance of Lincoln for the future of America.

It was Lincoln's greatness that he did the work of Alexander Hamilton, on the basis of the principles of Thomas Jefferson; and thus united, in his leadership and career, the two strands of political philosophy that had divided our country: united them, let us hope, for our whole future.

With six such stars shining in our spiritual firmament, with six such leaders in our wonderful heritage from the past, have we not reason to be proud, and humble, to regard that heritage, not as something merely to be gloried in, but as a challenge, to us, not to sit down, but to get up and go forward, to see to it that the aim of our forefathers is not defeated, that the American experiment does not fail, that America becomes the Beacon Light among the nations, they one and all dreamed she was to be; until in the end, to use Lincoln's great phrase, "Government of the people, by the people, and for the people" shall prevail, not only completely within the nation, but in the relations of all the nations of mankind?

The challenge in our heritage to present day America.

BOOK LIST

Books starred are of special value in relation to the subjects of this volume; those double-starred are texts for study or are otherwise of first importance.

ADAM, G. Mercer, *The Life of General Robert E. Lee*, pp. IV+321, A. L. Burt & Co., New York, 1905.

ADAMS, Charles Francis, **Lee's Centennial: An Address at Lexington, Va.*, Jan. 19, 1907, pp. 76. Privately printed.

ATHERTON, Gertrude, *The Conqueror: A Dramatized Biography of Alexander Hamilton*, pp. XII+536. Frederick A. Stokes Co., New York, 1902.

ATHERTON, Gertrude, Editor. *A Few of Hamilton's Letters*, pp. XXI+227. The Macmillan Co., New York, 1903.

BACHELLER, Irving, *In the Days of Poor Richard*, pp. 414. Bobbs-Merrill Co., Indianapolis, 1922.

BARTON, William E., **The Life of Abraham Lincoln*, 2 vols., pp. XVI+517 and 516. Bobbs-Merrill Co., Indianapolis, 1925.

BARTON, William E., *The Soul of Abraham Lincoln*, pp. 407. George H. Doran Co., New York, 1920.

BASSETT, John Spencer, *The Federalist System*, pp. XVIII +327. Harper & Bros., New York, 1906.

BINNS, Henry Bryan, *Abraham Lincoln*, pp. XIII+379. Temple Biographies, J. M. Dent & Co., London, 1907.

BOWEN, John Joseph, *The Strategy of Robert E. Lee*, pp. 256. Neale Publishing Co., New York, 1914.

BOWERS, Claude G., **Jefferson and Hamilton*, pp. XVII+531. Houghton Mifflin Co., New York, 1925.

Bowers, Claude G., *The Party Battles of the Jackson Period*, pp. XIX+506. Houghton Mifflin Co., N. Y., 1922.

Bradford, Gamaliel, Jr., *Lee the American*, pp. XVI+324. Houghton Mifflin & Co., Boston, 1912.

Brooks, Noah, *Abraham Lincoln*, pp. XIV+471. Heroes of the Nations, G. P. Putnam's Sons, New York, 1894.

Bruce, Philip Alexander, *Robert E. Lee*, pp. 380. George W. Jacobs & Co., Philadelphia, 1907.

Bruce, William Cabell, *Benjamin Franklin: Self Revealed*, 2 vols., pp. III+544 and III+550. G. P. Putnam's Sons, New York, 1917.

Channing, Edward, *The Jeffersonian System*, pp. XII+299. Harper & Bros., New York, 1906.

Charnworth, Lord (Godfrey R. Benson), *Abraham Lincoln*, pp. VIII+479. Makers of the Nineteenth Century, Henry Holt & Co., New York, 1926.

Conant, Charles A., *Alexander Hamilton*, pp. 145. Riverside Biographical Series, Houghton, Mifflin & Co., New York, 1901.

Curtis, William Eleroy, **The True Abraham Lincoln*, pp. XIV+409, J. B. Lippincott & Co., Philadelphia, 1904.

Curtis, William Eleroy, **The True Thomas Jefferson*, pp. 395, J. B. Lippincott & Co., Philadelphia, 1901.

Drinkwater, John, *Abraham Lincoln: A Play*, pp. XII+112. The Houghton, Mifflin Co., New York, 1919.

Drinkwater, John, *Robert E. Lee: A Play*, pp. 95. Sidgwick and Jackson, London, 1923.

Fisher, Sydney George, **The True Benjamin Franklin*, pp. 381. J. B. Lippincott & Co., Philadelphia, 1898.

Foley, John P., Editor, **The Jefferson Cyclopedia*, pp. XXII+1009. The Funk & Wagnalls Co., New York, 1900.

Ford, Henry Jones, **Alexander Hamilton*, pp. VIII+381. Figures from American History. Charles Scribner's Sons, New York, 1920.

Ford, Paul Leicester, **The Many-Sided Franklin*, pp. XX +516. The Century Co., New York, 1899.

Ford, Paul Leicester, Editor, **The Sayings of Poor Richard*, pp. 288. G. P. Putnam's Sons, New York, 1889.

Ford, Paul Leicester, **The True George Washington*, pp. 319. The J. B. Lippincott Co., Philadelphia, 1896.

Franklin, Benjamin, ***Autobiography*, with an Introduction by Woodrow Wilson, pp. XIX+299. The Century Co., New York, 1910. Numerous other editions.

Franklin, Benjamin, ***Complete Works*, 10 vols. G. P. Putnam's Sons, New York, 1887.

Freeman, Douglas Southall, *Lee's Dispatches*, pp. LXIII +400. G. P. Putnam's Sons, New York, 1915.

Gerwig, George William, *Washington, the Young Leader*, pp. XII+144. Charles Scribner's Sons, New York, 1923.

Gilman, Bradley, *Robert E. Lee*, pp. IX+205. The Macmillan Co., New York, 1915.

Hamilton, Alexander, ***The Federalist*, edited by Henry Cabot Lodge, pp. LIX+586. G. P. Putnam's Sons, New York, 1888.

Hamilton, Alexander, ***Works, Constitutional Edition*, edited by Henry Cabot Lodge, 12 vols. G. P. Putnam's Sons, New York, 1903.

Hamilton, Allan McLane, **The Intimate Life of Alexander Hamilton*, pp. XII+482. Charles Scribner's Sons, New York, 1910.

Hapgood, Norman, *Abraham Lincoln: The Man of the People*, pp. XI+433. The Macmillan Co., New York, 1913.

Hapgood, Norman, *George Washington*, pp. XI+419. The Macmillan Co., New York, 1901.

Harrison, James Albert, *George Washington*, pp. XXIII +481. Heroes of the Nations, G. P. Putnam's Sons, New York, 1906.

HERNDON, William H. and Weik, Jesse W., *Abraham Lincoln: The True Story of a Great Life*, pp. XXVIII +331 and VII+348. D. Appleton & Co., New York, 1913.

HILL, Frederick Trevor, *On the Trail of Grant and Lee*, pp. XIV+305. D. Appleton & Co., New York, 1911.

HILL, Frederick Trevor, * *On the Trail of Washington*, pp. XIV+276. D. Appleton & Co., New York, 1922.

IRVING, Washington, *The Life of George Washington*, 5 vols. G. P. Putnam & Co., New York, 1855-1859.

JEFFERSON, Thomas, ***Writings*, Definitive Edition, edited by Andrew A. Lipscomb, et al., 20 vols., Jefferson Memorial Association, Washington, 1905.

JOHNSON, Bradley T., *General Washington*, pp. X+338. Great Commanders, D. Appleton & Co., New York, 1894.

JONES, J. William, **Life and Letters of Robert Edward Lee, Soldier and Man*, pp. 486. Neale Publishing Co., New York, 1906.

JONES, J. William, *Personal Reminiscences, Anecdotes and Letters of General Robert E. Lee*, pp. XVI+509. D. Appleton & Co., New York, 1875.

LAMBETH, W. A. and Manning, W. H., *Thomas Jefferson as an Architect and Designer of Landscapes*, pp. IX +122+plates. Houghton, Mifflin & Co., Boston, 1913.

LEE, Fitzhugh, **General Lee*, pp. 432. Great Commanders, D. Appleton & Co., New York, 1894.

LEE, Captain Robert E., **Recollections and Letters of General Robert E. Lee, by his Son*, pp. XII+461. Doubleday, Page & Co., New York, 1904.

LINCOLN, Abraham, ***Writings*, edited by Arthur Brooks Lapsley, 8 vols., G. P. Putnam's Sons, New York, 1905, 6.

LODGE, Henry Cabot, *Alexander Hamilton*, pp. VIII+317. American Statesmen, Houghton, Mifflin & Co., Boston, 1898.

LODGE, Henry Cabot, **George Washington*, 2 vols., pp. VI+341 and 399. American Statesmen, Houghton, Mifflin Co., Boston, 1917.

LONG, A. L., *Memoirs of Robert E. Lee*, pp. 707. Sampson Low, Marston, Searle, and Rivington, London, 1886.

LOSSING, Benson John, et al., *Harper's Encyclopaedia of American History*, revised edition, 10 vols. Harper & Bros., New York.

MACCHESNEY, Nathan William, Editor, *Abraham Lincoln: The Tribute of a Century*, pp. XXVIII+555. A. C. McClurg & Co., Chicago, 1910.

MAURICE, Frederick, Editor, *An Aide-de-Camp of Lee, Being the Papers of Charles Marshall*, pp XXIX+287. Little, Brown & Co., Boston, 1927.

MAURICE, Sir Frederick Barton, *Robert E. Lee, the Soldier*, pp VII+313. Houghton, Mifflin Co., New York, 1925.

MCMASTER, John Bach, *Benjamin Franklin as a Man of Letters*, pp. IX+293, American Men of Letters, Houghton, Mifflin & Co., Boston, 1900.

MERWIN, Henry Childs, *Thomas Jefferson*, pp. 164. Riverside Biographical Series, Houghton, Mifflin & Co., Boston, 1901.

MORE, Paul Elmer, *Benjamin Franklin*, pp. 139. Riverside Biographical Series. Houghton, Mifflin & Co., Boston, 1900.

MORSE, John T., Jr., *Abraham Lincoln*, 2 vols. pp. VI+387 and VI+373. American Statesmen, Houghton, Mifflin & Co., Boston, 1893.

MORSE, John T., Jr., *Benjamin Franklin*, pp. VI.+428. American Statesmen, Houghton, Mifflin & Co., Boston, 1896.

Morse, John T., Jr., *The Life of Alexander Hamilton,* 2 vols., pp. IX+425 and 384. Little, Brown & Co., Boston, 1876.

Morse, John T., Jr., *Thomas Jefferson,* pp. XIII+326. American Statesmen, Houghton, Mifflin & Co., Boston, 1898.

Muzzey, David Saville, *Thomas Jefferson,* pp. VIII+319. Charles Scribner's Sons, New York, 1918.

Nicolay, John G., *A Short Life of Abraham Lincoln,* pp. XVI+578. The Century Co., New York, 1902.

Nicolay, John G., and Hay, John, *Abraham Lincoln: A History,* 10 vols. The Century Co., New York, 1890.

Oliver, Frederick Scott, *Alexander Hamilton: An Essay on American Union,* pp. XIII+502. G. P. Putnam's Sons, New York, 1906.

Page, Thomas Nelson, **Robert E. Lee: Man and Soldier,* pp. XVIII+734. Charles Scribner's Sons, New York, 1911.

Parton, James, **The Life and Times of Benjamin Franklin,* 2 vols., pp. 627 and 707. Mason Bros., New York, 1864.

Phillips, Wendell, *Speeches, Lectures and Letters. Series I,* pp. IV+562, Walker, Wise & Co., Boston, 1864. *Series II,* pp. V+476. Lee and Shepard, Boston, 1892.

Pierson, Hamilton W., *Jefferson at Monticello,* pp. 138. Charles Scribner, New York, 1862.

Putnam, George Haven, *Abraham Lincoln,* pp. VIII+292. G. P. Putnam's Sons, New York, 1909.

Randall, Henry S., *The Life of Thomas Jefferson,* 3 vols. Derby and Jackson, New York, 1858.

Russell, Phillips, *Benjamin Franklin: The First Civilized American,* pp. X+323. Brentano's, New York, 1926.

Sandburg, Carl, *Abraham Lincoln: The Prairie Years,* 2 vols., pp. XVI+480 and VI+482. Harcourt, Brace & Co., New York, 1926.

SCOTT, Winfield, *Memoirs, Written by Himself*, 2 vols., pp. XXII+653. Sheldon & Co., New York, 1864.

SHEPHERD, Henry E., *Life of Robert Edward Lee*, pp. 280. The Neale Publishing Co., New York, 1906.

SHIRLEY, Ralph, *A Short Life of Abraham Lincoln*, pp. 188. Funk & Wagnalls Co., New York, 1919.

STEPHENSON, Nathaniel Wright, Compiler. **An Autobiography of Abraham Lincoln: Consisting of the Personal Portions of His Letters, Speeches and Conversations*, pp. 501. Bobbs-Merrill Co., Indianapolis, 1926.

STEPHENSON, Nathaniel Wright, **Lincoln*, pp. 474. The Bobbs-Merrill Co., Indianapolis, 1922.

SUMNER, William Graham, *Alexander Hamilton*, pp. X+281. Makers of America, Dodd, Mead & Co., New York, 1890.

TARBELL, Ida M., **In the Footsteps of the Lincolns*, pp. XI+418. Harper & Bros., New York, 1924.

TARBELL, Ida M., **The Life of Abraham Lincoln*, 2 vols., pp. XXXVI+426 and 475. The Macmillan Co., New York, 1917.

THAYER, William Roscoe, *George Washington*, pp. IX+274. Houghton, Mifflin Co., Boston, 1922.

TRENT, William P., *Robert E. Lee*, pp. XVIII+135. Beacon Biographies, Small, Maynard & Co., Boston, 1899.

VANDENBERG, Arthur Hendrick, *The Greatest American: Alexander Hamilton*, pp. XX+353. G. P. Putnam's Sons, New York, 1921.

WASHINGTON, George, ***Diaries*, edited by John C. Fitzpatrick, 4 vols. Houghton, Mifflin Co., New York, 1925.

WASHINGTON, George, **Writings*, edited by Lawrence B. Evans, pp. LXIX+567. G. P. Putnam's Sons, New York, 1908.

WASHINGTON, George, **Writings, collected and edited by Worthington Chauncey Ford, 14 vols. G. P. Putnam's Sons, New York, 1889-1893.

WATSON, Thomas E., *The Life and Times of Thomas Jefferson*, pp. XXII+534. D. Appleton & Co., New York, 1903.

WATSON, Thomas E., *Thomas Jefferson*, pp. XV+150. Beacon Biographies, Small, Maynard & Co., Boston, 1900.

WHITE, Henry Alexander, *Robert E. Lee and the Southern Confederacy*, pp. XIII+467. Heroes of the Nations, G. P. Putnam's Sons, New York, 1897.

WILLIAMS, John Sharp, *Thomas Jefferson, His Permanent Influence on American Institutions*, pp. IX+330. Columbia University Press, New York, 1913.

WILSON, Woodrow, **George Washington*, pp. VIII+333. Harper and Bros., New York, 1896.

WOODWARD, W. E., *George Washington: The Image and the Man*, pp. 460+XXXV. Boni & Liveright, New York, 1926.

INDEX